The Deeper Arts of the Völva

The Deeper Arts of the Völva

Self-Discovery Through Ancient Paths in the Modern World

Ivy Mulligan

Hubbardston, Massachusetts

Asphodel Press
12 Simond Hill Road
Hubbardston, MA 01452

*The Deeper Arts of the Völva: Self-Discovery Through
Ancient Paths in the Modern World*
© 2020 Ivy Mulligan
ISBN 978-1-938197-28-4
Second Edition

Cover Art © 2019 Joan Howe

All rights reserved. Unless otherwise specified,
no part of this book may be reproduced in any form
or by any means without the permission of the author.

Distributed in cooperation with
Lulu Enterprises, Inc.
860 Aviation Parkway, Suite 300
Morrisville, NC 27560

I dedicate this book to all the Seiðr-folk, Northern Shamans, Vitkis, and Völvas who put to pen and paper the Great Work of their paths, so that others may find a light in the dark. I especially dedicate this work to my Landvaettir, my Ancestors, Loki, and Odin, whose kinship and involvement with my life inspired this book.

I dedicate this book to my mentors who have passed: Valerie Walker (Veedub) and Ailo Gaup, whose wisdom shaped my understanding of all things mystic and shamanic, and to my living mentors Inger Johanne Syverud, Lindy Fay, and Stephan Gunn. Without your friendship and guidance I would still be in the dark on many concepts.

I also dedicate this book to the mavericks of the 21st century who have brought the ways of Seiðr and Northern Shamanism back into the reclaiming process in their own powerful and unique ways: Evelyn Rysdyk, Diana L. Paxson, Freya Aswynn, and Raven Kaldera—thank you for bravely blazing the trail to reclaiming these ancient ways!

And, of course, I dedicate this book to my Husband and best friend of 33 years; without your support, John, I wouldn't be the Völva I have become. And a shout out to my "little brother" Kurt Hoogstraat, whose friendship has been, truly, a candle in the wind.

The Gods of Old encourage everyone to take the Eddas and the Sagas, with all the lore of the ancients and our Ancestors, and make them their own; by reading them, telling them, and then visiting all the Nine Worlds while getting to know some of the beings who reside there. Hail to my Seiðr and Völva kith, who have viewed Yggdrasil in time-honored ways, then brought those visions back to aid our Kindred. I am honored to have been blessed with a glimpse of those places, and to report back what I have found.

Contents

Foreword .... *i*
Introduction .... *iii*

Arts of the Völva
  Month 1: The Art of Ritual 1
  Month 2: Journey Into Yggdrasil 29
  Month 3: Journey to the Well of Urd 48
  Month 4: Odin and His Ravens. 69
  Month 5: A Walker With Many Skins 90
  Month 6: Wyrd Weaver, Spinner of Fate 108
  Month 7: Movement into the Ecstatic. 120
  Month 8: Mastering the Self 140
  Month 9: Time and Seasons. 176

Sacred Ceremony
  Sacred Calendars 192
  Blóts and Sumbels 212
  Tools of the Trade. 214
  Seasonal Rituals 216

Appendixes
  Appendix I: Required Reading List 268
  Appendix II: Rune Meanings 269

About The Author 280

Foreword

This workbook originally started off as my advanced distance course to follow my year-long distance apprenticeship of the 101 level of the Arts of the Völva, the Vitki, the Norse Shaman and the Seiðkona.

This workbook is an anthology of sorts. By compiling it, I am simply a guide (or Sherpa, if you will), bringing you gathered knowledge from all over which I hope will make this trek into the wilderness easier and more productive.

I wish anyone reading this to understand that I am not trying to assume the role of an authority figure or scholar. I do not intend to become your "teacher"; I am simply your guide. I view myself as a Sacred Sherpa, because I know this trail well, and I vow while you are under my care that I will show you the trails that I have found best for ease of travel. I will show you how to make fire, gather food, and make shelter as you fare forth. I will even carry your gear and administer first aid along the trail up the mountain, if that's what you require. But the most assured way to have a successful expedition is through the troop with whom we are exploring. Your climbing partners—including the many voices of wisdom which have come before me, as an anthologist—are just as crucial as your Sherpa. Within this workbook, you will find some very experienced travelers whom I hope to honor by including them in this "base camp". I hope you will share in their past expeditions, their trail maps, and their collective kennings, as it is via collective wisdom that we grow stronger in our resolve when the trail gets steep. I want you to reach the summit. Moreover, I have tried to use and include *many* other people's work (with permission) since that gives each reader a sense of the wide variety of adaptations other advanced practitioners have come to discover.

This collection is about building a new Kindred of worthy voices: we are stronger together than we are alone. *Skal* and hail to each and every reader of this anthology, and to all of the brilliant minds quoted and shared within it! I encourage all of you to be fearless in letting your individual lights shine, so that everyone might find the way! As always, use what serves you and leave the rest behind.

Due to the time restraints and the massive work involved (as well as the cost of the original online course), I have hearkened to Those Whom I Serve and decided to turn the curriculum from its original construct as an online Power-Point format into an accessible book format available for anyone who is looking for deeper insights and practice concepts reclaimed by modern practitioners of today.

The book's chapters are the original nine months' lessons, so each chapter is divided into subcategories of the material and information any immersion student I have taught would need to cover. However, if you feel each chapter needs more than one month to understand and execute, then by all means take the time you need to work through it. This is a *read/do* course load and workbook, meaning that you read the information, then you apply it to your practice by actually doing it. It's a *work*-book.

You will need to acquire extra reading material—i.e. specific books from other Authors to fully get what I intended from this course; but in the end it will be worth it to you to do so.

As this originally was an online long-distance course, I have kept many of the weblinks included, as these add much background information to the concepts I (and others) are trying to share and convey. However, I realize that the Internet is an ephemeral place, and links often vanish over time. If this happens, I apologize in advance; you might try running the title phrase above each quote through a search engine in case it is elsewhere on the Internet.

I wish you the best on this journey. Only you will know the way you are best at serving the Nine Worlds, but I hope this book gives you more of a focused, empowered, and wise place to travel from.

Skal!

Ivy Mulligan
June 2018

Introduction

What is a Völva?

A Völva is/was the Scandinavian equivalent of a Witch; a Healer who was also a Sorceress. A Völva, in other words, was/is a Norse Witch who did holistic, organic root work and was most often a *seer*. In the past, a Völva was the equivalent of a medicine woman and often a spiritual priestess as well, though her lessons would be impromptu, informal, and highly practical. Historically, the Norse practitioners of the various arts of magic were respected professionals whose services were valued by their communities. In the Norse literature, men as well as women appear wielding the arts of magic. Since Norse magic was mostly a woman's art, throughout this book I will deal with magic as practiced by women, using the feminine pronoun, but it should be remembered that men as well as women practiced the arts as recorded in the sagas.

- ❖ She would usher new life into the world, and she would give plant remedies to those of the living who ailed.
- ❖ A Völva could also end life, if need be.
- ❖ A Völva was known to sometimes help "ailing" spirits as well as living humans.
- ❖ The Völva would lend a keen ear to her tribe's soul worries and all the tribe's maladies as well, knowing that a person needs to be hale in all parts of themselves, both seen and unseen.
- ❖ Sometimes the Völva would need to find answers just outside of this physical kenning, so the Völva would do Spá. She became a master of communicating with the land-wights and the ancestors (or sometimes even the gods themselves), looking for deeper answers.

A Völva is the term for practitioners of Spá, usually translated as "prophetess", "witch" or "sybil". The word *Völva* dates back to the early Germanic tribes, where the term is found in the name or title of some tribal seeresses; it comes from a root meaning "magical staff", and throughout Norse literature one sees female prophetesses and witches bearing a staff.[1] The term Spá or Spae is a second type of magic, which differs slightly from Seiðr. A Völva's Spá work consisted of prophecy, channeling the spirits' words or voices through a human medium. Seiðr goes deeper into manipulating Wyrd (destiny) and is usually done within a trance state; it can include performing magic that affects weather or animal movements, as well as a wide range of malefic magic. Archaeologist Neil Price has provided an excellent summary of the known uses of seiðr:

> *There were seiðr rituals for divination and clairvoyance; for seeking out the hidden, both in the secrets of the mind and in physical locations; for healing the sick; for bringing good luck; for controlling the weather; for calling game animals and fish. Importantly, it could also be used for the opposite of these things—to curse an individual or an enterprise; to blight the land and make it barren; to induce illness; to tell false futures and thus to set their recipients on a road to disaster; to injure, maim and kill, in domestic disputes and especially in battle.*[2]

Magic as described in the Norse sagas was not a single art: there was seiðr, spá (spae), Galdr, and runic magic. Of these terms, seiðr is the most common, as well as the most difficult to define. The term seiðr is what I refer to most in my writing, as it is the term closest to what practices I use. Seiðr is believed by many practitioners to be a late form of northern European shamanism, and is used by them to describe actions ranging from shamanic magic (such as spirit journeys, magical healing, or removing harmful influences) to magical psychological treatment in the form of recovering lost portions of the soul-complex, etc.

In my personal experience, the Norns are the foremost masters of Seiðr; however much destiny may be altered by gods, humans, and other beings, the initial framework is established by the Norns. To do this, they

---

[1] Mercatante, Anthony S. & Dow, James R. (2004): The Facts on File Encyclopedia of World Mythology and Legend, 2nd edition, p. 893.
[2] Price, Neil S. 2019. The Viking Way: Magic and Mind in Late Iron Age Scandinavia. p. 64.

use the same means as any "norn" with a lowercase "n" (which I and some modern practitioners use as a synonym for Völva): weaving, carving runes, and other mainstays of the toolkit of pre-Christian Germanic magic.

A Völva can (and does) become a seiðkona, and in doing so takes on the task of learning to sing the songs of enchantment. She learns to work, befriend, and honor the "re-wilding" of the Ancestral magic of seið, which is available to everyone via the wights (spirits) of Nature, and by connecting with the essence of the ancient people who lived still connected to the great web of Wyrd. These are the deep mysteries, the mysteries of our connection to soul.

By doing seiðr, the Völva can gain invaluable insight, and then pass on the information to the Folk she is serving; as kindred and as a Medicine Woman, thereby fulfilling the sacred role of the "thrice-burned witch".

Fast-forward to today, and you begin to see that the world is witnessing a "calling out" for many shamans and shamanic practitioners to take up Stav and Drum and other tools, and begin to sing a song of strength, wisdom, perseverance, hope and cohesive evolution similar to what was once sung by their ancient ancestors. This calling appears to be worldwide, and many indigenous ancestors are being awakened and asking to be given voice by their shaman/witch descendants. That includes me, and those whose genetic lines are European. Back then, our ancestor probably didn't have a name for labeling what they believed or practiced spiritually. Religion wasn't an experience people added on to their ordinary lives; it was a daily part of living their Earth-based existence. However, as time passed after the domination of Christianity, the Germanic/Teutonic pagan form of spirituality was called "heathen", meaning "Heath Dweller", and the name has been taken up today as a non-insulting label for this religious cosmology.

Most (although not all) Völvas consider themselves to work within Heathenry (or Asatru, a subsect of Heathenry, whose name means "true to the Aesir"); which is a modern faith made up of folk who are trying to reconstruct the spiritual aspect of their collective Germanic/Nordic cultural heritage and cosmology. Another Heathen denomination is Vanatru, whose practitioners primarily honor the Vanir or pantheon of Earth-Gods. Outside of the Heathen umbrella demographic, a tradition known as

Northern Tradition Paganism has grown up alongside, which is less reconstructionist and more centered in personal revelation; one subsect of this tradition is Rökkatru, which primarily honors the third pantheon of Norse/Germanic "Dark Gods". Each of these various groups is producing their own mystics and spiritual practitioners.

But not everyone in Heathenry is called to the path of the Norse mystic, nor is every Völva called to be a Gythia (god-woman or priestess) to a tribe of folk. Sometimes, a Völva isn't even called to do deep Spa, especially when it involves the High Seat Ritual (as described in *Erik the Red's Saga*). Her vocation is that of a healer, and even though she is devoted in her own sacred practice of how she communes with the Holy, this Healer-Völva doesn't necessarily feel the need to share ritual work with other human souls on a regular basis. Even her divination and bone-casting might be kept to a minimum, as a big part of this Völva's practice would be the desire to live her mystical path as it comes each day. A Healer-Völva takes pride in her skillsets of "taking care of business", as it arises, from a hedge-witch or folk-healer perspective. This Völva is a Priestess of the Woodlands, and her magic is deep, primal Earth work.

At times, we might also find a Völva who is more adept as a rune singer, a Skald, or as a psychopomp/soul worker. Each of these callings is a scared path into Yggdrasill, and each path brings to this Tradition different specialties required for proficiency within each calling of a modern 21st century Völva.

This workbook is a way of kenning this Northern Path of Witchcraft and Shamanism as I have tried to reclaim it, both as a healer and as a Priestess. Within its pages, you too will learn each of these magic modalities, and within the next nine months what you find should allow you, the reader, a renewed sense of what your calling and talents are as a Völva or seiðkona.

I would hope that whoever reads this workbook would already be familiar with Norse Paganism, as well as its mystical, esoteric side which include the arts of the Völva (and Vitki to some extent) as Healer, the Seiðkona (and seiðmenn), the Galdr-singer, and the Skald.

In the next nine chapters which are titled "Months", I will attempt to take you deep within a multitude of worlds: the world of runes, the world of inner space (which is the world of potential and the in-between, the world of written prose, the world of song and sound, as well as the world of our bodies within the physical world of nature. This is a book about *doing* as much as it involves study and reading. To be adept at any art one must *do* as much as one must study, so expect to roll up your sleeves and actually participate in these activities.

With that being said, this path also requires much study and in-depth investigative work on behalf of the practitioner, so I have come up with various reading material to accompany this one, ensuring a solid well-rounded understanding of this book's concepts. I have added many websites that underline the images I am trying to bring to life within these concepts, as well as a handful of additional books to work through simultaneously. Heathenry is said to be "the religion with homework", and the Norse mystical arts are no exception.

Therefore, each chapter (month) we will explore and delve deeply into the five major components that comprise a Völva/Viki's practice and make it unique to any other form of world-wide mysticism; the Self, the Staff, the Song, the Seat, and the Spirits. We will accomplish this by using timed tested techniques that address the categories of Mind, Body, Luck, Magic, and Calling. This will be done by the following ways:

1. How to build and charge a Seiðrstallr (your high seat and the area around it).
2. What is Vé, and how to create it and use it.
3. Basics of Utiseta (Out-sitting).
4. Creating Galdr and other traditional songs used by our ancestors for trance work.
5. Omen journal (developing your own omen-taking system). Not just the Futhark runes, although we will be working with them thoroughly.
6. What are "soul parts", and how we use them.
7. Active and personal ritual creation, both in Blóts and seiðr work.

Also, we will journey through the Voluspa, with one line per week to understand. We will designate one day a month to Utiseta (out-sitting) on the full moon, whereby we receive our deep kennings, and we will journey into inner space, the world of sound, the world of in-between, and the world of potential; thereby truly learning as well as re-claiming the arts of the many Völva's songs and methods which we use in seiðr and spá. This will be shown later in this month's lesson how to perform this type of mini-"vision quest", and throughout the year we will learn the various songs and chants or ancestors used as well as why. We will learn examples of these forms of invocation, but it is up to each participant to settle on their own unique style and method for effectiveness and ease of use.

This book will be laid out as each chapter being a month's worth of lessons, building from the last lesson and adding more information and practices as needed. This format keeps you progressing and moving forward in your practice.

We will include work with the Futhark runes as a journey; we will spá to start our monthly work on the first of each month, using the intention we wish to be shown our Wyrd, and what concept, practice, Orlog, or direction we are to focus on for our immersion work that month. Then, each day upon rising, we will use the Futhark runes we received (one at a time at first, then in combinations of twos or threes) to begin our day; by creating our own Galdr and Galdralag to manifest our Wyrd the way we want or need it to unfold. Finally we will journey through the five laws of the Witch, which I believe are universal no matter what ancestry we have inherited. These laws are *to know, to will, to dare, to be silent, and to manifest*.

What you will need:

❖ A private space in which to do your work, a place that is sanctified for your seiðr and spá.
❖ A head cover.
❖ A Stav.
❖ A Drum.
❖ Futhark or (Futhorc) runes, or a set of your own symbols.

- ❖ A journal to record your progress. It is through careful documentation that a Völva/Vitki can check their progress, remember their visions, and compare their everyday energy levels.
- ❖ Books on the reading list in the appendix at back. You must read all the material! I will recommend some additional online reading material, but at this point, I am assuming most of you are very familiar with the Eddas and the Sagas, as well as you have your own favorite books on runes and seiðr. Please read over the list now.
- ❖ Time! Each month you will need to really commit to this as a way of life, and find the time to add daily work in the morning, weekly work for the process of working though the paradigms and the Voluspa, and your monthly time of out-sitting. If you don't commit to this work and make it a priority, you will not grow in wisdom, proficiency, or power.
- ❖ A special outdoor location for your monthly sessions of Utiseta. This is mandatory, as being outside is the only way to connect deeply with the wilderness and the wisdom of the earth. The whole propose of out-sitting is to be seated upon a sacred and powerful spot on the earth; a sort of portal if you will. Traditionally it was on a grave or burial mound; but a spot in nature with its primal energy will work just as well.
- ❖ Internet access. At some point it will benefit you to look up the links I share, as this gives a collective overview of how others approach the concepts I explain.

I hope that in the end, after completing this book, you will have a functioning and effective practice as a Völva or Vitki. My aim is to have any serious seeker be able to take the kennings of our Ancestors and weave that wisdom and power into today's modern 21st-century world.

Skal!

Arts of the Völva

Month 1: The Art of Ritual

Why do we do ritual and what is the purpose? Why is ritual so important for us to access in our path of spiritual pursuits, and why should we be doing them on a regular basis as a 21st-century Völva or Vitki?

Ritual is important and it is not often done on a personal level by many new to Heathenry. I believe that rituals can help us on a deep level to process issues and aid our healing and recovery from loss. They facilitate urbanized people to reconnect with the Earth and her changing seasons. They allow us opportunity to honor the many rites of passage we experience in our lives. More importantly, ritual participation keeps us connected to the vast energies of life—it is our means of linking ourselves to the vast web of Wyrd, which is what we seek foremost as Norse mystics. In short, ritual is something that people have always done, still do and must continue to do.

Rituals take an extraordinary array of shapes and forms. They can be performed in communal or religious settings, or in solitude; they can involve fixed, repeated sequences of actions or not. People engage in rituals with the intention of achieving a wide set of desired outcomes, from reducing their anxiety to boosting their confidence to alleviating their grief. It is a way of communing as humans with the unseen forces of Wyrd, of the Wilderness, and with our Gods. Ritual is utilized by those who are in tune with their soul's work and the multi-universe for a plethora of objectives as complex as dedicating one's life to a new endeavor to as straightforward as making it rain.

When the beginner thinks about ritual, the image that comes to mind may be elaborate steps, staged settings, and large group participation. However, many of the most profound and sacred rituals I have experienced have been done alone, impromptu, and deep within the forest with no tools, props or fellow practitioners. Ritual then becomes as it is intended: an intimate weaving and sharing of human life, experience, love and reverence (as well as gratitude) with those forces beyond man-made life; those mysteries that we might try to understand, yet that are truly unfathomable to us.

As we work toward reclaiming the sacred arts of the Norse mystic, it is very easy to get entrapped by all the "correct procedures" available to us in an overwhelming influx as 21st-century people. We are conditioned to get online, read that stack of books, and follow the lead of others who are blazing their own trails through the Nine Worlds. We spend so much of our time trying to regurgitate the proper way of doing what is already instinctual that we then miss the opportunity that is always present for our real growth and evolution as Norse mystics, healers, and visionaries, which is participation in frequent individualistic ritual. When we begin to trust in ourselves, our inner wisdom, and our natural connection to the universe, we begin to forge an intimate and very personal bond with these forces, and this can only happen during our sacred rites. Through ceremony we intuitively seek connection and interaction in real time with those things we call Gods and Wights.

Ritual can be as simple as saying a heartfelt "prayer" and leaving an offering to as grandioso as a full on Asatru Handfasting. Ritual can be a Völva out-sitting to absorb the energies and wisdom of her Landvaettir, to weaving a spell for healing of her neighbor. Ritual can also be lighting a candle at your altar space and communing with the Gods you serve, or by writing a poem for your ancestors and reading it to them as you visit the family homestead for your yearly reunion. The crucial thing is that you understand its importance of its application into your life as a Heathen/Norse Mystic and take the initiative to include it regularly in your spiritual life. You will be a much happier Völva or Vitki for the effort, I promise.

Lesson 1/1: Runes

What we call "runes" today in modern Heathenry—the Futhark or Futhorc symbols—are very important symbols of power. However, my understanding of "runes" is very different from that of most modern writers and practitioners, and I need to explain it here.

Over time, due to my own deep awakenings as well as correspondence with non-American Seiðr-workers, I've come to understand that the word "rune" does not just refer to the Futhark (or Futhorc) symbols used in Heathenry and Norse Paganism for divination and magical work.

Etymologically, the word "rune" could refer to a hidden secret, a spell, an incantation, or any mysterious or "occult" symbol. A "rune" could be a symbol or sigil you created yourself, and it can still be anything of that description.

In the last three decades, many noted writers have put out a number of books on Norse runes, almost always referring to the study of the Futhark runes. Over time, these works have made the word "rune" synonymous only with the Futhark (or Futhorc) symbols. I believe, however, that when the ancient Norse people referred to "runes", they were using the broader meaning referred to above. and that this is the meaning of "runes" in Snorri Sturluson's writings. Anyone could create a magical symbol and call it a "rune". Anyone could put together an incantation and call it a "rune". Anyone could make a charm and call it a "rune". This is how I use the word, and throughout this book when I say "runes", I am referring to any of the above.

I do not believe that the word "rune" had anything to do with the Norse letters; I believe that they were just an alphabet. I have found nothing in any historical references which state that the Norse letters were used for divination; I believe that in the past fifty years modern man has done an awesome magical feat by turning those letters into occult sigils, and the focal point of 20th and 21st century Heathen and Norse Pagan divination. I generally find that the Futhark runes are best used as sigils for magical working; truth be told, even our own Roman alphabet can be used to create powerful sigils just as effectively. However, since many of you will want to learn modern Futhark (or Futhorc) "runic" divination, I am including (in the appendix of this book) a list of the divinatory meanings of the Futhark and Futhorc symbols as used by the Northern Shamanism Guild.

In my informal blog I now tend to refer to the Old Norse letters as "futharks", but for purposes of clarity this book will refer to them as "Futhark runes" (or "Futhorc runes") since they are now technically occult symbols. (In writings donated by others, the word "runes" will refer to their own understanding of the Futhark or Futhorc runes as synonymous with "runes".) However, I also encourage you to create runes of your own, symbols with their own meanings that are special to you, and use those as well. These can be used for divination just as well as the Futhark (or Futhorc) runes. Looking at comparative evidence of all the surrounding countries and cultures, the way of casting lots for divination purpose generally used natural objects, as they were found within nature—bones, shells, entrails, bird-flight patterns, weather and astrological events, etc.

This is a profound kenning, this mystery I am sharing with you which I myself just recently discovered via synchronistic events, divine kennings, and re-membering. I was shown that this understanding is usually reserved for those deeply adept, those who have a sacred understanding of what the lore is really telling their spiritually-Norse soul. The early Heathen/Asatru authors are welcome to their own souls' discovery, but we each must learn to find our own authenticity and trust it. Much like our ancestors expect us to do, we are to search fearlessly for those old ways in a self-sovereign and personal way, and make sure those truths work for our personal evolution, which in turn helps the world evolve. We do not need other human beings to validate our souls' truths, as they have been handed down to us via the thousands of lives and loves our Ancestors lived to make us who we are in this moment.

To adequately and successfully do any of our rituals, you will need a sacred space allotted and hallowed for the specific purpose of our seiðr/rune/spá work. This is sometimes referred to as a *hörgr* (stone cairn altar) or if a entire building, a *Hof*. When doing Spá our sacred space is known as a Seiðrstallr (the high seat and the area around it).

Practice: Daily Rune Reading. Tonight (and every night hereafter) before going to bed, simply draw a Futhark (or Futhorc) rune after hallowing your sacred space (*hof* or *hörgr*). This first month will be just getting familiar with using the Futhark runes as actual allies for your daily actions. This month (if you haven't yet) begin to view the runes as living deities, demi-gods if you will, or better yet as the vocal cords of the spirits of the Well of Urd. (At the same time, if you want to create your own divinatory symbols and use them, you can do that over these months as well.)

To form a bond with the Futhark runes by realizing they are a unique intelligence with a life force all their own gives every Völva/Vitki the advantage of truly seeing that our Wyrd and our destiny is very mercurial. The Futhark runes are much more to us than simply a tool for seeing in to the future; they are the voice and the language of the Norse cosmology.

Using your journal, after your daily work with the Futhark runes, take one Futhark rune from your reading for that day and meditate on its meaning. If you can, visualize a journey to your "inner space" using the Futhark rune's image and meaning as your vehicle. Sit quietly with the Futhark rune in your inner space and observe all the traffic in your mind, letting the Futhark rune's energy work as a "filter". Note how the presence of that Futhark rune traveling with you changes your perception of your inner workings. This exercise should take about five to ten minutes. Note that if "being with" a Futhark rune helps you to still and settle your inner "busy ness", how does it facilitate the process and why? Write down your observations in your journal and compare them.

This Futhark rune will also be the "forecast" for the following day, so it's worth it to you to learn its meaning. As you go on through the month, if you first draw a Futhark rune you've already meditated on and learned, consider that your "forecast" and draw another one to meditate on.

Spá: What It Is and How to Do It.

We find that the main draw of the path of seiðr is the use of prophecy and divination. There are a few techniques which a Völva might use to "ken" information as to the workings of the world, both seen and unseen.

The best well known is the seiðr seance, which is usually called "the rite of high seat", and that form of Spá entails a Völva going into to a trance state to journey to the unseen worlds of Norse cosmology for the purposes of being an oracle for a community. There is also the form of spá that uses tactical tools to perform divination, which is also known as reading signs, augury, or omen-taking.

Many people who do seiðr will use Futhark (or Futhorc) runes for divination, but I feel that the Bones, scrying, and nature augury are just as important (and sometimes clearer) for the use of divination. I personally use Bones as well as nature augury most frequently as my divination tools, and although both methods takes a while to master, the information I glean from them is a very accurate and thorough in its divinatory picture. I find that the Bones work better for me than Tarot or other human-generated imagery-based divination tools, as they remove the need for analytical "right brain" translations of the symbols.

Methodology for Bones or Augury.

To Read the Bones: There are two types of bone reading; one is called "freestyle", meaning it is a collection of bones and other items thrown upon a mat with a circle divided up into directions or time correspondences. The other is using a set of knuckle bones from a sheep, and reading them like dice. I use the "freestyle" method, as described by a wonderful witch named Britton on her blog.[3]

To understand bone reading through the use of Shagai, a form of gaming and divination used by Mongolian shamans, I recommend that you consult Sarangerel's book *Riding Windhorses* (Destiny Books, 2000), which describes the process in detail.

To perform Augury, it is essential to spend much quality time outdoors in Nature. Augury is often a misused word, possibly because true augury has been largely lost. Over time the word has come to be used as a word for divination, often associated with the flight and behavioral patterns of birds. It is that, but not only that. By the study and patterns of any living creature in a wilderness setting, we can begin to get a understanding of how certain events, collective situations, and dimensional time analysis affect our human lives, as we are all connected via the web of life. Just as we learn in the world of science, an ecosystem relies on many organisms acting as a cohesive unit; what affects one organism affects another.

When I do Nature Augury, I am not just looking for metaphysical answers to my query of what I should be aware of. I also look to the beings I am "divining" for solid proof, physical Midgard proof, that environmental, ecological and atmospheric events I feel are beginning to transpire are actually happening. I feel that the best way to do that is by observing Nature and its inhabitants—not just birds, although they are the most common animal form to use while practicing augury.

---

[3] http://archaichoney.com/blog/2016/5/1/bone-reading-intro-starting-guide

By taking what we collectively know of their habits and behaviors, we can begin to form a picture of what is transpiring energetically in the world around us. By immersion in Jord's ways as She is—being one with the natural world—we come to the deepest understandings of "seeing" as Norse Shamans. There are many websites that discuss at length the purpose of augury and how to do it. I suggest if you are called to this form of Spá, look into the habits and patterns of any living creatures that resonate with you.

Lesson 1/2: Self

I recognize five "parts" of the Norse mystic, and we will use these "parts" to find ourselves. Each month we will go over in depth what role each "part" plays in our modern life as well as historically, and then for the last couple of months we will learn to integrate and use all those parts as a cohesive whole. These parts are:

1) The Individual (the Healer)
2) The Seidkona/Seidmann (the Shaman)
3) The Staff Carrier, or Völva/Vitki (the Witch)
4) The Spakona (the Seer/Oracle)
5) The Fjölkyngi/Fjolkunner (the Magician)

As Norse Mystics, we all have this construct of soul parts. Having a soul constructed of different parts is actually a foundational belief in all forms of shamanism worldwide. In the Northern Tradition, the way a human's essence of "soul" composition is made up is very complex. Some Norse/Germanic groups use a model with nine interacting component "parts" that make up a human being; others use as many as seventeen.[4] In many outside traditions there are simple three, labeled "Body, Mind, and Soul." The nine-fold model contains the following soul parts:

---

[4] For the seventeen-fold soul model used by the Northern Shamanism Guild, see *Wyrdwalkers* pp. 184-207. (Raven Kaldera, Asphodel Press, 2007.)

- ❖ The *Hamr*: Literally translates to "shape" or "skin," which is the energetiic and measurable auric field that surrounds every living creature.
- ❖ The *Hugr* and *Minni*: Translated as "thought" and "memory," which equates with the mind.
- ❖ The *Fylgja*: The astral body, translated as "One who Follows". Also called the "fetch".
- ❖ The *Hamingja*: Luck.
- ❖ The *Ek*: Ego.
- ❖ The *Lyke*: Physical body.
- ❖ The *Öðr*: Divine Consciousness.
- ❖ The *Önd*: Sacred breath.

Throughout this book, we will explore, as well as implement, each of these facets to our deeper work. Let us examine the beginning element of coming to know the Self: the world of inner space.

Some scholars classify people who do "sacred work" into separate categories by the types of ritual the sacred person is associated with (as well as the types of religious experience that they undergo). Sacred practitioners become categorized by the types of authority structures within which they function. In this view, the title of "shaman" as a sacred practitioner is sometimes categorized under the term "experiential expert", meaning that the religious experiences of a shaman may be different from all other forms of religious experience. This is because each practitioner learns the various stages of religious experience through experimentation within parameters of following specific steps that are the same worldwide and recognized as "shamanic", but each one can venerate different spiritual bodies, cosmologies and theologies, and still come to the same conclusions and results in their spiritual work.

This does not imply that a Norse/Germanic shamanic practitioner (specifically a Völva or Vitki, whom I consider to be a Shaman-Witch who practices seiðr in a Norse/Germanic tradition) is entirely experimental, nor do the various foms of Norse/Germanic shamanism lack specific ritual functions or fail to fit into an "authority structure". Norse Pagans accept that there is a specific cosmology with an order to it. This is proven by the evidence left to us in literature as to how the Norse mystics went about their practice of seiðr.

This is the point of this book: to master the actual structure, given authority by those who developed a specific practice (in history as well as today) through trial and error, thusly forming a tradition that worked consistently, and thereby delegated the successful elements to this form of Norse mysticism as we practice it today. Just as our ancestors have done, through deep immersion, discipline, and unflinching self-awareness, we will experience in the mythology, techniques, and regular application the viability of these timeless arts to our daily lives.

One of my favorite modern writers on ecstatic spirituality is Mircea Eliade (1907–1986). Eliade's studies focused on the ability of the shaman/mystic to practice spiritual veneration ecstatically, as well as each practitioner's ability to send the soul on a journey outside the body to transcendental realities. Eliade's interpretation of shamanism is universalistic (what the late Michael Harner later termed "Core Shamanism") and Eliade used the term "ecstasy" exclusively to indicate the ascent to a god-world motif, which he believed to be the core concept of "pure shamanism". Eliade further saw "ecstasy" as a condition which was controlled by the shaman; he understood that through his power of "walking between all worlds", the shaman had the ability to control not only outside unseen forces but also alter his own inner landscapes, thereby being a intercessory of spirits and of physical manifestation in the body, the mind, or on the land.

So we begin with the concept of inner space. What is inner space? According to *The Inner Journey Home*[5], A. H. Almaas states: "Our inner field is pure consciousness that is also pure potential for experience. How does this potential become actuality? How does the seed become a tree? To explore this we first need to remember that our soul is not a particular state or condition; it is the medium and locus where all states and conditions arise. The fact that all inner states and events are forms within and part of the soul means that the soul is in constant change ... One

---

[5] A.H. Almass, The Ridhwan Foundation, Shambhala Press, 2004, pg. 77.

thought follows another, one feeling leaves only to vacate the space for another. Inner sensations and movements are never still. Our inner space is like a multiple intersection at the center of a major city, where all streets and lanes are busy most of the time, with an incessant flow of traffic of various kinds and sizes of vehicles. Our inner space is not only busy with content, it is in incessant movement, transformation, development, evolution or devolution, expansion or contraction, and so on. These are the external forms of our soul's field of consciousness; s/he is rarely at rest, rarely settled. And when s/he is settled, this is only a momentary state like all other states."

This month our goal is to begin to simply notice our inner space and all that is happening with in it.

Lesson 1/3: Spirits.

Faring forth to the world of spirits is one of the most crucial and profound paths we as Norse Witches and Shamans will ever take. There are many methods to use in this skillset, and in the upcoming year we will experiment with a variety of them to get there. Traditionally, faring forth was evoked by inducing a trance state, during which one sent their Fylgja (Norse word for the soul part we all have that most resembles the Neo-Pagan term "astral body") where needed. The Völva would send her Fylgja forth into whatever worlds she thought an answer might be found; often the Well of Urd. Other techniques might be rhythmic movements and aggressive dancing, stomping, shaking or spinning a distaff, as well as chanting/singing simple songs. Through this, a Völva or seiðkona would induce a state of being where she would only be aware of her spiritual senses, giving her "Fetch" (Fylgja) her undivided awareness and attention.

But it's not just ways in which we can induce trance states that is our concern; we need to know how to deal with spirits we meet, where we are going to find them, and why we are seeking them out in the first place. We will work on faring forth each month during the full moon by participating in a Utiseta, which means in Old Norse "sitting-out".

Utiseta

Utiseta or "sitting-out" (also known as going under the cloak) is accomplished by a Völva or Vitki withdrawing to a secluded location and covering up with a hood, cloak, hide, or blanket, and then sitting upon a place of power like a burial mound, a grave site, or a power spot in nature, with the intention of faring forth and getting divine information.[6]

In this place of power, the Völva uses the solitude and the powerful energies to meditate and chant her way into trance-induced spells, Galdr and sacred songs, while seeming asleep, or (according to legend) even dead. According to historical accounts, during this process, it was important that no one spoke to the Völva. Most importantly, the Völva's name wasn't to be said out loud, as she was in a deep trance state and calling to her would interrupt the working, possibly with dangerous consequences.

In some of the accounts, the trance was entered by a huge and unnatural yawn, and the end of the trance was acknowledged in the same manner, suggesting that the practitioner's consciousness (or Fylgja) was issuing out through the mouth and returning the same way. This technique of trance work by "going under the cloak" was often practiced by men as well as women, and seems to be a part of the art of the Völva, the Vitki and the skald for seeking out hidden truths, foretelling the future, creating/sending malevolent will to attack others, or to seek out information in both Midgard or the other eight worlds.

The Sagas mention that through Utiseta, it was possible to cast spells which would cause physical events in Midgard such as drought, landslides and crop failure. Utiseta, sitting out) is also known as *sitja á haugi*, which means to "sit on a barrow". Why did it seem that the most effective location for this "under the cloak" technique was atop a barrow or grave? Probably in order for the practitioner to receive wisdom from the dead. It was said that there was always danger in Utiseta, as the person who dared

---

[6] For more information about Utiseta, I recmmend Evelyn Rysdyk's book *The Norse Shaman: Spiritual Practices of the Northern Tradition* (Destiny Books, 2017) or the Utiseta section of Raven Kaldera's book *Wightridden: Paths of Northern Tradition Shamanism* (Asphodel Press, 2007, pp, 43-60).

it might be attacked by the ghost (or the reanimated corpse who still stayed in the grave), or they might be found to be insane the next morning as their Fylgja never returned.

To be sure, I have out-sat many times with only good benefits, so I don't hesitate to do it. Moreover, a gravesite is not a required place to perform Utiseta; any quiet, secluded, power-rich place in nature can be utilized.

Rituals of Gratitude

As you know by now, the path of the Völva/Vitki is polytheistic, centering on a pantheon of deities from pre-Christian Norse/Germanic Europe. It adopts cosmological views from these regions, but it is important to remember this includes an animistic view of the cosmos in which the natural world is imbued with spirits, called *vaettir* in Old Norse and *wights* in Old English.

Deities and spirits are honored in sacrificial rites known as Blóts. A Blót is a ritual where food, drink, and other libations are offered freely as a form of sacrifice. Blóts are often accompanied by a Sumbel—the act of ceremonially toasting the gods or ancestors with an alcoholic beverage. As Norse Mystic practitioners we are familiar with engaging in rituals designed to induce an altered state of consciousness and visions (most notably seiðr) with the intent of gaining wisdom and advice from the deities, but practicing the ceremonial action of proffering regular offerings of gratitude and sacrifice as a form of gift exchange can be lost on many new Heathens coming to the path of the Norse Mystic.

In keeping with this idea of regular offerings and rites, I have to challenge you: How often do you honor any spirits in structured regular rites, offering freely gifts of sacrifice, without asking anything in return? Did you realize that it is through this act of regular sacrificial giving that you begin a lifelong rapport and relationship as co-creating partners with the Wights and the Gods? Although many solitary practitioners follow the path of the Völva/Vitki by themselves, they sometimes forget that this world view is actually polytheistic and animistic, and that they receive their power and gifts from all the nine worlds of the Norse Cosmos and the spirits who inhabit them. It is crucial that you hold regular ceremonies showing reverence, veneration, and gratitude for the spirit world you visit for messages, omens and healing. This regular act will keep you within the "flow", just as it does all shamanic practice, and even though you may not belong to a group of Kindred, you can still honor the seasonal times, as well as the Gods you serve in your own private space.

Practice: This month, besides your full moon out-sitting, pick a day and create a ritual which includes a Blót to the patron deity you serve, as well as to Odin and Freya, and to your Disir. Be sure to include the Landvaettir and your spirit guides or totems if you have any.[7]

Lesson 1/4: Song

Every indigenous shamanic path has some form or technique for which it becomes "known". In the Australian outback, the Aborigines are recognized by their use of dreamtime and their walkabouts. For Voodoo root workers it is the drawing of elaborate *veves* and the encouragement of full spirit-possession. In Scandinavian seiðr, what sets it apart from other paths of shamanism is that our Ancestors used singing (instead of or along with drumming or percussion) to attain a trance-like state and to come into contact with the Otherworlds. besides your intention, this is the most authentic tool that you will use in your work.

If we refer back to the saga of the Völva in Erik the Red, Thorbjörg explains to all present that she needed "those who could sing the song of the Völva." The Song helped to put her in to trance, and also "lured" in the Wights to aid in her spá.

As stated in the saga, "Sweet was the chanting; no one present had ever heard a fairer song." Even though the details of what the songs were comprised of are lost to history, we can still read that the Songs were described as "strong" or "harsh." Both then (and now) the songs used in

---

[7] To better get to know the spirits of the Norse cosmology, we will work through the book *Elves, Wights, and Trolls* by Kveldulf Gunderson, one chapter per month. Through his experience and insight, you will come to understand the personas of the spirits who inhabit the Nine Worlds, and the way we as seiðr-workers should approach them.

seiðr are known to often be of an ecstatic nature, and sometimes are created spontaneously.

However, since no ancient seiðr songs have been handed down to us to decipher, we must look to the folk songs of the surrounding areas still known to us today. In these forms of songs we can find some idea of structural possibilities. We have *Galdr* (singing runes) and *Galdralag* (magic-spell poetic meter), Saami *joik* (spontaneous shaman songs), the *Kaud* (or "*kvad*", which is basically poetry performed in front of an audience and set to music). I feel that the *varthlokkur* may still survive in the Swedish art of cow-calling known as *Kulning*).

How can song help us to access the spirit realms? We must re- learn the forgotten skills of magic singing left to us as a cultural heritage. Traditional mystical singing or "chanting" (i.e. the word en-chantment) is characterized by lengthy repetition, facilitating a trance state or a change of consciousness similar to the way drumming works. If you have ever heard Tibetan monks chanting, you will know what I am talking about here. That is the old, literal meaning of the word en-chantment. Today this can still be experienced by both the Völva trying to gain access to the Nine Worlds via the High Seat séance, as well as by her "posse" of singers in the circle. When we re-learn the basic human experience of letting go completely into singing, we come to see the true power of Song.

Sung messages, unlike simply "spoken" words, have a way of going directly to the heart of the listener without being first filtered by the brain. (Just think how your favorite song can come on the radio and suddenly change your mood, or inspire you to action!) Song is a way of moving power, strengthening the impact of the magical intent. It is a sure-fire way one can deeply touch the emotions of the listener, which in a High Seat séance means the otherworldly beings.

Both Norse and Celtic spiritual traditions have terminology given to the Songs of Magic. These Songs are known to come from a place of inspiration (in the literal sense, called *Odr* in the Norse, and *Awen* in the Celtic path, which come to the practitioner during states of ecstatic altered consciousness. This form of ecstatic singing can be seen worldwide in shamanic rituals of all traditions, as singing easily enhances and empowers rites of healing and other shamanic work. In the following months we will take an in-depth look at each of the practices and techniques of voice and song used by Norse witches, seiðkonas or spákonas.

Practice: For this, I am indebted to Kari Tauring[8], creator of the Völva Stav Manual. Ideally you should own and check out her entire manual, but for now you can start with her Stav voice exercises which she has generously made available to the public through Youtube. Please go to: https://www.youtube.com/watch?v=0G-0vC0wG40&t=39s

Lesson 1/5: Stav and Dis-Staff

In Nordic History there have been two kinds of magic practiced among the peoples of the Ancient North. One was Galdr, and the other was seiðr. Galdr develops one's will and self-control of one's *conscious* thoughts and perceived environment. It implements the use of symbols (not just language) for communication, spell-casting or divination. The symbols are usually the Futhark (or Futhorc) runes (although they can be any magical symbols), and those who use them with proficiency are known as *runemal* or Rune Masters. Someone doing Galdr will work in such a way that they are assured their will is heard by the Nine Worlds by forcefully yelling their willed intention into the cosmos. The Galdr work is almost always combined with a Runemaster's understanding and use of Runes as the magical cosmic vehicle of the Norse universe. (We'll learn more about Galdr in a future chapter.)

Seiðr, however, is about the voluntary loss of one's control of self, *conscious* awareness via a self-induced trance. It is about the uninhibited submersion of one's self into something outside the practitioner's known and recognized persona. (We'll talk more about this in the next section.) The practitioner has a different sort of understanding and control of themselves, of their parts, their capabilities, and all the tools they use at their disposal.

Back in the Iron Age, when Seiðr was a practiced form of occult work, as was the sybil work of a Volva, each station held different yet subtle specialties. These specialties could overlap, but each skillset or occult

---

[8] http://karitauring.com/

practice had a specific "tool of the trade" if you will, to designate what Art the Scandinavian esoteric practitioner was actually performing, and these tools also doubled as a outward symbol they carried when performing their chosen craft. They were known as the staff (Stav/Wand) of the Volva, or the distaff of the seidkonna.

The Stav was a long walking stick, probably dressed up with power objects that the Volva would use to "ride" into her journeys to the Otherworlds. The Stav was also seen by the Volva as Yggdrasil, a touchstone to keep her within reach of any of the Nine Worlds—and especially Midgard, when she needed to return from her oracle session.

For the seidkona, a Dis-staff was a long iron or wood stick bearing a round cage-like feature on the end, like a basket; it was sometimes made of bent-over branches (if on the end of a wood staff) or wrought iron. In the life of the everyday woman of the time, a distaff is used for spinning, and weaving or spinning is what the Norns do with our wyrd. It is also via the Norns that we might gain permission and access to see and touch these "strands of life and fate". So the seidkona's stick was shaped like—or in some cases, actually was—a distaff, as it mimicked a tool used in everyday life for spinning threads of twine. When a seidkona was going to alter reality, she sought the aid and blessings of the Nornir, so this staff was a representation of the weaving power she was gifted by the Wyrd sisters from the Well of Urd. Due to her ability to manipulate ongoing events around her—be it weather, fertility, or the cursing of a neighboring tribe for protection or malice—to see a woman holding a distaff was awe- and fear-inspiring.

The first of the Norns is Urd ("What Once Was"). Urd is the one who begins the thread of each of our Wyrds and stretches it out to hand to Her sister Verdandi. Verdandi means "What Is Coming into Being", and she is in charge of giving the length and knots to each strand. Finally, the Wyrd is handed off to Skuld ("What Shall Be"), and after adding whatever tangles, knots or fiber is needed to complete each strand, Skuld then cuts it; signifying an end to that particular persons Wyrd and life.

To hold a distaff and then to purposely journey to the Norns at their Well of Urd is a huge responsibility and requires precise skills in trance, as well as an understanding of Wyrd and weaving and spinning.[9] I wish for whomever reads this to know that they can choose what skillsets they are learning, which means their own choice of a Stav or a distaff. For me, a Volva is both a seer and a Witch, so she would use a Stav to wield her power much like a modern witch uses a wand. Each person called to this path might be both a Witch *and* a Shaman, so they might have a staff for each practice, depending upon the path they choose to work within at the time.

Lesson 1/6: Focused Surrender

Today's 21st century people who are heeding the call of the "shaman" often say they want to be true to their ancestral heritage. Perhaps they have been introduced to "core shamanism", but that may lead them to the ambivalent practice of cultural appropriation of the traditions and customs of indigenous peoples, or a mix of practices that does not seat them in a coherent cosmology. How many adept practitioners come into their true calling and power is done by finding *authenticity* in the Shamanic path they wish to learn.

One way to be authentic as a shaman is to work through the cultural heritage that one's Ancestors were tied to demographically and generationally. For me, working with my blood-line Ancestors is how I anchor my practice in a spiritual tradition combined with the genetic connection passed down through my DNA, with all the talents and family tendencies that DNA carries. A shamanic tradition that is a part of one's own "native" cultural heritage is the most powerful Tradition a person so inclined to this work can access. By staying within our bloodlines of Ancestry we get a direct line to the ancestral power found in our very

---

[9] For more on how the Volva's staffs resembled distaffs, check this article on the website of Solekoru: https://solekoru.com/en/2017/10/iron-age-seeress-and-magic-wand/. Daniel McCoy also mentions the distaff at: https://norse-mythology.org/concepts/Seiðr/

blood, bones and breath. As with other ancient cultures, our Norse/Germanic forebears were very in tune with nature. The "chain of command" of worship was first the Land, then the Ancestors, and *then* the Gods, in that order. Like all Pagan and shamanic paths, seiðr is inseparable from wild nature.

In reclaiming these arts, we are starting with Utiseta, and we will use a Stav (staff) which is a representation of Yggdrasil, and is also our physical axis or "touchstone" to our "portal" between the worlds. Your Stav can be a simple wooden stick or something more decorated; it should be between hip and shoulder height. Once you have your Stav, you will perform your own Utiseta on each month's full moon amongst the hills and trees. We will attempt to learn and sing the powers of earth and sea, of fire and ice, and of still air or howling wind. This offers a meaningful way of literally accessing our spiritual and magic practice via tradition and our Ancestral roots, while being wholly present in our own landscape and in our own time.

The Industrial Revolution, with all its eventual artificial intelligence, the machines that do our work, the electronics which do much of our thinking, and our "civilized" way of living as domesticated animals has removed us far from our natural instincts, not to mention the skillsets that would have been required if we still had our homes in the wild places outdoors. We don't hear or see the Landvaettir very well, as we have forgotten what they look like, sound like and feel like. We as a species have come to fear our very natural and primal home. It will take work and persistence to re-acclimate to the wild places outdoors, but you must re-learn that you are a creature if the Earth, just as the animals of the forest are. When you begin to get outside on a regular basis and become familiar with its patterns, its smells, and its rhythms, you will be amazed at your growth, how happy you feel, and how tuned in to all things you become. Your mistrust (and fear) of Jord and Her wild places will disappear with time.

Note that usually when you are out in nature and doing seiðr, you will experience natural power in a way that is a gentle and cleansing form of spiritual awareness and healing. However, there will be times during your practice when you might encounter a raw, wild power of Nature coming from the earth itself, harking to your song. These spirits are known as Jönar or Jotunfolk. They are not "bad' entities; just wild, raw ones. They might recognize your Stav as your outward tool of power and your station as a Völva, and try to gain access to you via your Utiseta. Do not fight it or be afraid; this is a good thing! The Jötnar are powerful spirits who understand the mysteries of Nature. Known as Etins, Thurs, or Risi; these ancient beings are the building blocks of life as we know it, so when they hearken to your out-sitting it is a very auspicious moment. But the point is that your Stav lends extra tactile, *physical* energy, as it literally becomes your conduit to the Worlds. That is why so many staves were found in graves of now-known seiðkona and Völvas.

So what is the best way to use your Stav while doing Seiðr? A tricky concept called *focused surrender*.

Focused surrender means letting yourself go into a mystical experience while staying focused on the intent and outcome. This concept was named *ergi* in Old Norse. The word *ergi* is often misinterpreted as a derogatory term meaning an effeminate male practicing Seiðr. *Ergi* actually meant handling spirit power through a voluntary loss of control, uniting ecstasy and consciousness. In the Viking Age, this was seen as unmanly, which meant being a Völva or seiðkona was in the realm of "women's work." Historically and today, in most circumstances of our daily lives, the female of our species could more easily surrender to the power of strong emotional tides, as women tend to be receptive in their make-up and physiology. Men tend (then and now) to run the other way from strong emotions, unless they were/are in battle. Moreover, many "manly-men" abhor the thought of "surrendering" themselves to be a receptive vehicle for strong, overpowering, frightening, and perhaps overwhelming emotions and sensations.

Unfortunately, folks today don't have a good understanding of what the Norse people were like, and the term *ergi* can be misinterpreted as a detrimental title for men able to practice this art of Norse mysticism. If a man could be more in touch with their "feminine side," then the male practitioner would be better able to surrender to the feelings, insights, and power only strong (ecstatic) emotions can provoke. For a man in the Viking Age (and even nowadays), to cultivate their ability to access the ecstatic via a form of opening and surrender to divine and esoteric powers can be seen by other "manly-men" as weak, vulnerable, and not "warrior-ready". By demonstrating the *receiving* qualities of seiðr, a Viking Age man would be classified as *ergi*. Even today we will find modern males for whom the idea of being a "man's man" *and* being receptive and open to emotional ecstatic experience during spiritual work might be looked down upon as a bad thing. It's fear of the unknown, and ignorance.

As we well know, in today's world not being a macho peak-condition manly warrior isn't a death sentence. (Back in the Viking Age on the other hand, if one was called "ergi", they were probably viewed as an emotional misfit and burden to their fellow warriors, and best left at home with the women and weaker folk.) Moreover, in that world, it would have been viewed as shameful for someone that should be out pulling their weight by pillaging and fighting to have to stay back with the "more fragile" villagers. Even today, with all the confusion over what gender roles each sex is to have or not have, men by nature have a strong aversion to appearing vulnerable or emotionally open.

Today men are trying to re-forge their own mysteries within Heathenism, but many are mistrustful about attempt seiðr practice because of the stigma of *ergi*, which isn't about sexual preferences or habits, and is all about simply being proficient at the skill of focused surrender. Thankfully, this misnomer doesn't stop numerous men from engaging in seiðr! I know some Vitkis who have chosen seiðr as a profession, and although the title they are reclaiming is "Vitki", the proper terminology would be *seiðmenn*, as the name *Vitki* means sorcerer. To finish up this topic we must remember that the foremost "ergi" deity we have to study among seiðmenn was, of course, none other than Odin himself—and as we see, God or not, The Old Man was taunted with the accusation of being "ergi". This taunt by Loki towards Odin in the *Lokasenna* was loaded with contradictory ideas, as Loki was also known to "gender bend" to get what he wanted. Unmanly as seiðr may have been seen as being, it is a great source of power, given that it could change the course of Wyrd itself, so Odin unabashedly learned it and used it, and ever after is understood as a force to be reckoned with in spite of being a seiðmann!

In view of this, the sacrifice of being maligned by others for the ability to alter Wyrd wasn't too bad of a tradeoff. After all, because Odin decided it was worth the ribbing, men (and women) can now look to Odin, the All-Father of the Aesir, as a prime example of a what a seiðmann can accomplish. The Old Man sought out seiðr training in this skill by Freya, the epitome of ecstatic mysteries embodied in female form. Odin is not just a Master of the Runes; he is the male patron of Wyrd weaving!

Practice: This month, take your Stav and begin the art of Stav in your outside location. Sit comfortably and hold your Stav in front of you, with the end embedded in the Earth in front of you. Ground and center; send your roots down into the Earth.[10] Close your eyes and visualize that the Stav between your hands is the World Tree. Extend your consciousness mentally into the Stav and downward—feel it extend downward through the roots of Yggdrasil—and then upwards, feeling the Stav open into branches and leaves, up toward the Sky and Asgard. Feel yourself becoming, for the moment, one with the Tree through your Stav. Open your mouth and let any vocalization out that wants to come through you, until the feeling subsides. Then pull your consciousness out of the Stav and back into the world. Pull up your roots, and thank the land-spirit and Yggdrasil.

Lesson 1/7: The Powers of the Magus

The concept of the Witch's Pyramid was first described in *The Ritual Book of Magic* by Clifford Bias, who states: "The Magus, the Theurgist, the True Witch stand on a pyramid of power whose foundation is a profound knowledge of the occult, whose four sides are creative imagination, a will of steel, a living faith and the ability to keep silent." This concept was expanded upon in T. Thorn Coyle's book *Make Magic of your Life*, which we will work through in this year. I ascribe to the same notion as Coyle: "The Witch's Pyramid as a five-sided model that helps us understand the interaction of five important magical principles: To Know,

---

[10] For a concise description of how to ground and center, see the "Beginning Place" chapter of *Neolithic Shamanism* (Krasskova and Kaldera, Destiny Books 2012).

To Will, To Dare, To Be Silent, and To Manifest." The Clifford Bias concept is pertinent whether you are a Norse Witch or a Witch from *any* tradition. Each of these principles are hinging upon each other, as together, unified, each concept forms a functioning cohesive flow of "complementary axioms".

Imagine that each of these five principles forms a side of an enclosed box. If any one of the sides to the box (as well as the top or bottom) is missing or has holes in it, the magical energy enclosed within this box will escape and the resulting intended magic will be ineffective. A modern-day Völva/Vitki fearlessly examines her/his "box" on a regular basis to seal up these holes or missing sides. At the same time, s/he corrects the missing sides in her/his own character.

One of the biggest sides of our magical box most Völva's or Vitki's overlook is the power of silence. "To Keep Silent" does not mean "to keep your rituals secret". It means to learn to become still within and without. Only in Silence can we have awareness of the subtle energies and kennings that are all around us. We use Silence to clear our mind of distractions in meditation. To fully become aware of subtle currents, instincts, emotions, and messages during Spa, it obviously requires us to have easy access to Silence.

Unequivocally, it *is* important to keep your powerful magical workings to yourself in silence so that a tender magical intention can't be crushed or thwarted by ill-wishing or negating thoughts; however, Silence means much more to a Witch than simply "not telling all". Silence therefore represents knowing and awareness, not just secrecy.

So we will take a chapter a month and work through the witches' box of power by doing every exercise presented in Ms. Coyle's book *Make Magic of Your Life*, as well as the book *A Witch's Book of Silence* by Katrina BlackHeart.

Please acquire both of these and begin exercises. Do all the rituals given in these two books, picking a chapter a to work through each month. Be sure to document in your journal what results you get working through these exercises.

Lesson 1/8: Your Body.

In this next year, we will discover how to use our body in the way it was designed: to be the interface for healing as well as a conduit for moving healing energy to the outside world. I will begin to teach you how to use different body postures taken from Scandinavian images to invoke specific energies in trance, inspired by the information I have found in the books by Belinda Gore found in the Optional Reading list in the final appendix. One reading this book might wonder how ritual postures or poses would further our work with Norse Mysticism. However, as Belinda Gore states, "artifacts left us a wide array of artwork that depicts ritual postures," which is true all over the world. She goes on to say, "In fact, like many other ritual postures from around the world, they appear to be designed to induce particular states of mind, especially trance states in which we can receive healing, learn about ourselves and the divine, and undergo spiritual changes for the better." Therefore, from the depictions of Freya holding the cup of mead with both hands, to how Odin is often depicted in holding his Stav—even in the Norse tradition we can find some very useful sacred ritual poses and postures.

In Seiðr, shaking, swaying, singing or even drumming alone is usually enough to induce a light trance state in most people. The rhythmic repetition of movement or sound has been shown to have a balancing effect on the human brain, bringing the two hemispheres in sync, thereby inducing varying states of altered consciousness. When you add to these proven forms of trance induction ritual poses that are mimicking the energies you are attempting to invoke, the process gets unexplainably much easier to facilitate. I have found, as others have, that by adding various ritual postures that are aligned with the intention of the body of work for the ritual being performed, the experience becomes significantly more "real" and powerful, since you are engaging the body in the ritual via sacred stance or postures.

As you will hopefully find, each posture brings a specific energy, intention, and "archetype" to the ceremonial process being worked. I feel it will add to your tool box to learn the very natural, but almost forgotten process of rediscovery of this method of activation and sacred pantomime while working in altered states of consciousness. So in most of the following month's chapters, I will dedicate a section on the adaptations of ritual postures into your curriculum. You will read about each one, then add them to your rites and out-sitting sessions, keeping the ones that work, and leaving the rest behind.

Finally, another aspect of my advanced studies or further immersion into our true power is one of balance, so in addition to the body postures for ritual, I strongly recommend that you begin a yoga practice with a very powerful intention—to create strong flexible bodies. It is essential to have a strong, capable, healthy physical body as this is the vehicle with which we travel through Midgard. Yoga is a very effective, easy, and safe way to bring unity to the mind and to the body, and even if you are very stiff, very overweight, or very non-physical, there is a yoga practice out there for you. If you want, you can look online for Howard D.'s practice of Viking Yoga.[11] It utilizes the Younger Futhark as body postures. I tend to prefer the Older Futhark, but it is still a great idea. (For those who prefer other forms of chi-moving exercise, t'ai chi and chi gong are also very good for helping with body consciousness and becoming adept at moving energy around the physical body.)

Lesson 1/9: Our Many Gods.

Norse/Germanic mythology has many, many Gods. This may take some getting used to if you are accustomed to monotheism, or the idea that the fewer the deities, the more advanced or sophisticated the culture. This is not true, especially as we are drawing on deity-names and personalities from over several centuries and a very large area. Different Gods would be more or less popular in different times and places, and this doesn't even take into account many lost local and tribal Gods.

In modern times, it's not that different in some ways; some Gods are more or less popular, and various Northern-religion groups honor their own selection within the array. most are grouped onto one of three pantheons: the Aesir (Gods of sky, war, and civilization), the Vanir (Gods of agriculture, food, sex, and love), and the Rökkr (Gods of wild nature

---

[11] http://vikingyoga.biz

and natural processes). Regardless of which pantheon you are or aren't drawn to, it's important to at least have a general idea of our Gods and their basic attributes. To start, go to the Northern Paganism website at http://www.northernpaganism.org and look in the sidebar. You will find online shrines to the Norse/Germanic Gods, including descriptions, prayers, poetry, rituals, and the ability to light a virtual candle. Every month you will choose at least five Gods and read about them. (You can do more if you like.) It doesn't matter which ones, although Odin and Freya should be read the first month, as they are the patron of Seiðr.

Lesson 1/10: Reading Material

This is the "meat" of this course, and is what will transform you from a seeker to an adept seer. You will be reading *The History of Runic Lore*, *Galdrs of the Edda*, and *Heathen Rites of Ancient Nordic Chronicles* by Swedish runologist Lars Magnar Enoksen.[12] You must also acquire *Neolithic Shamanism* by Raven Kaldera and Galina Krasskova, *Wyrdwalkers* and *Wightridden* by Raven Kaldera, plus *The Icelandic Book of Fuþark*.[13] All of these brilliant and talented Völvas/Witches/Northern Shamans/Norse Mystics have developed crucial concepts which aid in turning a seeker into a master.

For most of the books on this list, I suggest picking a book a day, and reading a chapter or section a night, taking notes on each book's subject matter. Kaldera and Krasskova's book *Neolithic Shamanism* is also a book of ninety exercises; for this first month, read and work on the introductory chapters and the first practice chapter, "The Beginning Place". Do all the exercises in that chapter this month

In addition, you'll find another list in the appendix at the back, labeled "Suggested Reading". While these are not required, I strongly suggest that you pick up a few of them and read them as adjuncts to your studies over the next nine months. Some of them are out of print and hard to find;

---

[12] Available through the website http://www.wardruna.com/shop/
[13] Available from The Icelandic Magic Company, https://www.icelandicmagic.com/collections/books

some aren't specific to a Norse/Germanic practice but are very useful for any spiritual practice in general, and some are specialist books for those who are drawn to particular practices within this field of study.

Lesson 1/11: Immersion Into the Voluspa.

For every chapter of this anthology, I will give you seven verses from the *Voluspa*. This mythic poem was created from the *Codex Regius*, but translations are also found in the *Hauksbok*, and the *Elder Edda*. Read the examples I share in this book as a part of each month's lessons as they appear, then cross-reference translations found in the *Hauksbok* and the *Elder Edda*. (Both are available online in multiple places; just use a search engine.) You will work, then, to create your own meanings and write them in your journal. Combined, all three texts give a good overview of the sixty-four verses via cross referencing and language glossary. You must do your own research to find the version of the Voluspa that works best for you, in your understanding of the written work. I will begin with verses 27, 28, 29 and 30, to begin this odyssey, but after that we will go in sequence.

Why study these verses? There is a great deal of value and enlightenment that comes when one begins the practice of thoroughly examining and ruminating on the *Voluspa* and the Meditative Paradigms as a main line to the mysteries of Seiðr. This astoundingly "simplistic" act of meditation and reflection on primary sources cannot be underestimated!

Read seven verses per month of the *Voluspa*, beginning the evening you begin a new chapter. After reading them repeatedly for one night a week (I pick Friday, Freya's day), on the last Friday of the month you then will begin to create your own versions. Make notes in your journal about how these words in a myth make sense to you as a Modern Völva/Vitki by applying these pictures transposed onto a 21st century Mystical way of living. Even if it's just a word or two, connect with these writings weekly, at night, before bed.

The goal and purpose of this immersion into written prose is to go with the writings and pull out the real meaning as they pertain to you, the living, breathing Völva/Vitki. These writings of deep wisdom are subtle, but with much investigation, they can open doors that might have been closed before. Feel free to cross-reference any insights with other historical texts or Norse-related material, not just my list of books.

May the fates bless our journey together and may you step into your power as a Völva/Vitki!

The Voluspa, Verses 27–30:

27. She knows that Heimdall's hearing is hidden
under the heaven-brightholy tree.
A river she sees flow, with foamy falls,
from Valfather's pledge.
Know ye yet, or what?

28. Alone she sat without, when came that ancient
dread Æsir's prince; and in his eyes she gazed.
"Of what wouldst thou ask me? Odin! I know all,
where thou thine eye didst sink in the pure well of Mim."
Mim drinks mead each morn from Valfather's pledge.
Know ye yet, or what?

29. The Host-father gave to her rings and a necklace,
useful discourse, and a divining spirit:
she saw wide and far over every world.

30. She saw Valkyriur coming from afar,
ready to ride to the gods' people:
Skuld held a shield, and Skögul another.
Gunn, Hild, Göndul, and Geirskögul.
Now are tallied Herian's maidens,
ready to ride over the earth, the Valkyriur.

1. For silence I pray all children,
great and small, sons of Heimdall
they will that I Valfather's [Odin's] deeds recount,
men's ancient saws, those that I best remember.

2. I remember Jötuns early born,

those who have reared me of old.
I remember nine worlds, nine wood-wives,
the great measuring tree, beneath the earth.

3. When time was young, where Ymir dwelt,
was no sand, no sea, nor cool waves;
earth existed not, nor heaven above,
A chasm gaped, and grass nowhere.

Month 2: Journey Into Yggdrasil

In the last chapter, we were introduced to our core concepts of the year: the Self, the Staff, the Song, the Seat, the Spirits, and in this chapter we will access these concepts via immersion through the Mind, the Body, Luck, Runes, and Calling. Here is how each for me these concepts equates with the other:

- Self/Soul Parts/Luck
- Staff/Body/Nature/Physical Location
- Song/Calling
- Seat/Mind
- Runes/Spirits

When we begin to use and combine these core concepts of adept seiðr practice, we begin to see how Wyrd is a fluid interwoven tapestry. If any of the elements are maligned or excluded there is a tangle in a thread of our Wyrd, and eventually a hole in the tapestry. During Month 2 we are going to begin to address these individual concepts while visiting one of the Nine Worlds via the world tree, Yggdrasil.

Lesson 2/1: Seiðrstallr.

In the last chapter we approached the idea of creating a special place in nature for your Utiseta, but this month it's now time to study the concept of a *hof*, a *hörgr*, and a *Seiðrstallr*. If you haven't done it already, it is very important to create a sacred, hallowed, space to perform your Spa and seiðr work. This can be a whole building, a room, or even a simple altar space at which you will do your workings. This is done for two reasons. First, it is useful to have a place set aside and slowly infused with your repeated magical work and intentions, thereby forming a familiar portal to the access to the other worlds. Second, it forms a microcosm in a macrocosm, which allows you the safety and security to hold an open doorway while traveling or faring forth to any of the Nine Worlds of Yggdrasil.

Making your *hof*, *hörgr* or your high seat area (called a *Seiðrstallr*) is a very personal and essential first step in your daily, weekly and monthly workings. To hallow a space, one could use salt water, recels incense, a candle, ringing bells, singing a song, a poem or invocation read aloud, waving a Thor's Hammer, Galdring runes in the various directions, or any combination of these activities. In the *Landnámabók,* it tells of how the Icelandic people would claim land by walking the borders carrying fire, and lighting fire in the center of the land.

Lesson 2/2: Divination Protocol.

The type of magic used for divination purposes was known as spá, (or in a slightly archaic English or Scottish term, spae) which I go over in Chapter 1. It is often referred to as spá-craft or spae-craft, and the practitioners of spá are called spá-kona's or spae-wives. Because Spa is such an integral part of Seiðr, we will again (briefly) address ways that today's modern 21st century Völvas or Vitkis use Spá.

Spá is the art of determining *ørlög,* (Ørlög is literally "ur", meaning ancient or primeval, and "lög" is law, so ørlög is the law of how things will be, laid down by Wyrd or fate by the three Norns, and is understood to include inherited destiny from past family members.) This is usually done by intuition or personal gnosis, with the aid of articles of divination, like the runes, bones, blood, or bird/nature augury. Also, many modern Völvas use divination tools like tarot cards and the pendulum.

Spá is one of the most useful tools we can access, as it allows us the opportunity to cross-reference and double-check our insights and trance visions. When we sit upon the high seat, it is imperative that we are clear on our visions and messages from the Nine Worlds. Sometimes we can be puzzled by the information we receive, and via Spá we can clarify much in the ways of mysterious or unclear kennings.

However, no matter whether you're using Futhark or Futhorc runes, Tarot, bones, or other methods, it's good to have some kind of opening ritual to use when you are doing a serious session of divination. The Northern Shamanism Guild has put together such a protocol, used here with permission. This will be one of your assignments for this month. Make this protocol a priority, because you will be doing divination on a variety of subjects over the next few months.

Our Guild finds this protocol to be extremely useful, and we've taught it to multiple people who aren't even part of the Northern Tradition. It can be adapted to any animistic/polytheistic worldview. Doing it every time before divining helps to focus, and eventually if you do it long enough, just beginning the prayers or song or chant will bring you into a space where you are open to the messages coming through.

While the structure of this protocol is the same for everyone in our Guild, the way we do it is different for each person. Some write spoken prayers for each part. Some of us sing a song that takes in all eight parts, or multiple songs. At least one uses multiple cloths, unfolded one at a time, with the words embroidered upon them. One young woman in another tradition who had severe learning disorders that interfered with her ability to remember words made a cloth with eight patchwork pieces, so that she could look at each one in turn and say a silent, spontaneous prayer. Decide what is going to work for you, with all eight steps.

1) Cleansing the Space. Words asking that this space be clean and clear, that all messages might come through. It's very useful to have a dedicated cloth that you spread out at this time, on which to do your work. Some people sprinkle salt water, some sweep the cloth symbolically with a tiny broom, some just blow on it.

2) Asking for a blessing from a Gate-Opening Deity. In the Northern Tradition, we have two: Heimdall and Mordgud. Appeal to the one who seems closer to you. (Every tradition has its gate-opening deity; one Pagan woman we taught this to uses Ganesha in this spot.) We do this because Gate-Opening Gods not only open the "doors" to your signal further than you can, They can guard that Gate so that nothing dangerous to you comes through it, into your head.)

3) Asking for a blessing from a deity who has agreed to aid you in this work. There are many Gods who can aid with your divination—telling you when you're messing up, advising you on how to be clearer and cleaner, etc. In the Northern Tradition, Vor (one of the Handmaidens of Frigga) is a specialist in divining. Frigga herself, it is said, knows much about the future. Odin and Freya are both patrons of Seiðr/spae. Hela, as Death, is wise and far-seeing. There are probably others—ask formally and see who shows up to help you. (If you're not Northern Tradition, ask deities in

cosmologies you work with.) Then ask for their blessing when you do this protocol.

4) Ask for the blessing of the diviners who have walked this road before you. They strove and experimented so that we have these techniques. If you are a diviner, you are part of that great lineage.

5) Ask for the blessing of the Ancestors. Honor our Dead who lived and died, invented great things and made terrible mistakes, and left us their legacies, so that the human race might still be here.

6) Bless the person who is asking. Even if that's you.

7) Bless the tools you are using. Runes, Tarot, shagai, I Ching—whatever they are, those spirits work hard for you.

8) Formally and ritually ask for clarity. You don't want your inner baggage getting in the way of the interpretations; you want to be as clean and objective as possible. Ask for this.

Try this protocol—you'd be surprised how much it will help! Good luck in piercing the veil of hidden knowledge.

Lesson 2/3: Yggdrasil.

The generally accepted meaning of Old Norse Yggdrasill is "Odin's horse", meaning "gallows". This interpretation comes about because *drasill* means "horse" and *Yggr* is one of Odin's many names, specifically referring to his aspect as the Sacrificed God. The Poetic Edda poem *Hávamál* describes how Odin sacrificed himself by hanging from a tree, making this tree Odin's gallows. This tree is generally thought to be Yggdrasil. The gallows has been called "the horse of the hanged", and therefore Odin's gallows may have developed into the expression "Odin's horse", which then became the name of the tree.

Another possible etymology uses the term *yggr* ("terror"), but not in reference to Odin's title, and so Yggdrasill would then mean "tree of terror". Yet another one is translated as "yew pillar", deriving *yggia* from *igwja* (meaning "yew-tree"), and *drasill* from *dher-* (meaning "support"). Yggdrasill is known sometimes as an Ash tree, and sometimes as a Yew.

For me, personally, Yggdrasil is all these things and one more: an actual portal for access to the Norse Nine Worlds. In my first book, I have the reader make a map of the Nine Worlds using a bedsheet to familiarize themselves with the topography. As many Traditions have a World Tree as an otherworldly entry, it is no accident that Odin chooses Yggdrasill as the place to offer himself to himself for the runic wisdom. He chose the World tree because it was the portal to all other states of consciousness, and to seek the runic wisdom there says volumes to the power and wisdom that's available if one simply chooses to make the entire tree a road way to otherworldly understanding. To make a map of the Nine Worlds in relationship to Yggdrasill's roots and branches is *the* surest way to learn your way around. It is my belief that you can't know where your heading to with much success if you don't have a map of the area.

For this month's work, I will share the way I learned to map out Yggdrasill, and I recommend you do the same, whether on paper, on fabric, or in the dirt. Make yourself a map of the Nine Worlds, and learn everything's positioning so you can easily move to and from Midgard and feel secure, safe, and deft with navigation.

Exercise: Making a Map of Yggdrasill.

This exercise has no time constraints, as it will hopefully become an ongoing project. You will be learning to create your Portal to the other worlds as a tree, with attention paid to the nine "directions" that branch off from this Tree, as well as influence life here on earth. Building your own representation of Yggdrasill will help you visualize and assimilate the concepts of Microcosm/Macrocosm. Moreover, you will gain proficiency at finding your way through the Norse cosmology, as this "picture" will become a map of what you have come to know within the direction of each world.

In this exercise, you will be physically creating where each World's elements lie, and what they contain for you, in the form of a large drawing/painting. The initial time frame will be about a week or so as you first begin to draw, paint, and explore what a sacred area holds for your practice at this time. Images, colors, and associated entities may change for you as you journey along your path. You will need a plain white bedsheet (king-size works best, but choose a size you can sit/stand within comfortably), fabric paints, and markers.

1) Take your canvas, spread it out, and sit in the middle of it. (This exercise is best done outdoors, but inside is OK too).
2) Use your marker and create an equal-armed cross over the entire space of the sheet. This cross will represent the world tree known as Yggdrasil.
3) Near the top of your cross, draw a large circle and write the word Asgard.
4) Next draw two circles on either side of the first circle, slightly lower down the sheet. Mark the left one Vanaheim and the right one Jotunheim. Be sure to leave plenty of room, as you will be filling in each circle with images or other artwork that represents any energies invoked by you on your sacred journey.
5) Make a circle in the middle of the tree, on the lines of the cross and name it Midgard.
6) Draw two more circles slightly lower than the one you drew for Midgard, one on the left and one on the right, naming the left Niflheim, and the right Muspellheim.
7) Finally draw three more circles on your tree, this time at the very bottom of the cross with the far-left circle named Svartalfheim, the middle circle named Helheim, and the far right circle named Alfheim.
8) When you have drawn your Tree, sit or stand in the middle of your sheet and attune yourself to this space. Visualize the Great Tree growing up around you, from the earth to the sky, with you as part of its trunk. You will do this every time before working on it.
9) Then start to fill in the blank spaces of each of the Nine Worlds with images that invoke for you the power and energies of each realm and all its associations, beginning with Midgard. These can be painted pictures, symbols, words and names; for example, colors, elements, animals, or Deities. You can also add people from the sagas or actual history, and you can include your own ancestors if you feel their presence adds power to bring these places alive for you. Continue this process with each of the World's until you have your entire Tree built

on this sheet adequately enough to truly feel, visualize and experience the entirety of your cosmos perimeters.[14]

There is no time limit, so take as many days as you feel you need to really fill in your portrait. Steep yourself in each place, symbol, animal, element, and associated entity that carries the power you seek to bring your Tree to life. It took me a few weeks to accomplish this exercise, and was of profound use in aiding me to manifest sacred space in a much more tangible way when I stepped into my Seiðrstallr to work.

Lesson 2/4: Soul Part: Hamingja.

As mentioned in the Introduction, today (especially in the world of Core shamanism) it is popular to think of the self as having three components: a body, a mind, and a soul. These three parts combined form a single being that can be clearly and cleanly separated into functioning parts that work to effectually interface within its environments (mundane world and spiritual world respectively); at least conceptually. We then come to see, as a Norse Shaman, the understanding of the importance of the lines that separates a self and its specified parts creates the concept of workable vehicles that are fairly absolute and viable.

Like all shamanic traditions, the Norse viewed a person as having many parts to their spirit and body that created the entity of a healthy functioning person. Luck, called the Hamingja (pronounced "HAM-ing-ya"), was very pivotal to the way a person lives a full healthy, productive life. It wasn't just viewed as simply "chance" or fate; it was seen as a part of that person, much like a spirit, and even could be passed down to family members, whether the "luck" was good or bad. When our Hamingja is good, all the rest of our existence is smooth and flowing; we are doing what we are called to do with very little resistance. Our Hamingja is

---

[14] You can fill in everything from the Eddas, or books of Norse mythologies, or the visual perspectives of modern artists. An alternate perspective can be found in the book *Pathwalker's Guide to the Nine Worlds* (Raven Kaldera, Asphodel Press, 2007).

directly connected to our Wyrd, and particularly our Orlog; so in the months to come, we will focus on working on these parts of our selves; thereby creating a hale, strong whole.[15]

Author Bettina Sejbjerg Sommer eloquently states about the Norse concept of Hamingja: "...Luck was a quality inherent in the man and his lineage, a part of his personality similar to his strength, intelligence, or skill with weapons, at once both the cause and the expression of the success, wealth, and power of a family."[16] We see "luck" isn't just about whether or not we are gifted by winning stuff or that we never seem to lose at games we play. Having a good hamingja is about owning a long running streak of joyous, calm, and abundantly vibrant living, with good fortune that follows generations of our family members due to the choices and actions we choose to play out. It is an extension of our Wyrd, and it behooves us to keep that "luck" good, by paying attention to the consequences of our thoughts and deeds to see if they might have bad ramifications to our descendants, reverberating generations down the road.

So what do we know about the Hamingja? *Víga-Glúms saga 9* mentions it as something that can be passed to unnamed family members, and in the Hávamál we read:

> Wealth will pass,
> Men will pass,
> You too, likewise, will pass.
> One thing alone
> Will never pass:
> The fame of one who has earned it.

The name Hamingja was also used to indicate happiness, and that is what it means in modern Icelandic. We also understand it is known as "luck" but I feel many folk are stopped short in today's world when trying to understand the Old Norse concept of Luck. Luck isn't so much about

---

[15] For more writings on Hamingja, I recommend the Pagan Princesses' blog post at http://www.paganprincesses.com/hamingja-the-embodiment-of-luck/.
[16] *The Norse Concept of Luck. In Scandinavian Studies*: Volume 79, No. 3. p. 275.

being "charmed" or "gifted" by a miraculous gift of Fate. I feel it is entwined into our Orlog, and it is more akin to the concept of "karma" and ancestrally passed traits, inherited in our very DNA. Hamingja is part of our genetic code, and luck can be earned as well as worked to be better!

Have you ever met some poor sod who seemed to be the epitome of the song "A Man of Constant Sorrow?" This person always has bad luck; he never can hold down a job, or a meaningful relationship, he has a drinking and gambling problem that leaves him in trouble with the law and his money lenders, etc. Even the few times our Sorrowful Joe would try to change his destiny,—for example, to go apply for that new job that would get him on the right path—his alarm clock wouldn't go off, and on the way to the interview he would get a flat tire (with no spare in the trunk), so he never got the job. It seems he can never get a break, and his life is consistently in the toilet. Unlucky Joe has even sought help, but when he is given very wise counsel, he turns a deaf ear and falls back into a life of trouble and unhappiness. So as an observer, we scratch our heads and wonder why Joe's life seems to be so full of bad luck.

As a Norse Heathen and Völva, I instinctually sense that Joe has bad inherited Orlog. He has inherited a family string of bad misfortune, bad behaviors, and bad life choices which started centuries back with a foolhardy and careless relative. This ancestor probably had some incident that set him on a path of dishonorable behavior—perhaps he stole something from a friend of his, which in turn led him to becoming unwilling to welcome this friend into his family home. (Not to show hospitality to your kindred was actually viewed as a very major social injustice back then.) This action, in turn, led the vile ancestor to become an outcast in his tribe, so he began to drink a lot to drown his disconnection from the village, which in turn lead to violent outburst, which lead to him in a fit of rage killing his wife, which of course led to him being punished to pay the blood debt to her family, which finally led to him dying bitter, reviled, and alone. Upon his death, his "luck" (Hamingja) was passed to his child, and this string of unfortunate events followed the entire family line to poor Joe whom we find today; sad, dejected, and defeated before he even started.

OK, so seeing as none of us want to be Unlucky Joe, how—if we recognize this sort of pattern—can we change it? Or can we? Yes, we can, via the process of working our Wyrd, as well as taking real-time steps each day of diligent change that will lead to improving a bad Hamingja.[17]

Lesson 2/5: The Power of Intention Put to Song

After attempting our second months' work of Utiseta (out sitting) as a journey to the well of Hvergelmir, we must now come understand the power of song to a Völva/Vitki and for the practice of seiðr. This month we will learn the art of "vardlokkur" and how this song was used by our ancestors to sing their way into weaving wyrd and into the other worlds.

> "The women now formed a circle around the platform on which Thorbjorg was seated. Gudrid recited the chant so beautifully and well that no one who was present could say he heard a chant recited by a lovelier voice. The seeress thanked her for her chant, adding that many spirits had been drawn there now and thought it lovely to lend ear- spirits who had before wished to keep their distance and give no hearing. And now many other things are apparent to me, which earlier were hidden "[18]

What is the vardlökkur? It is the chanting, or singing, that occurs during seiðr séance (and some other shamanic rites) in the Northern/Norse tradition. The word roughly means "spirit attractor" or "spirit caller". A vardlökkur is the song that actually lures in the spirts that witness a working Spá session. It gains us access to the well of Urd, where all Spá kennings come from.

Vardlokkur is a song, made up on the spot for the occasion, and is essential to the success of a Seiðr séance ritual that is performed. Remember, the key of seiðr is an altered state leading our Fylgja (fetch)

---

[17] For another look at soul parts, please see Diana Paxson on Hyge-Craeft at https://hrafnar.org/articles/dpaxson/norse/hyge-craeft/

[18] *Erik the Red's Saga.*

into other worlds, and singing a good vardlökkur gets us there. This "soul singing" is the Norse tradition's "direct line" to that state.

A vardlökkur also serves the role of guiding the Völva through the seiðr séance via a sung intention that was created at the time of the Workings for a particular reason. This sacred song helps a Völva (whether working alone or with a "posse" of Spá workers) through their trancework and journeying, allowing them to "see" more clearly while faring forth. The singing of a vardlökkur allows a Völva to tap into the roots of Yggdrasil in a more direct manner, and she then can get more productive resources from her access to the World Tree.

The final component to a *vardlökkur* (or for that matter any song sung out loud for seiðr) is that it involves breath (also called *Önd*) which is sacred and magical in the Norse Mystical tradition. By using your *Önd* via singing a *vardlökkur* of your magical intention, an impromptu song becomes a very powerful thing. The more involved a *vardlökkur* is in a ritual, the more it was traditionally believed to ensure the ritual would have success. I believe that the song of seiðr, the *vardlökkur*, has three predominant traits:

❖ It is sung while entering and then maintaining an altered state of consciousness, or trance state.
❖ It has a definite purpose and clear goal.
❖ It is not composed or constructed.

So what does this mean? How then does one *do* vardlokkur? I have found that the easiest way is to condense your intention into a three-syllable phrase and then intone those syllables, making your song a type of auditory sigil. For example; take a basic intention worded like this: "Disir come to me, at the well I wish to be; Disir aid me so, Niflheim is where I wish to go." Then reduce it to three syllable phrases: "Disir to me, Well I'll be, Aid me so, Niflheim I go!" That's your intention spoken in roughly three-syllable phrases. Now we'll alter it further, As you go into trance, give each phrase a melodic tone. This will allow you to easily carry the intention with you via song or intoned sounds. Choose a melody or set of tones you can remember that makes it easy to sing these phrases to a simple song, and sing for a period of time until you arrive in the other worlds and your journey begins. For example, you might sing the above three-syllable phrase to "I'm a Little Tea Pot", or a simple lullaby-type melody, or you can simply use intoned sounds. This involves extending the dominant vowel sounds taken from each word as shown in last month's lesson by Kari Tauring. (Example: The first line "Disir to me" would sound like: *DEE-sarrrAHtooomeeee*, all sort of flowing into one another, and so on.

Lesson 2/6: Sacred Postures.

How is your yoga practice going? Are you doing one regularly yet? If you recall, last month I informed you I was going to introduce ritual body postures. Each body posture can lead into the alternate reality—or a different field of consciousness—when performed in conjunction with the proper rhythmic accompaniment of approximately 210 beats per minute (this is 3-4 beats a second), performed with a drum or rattle. This method stimulates all senses, and helps to experience a deeper state of consciousness. These trance states generate longer-lasting feelings of euphoria, joy, and clarity as well as the certainty of being sheltered in the connectedness of all things. This method of ritual body posture is a very safe technique, which also stimulates one's own healing abilities.

To enter repeatedly and purposefully into a state of trance and to tune in to a different field of consciousness produces changes of the biochemical processes within the body. The experience of these feelings does have an effect on the unfolding of one's own being without being connected to conditions, demands, and dependency. In the state of trance, which is a higher awareness of the inner world, one is able to connect oneself with a different information field of consciousness that constantly creates itself anew, with new insights.

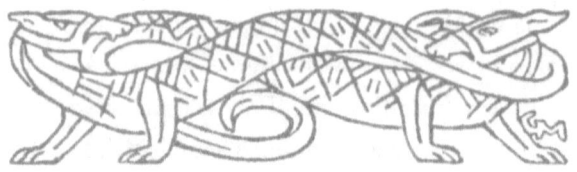

First Pose: Freya and the Sacred Mead Posture.

In Norse mythology, the Mead of Poetry is a mythical beverage that "whoever drinks of it, becomes a skald or scholar", thereby able to recite any information and solve any question. This myth was reported by Snorri Sturluson, who was a devout Christian, so I feel most of what the sacred mead really signified, was lost to him. The drink of mead is a vivid metaphor for poetic inspiration, often associated with Odin the god of ecstatic worship, be it a berserker rage or poetic inspiration (Óðr). But

when we dig deeper into the Norse mysteries, we see that the being who gave Odin that power was Freya, and to this day it is traditional in a Scandinavian Blót to have a woman pour out the mead in a horn and then hand it to a male to drink.

Why? Because by performing this physical ritual act, we are showing in a outward demonstration that we understand that in order to receive the gifts of divine understanding, inspiration, and ecstasy, one must be willing to surrender and receive the gifts as they come, via the term we learned in the last chapter—Focused Surrender. So when in ritual a woman fills the Horn with mead and then serves it, this is a ritualistic re-creation of how the Norse view the way Óðr is passed and received.

Freya is *the* goddess whom this understands this concept well, as seen in the story of the Brísingamen Necklace. The necklace Freya longs for is not simply a necklace. She decides to surrender sexually to each of the four dwarves (whom themselves represent the four elements that are the building blocks of life: earth, air fire and water) as they boldly request payment of enjoying her body for four consecutive nights of pleasure. By this story, we learn the compromise of desiring mastery of our environment through the act of focused surrender. With Freya and the Dwarves, we also learn of the sacrifice we must be willing to give for it, by the metaphors provided: sleeping with four powerful and scary dwarves, opening ourselves up to receive raw unbridled power, and then proudly displaying our hard-won "gifts" for all the world to see.

When we become an open vessel, we are able to receive the "Mead" of ecstatic inspiration. The necklace was, for me, simply a metaphor of the outward expression of those Folk who have drunk of the "sacred mead" and willingly yielded to the trials and tests one must surmount to drink of its sweetness. People who have tasted the "Mead" have a wisdom and kenning about them that is as obvious as a golden amber necklace worn on a flawless bare throat.

In most Norse Pagan rites, mead is used as a offering, so for your first posture, I wish to have that act understood, activated, and the doorway you use to begin every ritual and spiritual workings; thereby becoming the bearer of sacred Óðr.

Stand with a horn or large cup in both of your hands, ideally full of mead. As you gaze into the liquid, feel your connection via this physical item as a Sacred connection to all divine inspiration of our Norse ancestors. Hold the horn overhead and ask that it be imbued with the wisdom and inspiration of the Ancient Skalds, the seiðkona's, and for a moment link your physical being with the timeless magics of Spá and your Ancestors.

Lower the Horn, and hold it in front of you, visualizing all in your life you are attempting to transform with your Wyrd working. Blow your breath into the mead, and will your Wyrd to be transformed in the liquid imbued with Sacred Ond.

Give thanks for this magic and pour some of the mead out as an offering, then take a deep drink to bring the sacred mead's power into your body. You are now ready to continue your Spa work, whatever the intentions for the ritual might be.

Lesson 2/7: First Runic Divination

Throughout each chapter (month) we will begin the process of otherworld journeys. These are to be done during your monthly full moon Utiseta as an exercise to increase your experience (first hand) with many of the Nine Worlds.[19] After having developed and practiced your protocol, the next step is to do a divination to see if the following journey is for you.

Note: Otherworld journeys are a major path of growth and discovery, but they must be approached with reverence and seriousness. There are many entities out there who care not for our human kind, or our safety. The beings that live in the Nine Worlds, their protocols, and even the topography must be thoroughly addressed and understood when faring forth.

The Nine Worlds are not a Disneyland playground for us to wander around in without invitation and good reason. A journey there is not just wandering around in our own fantasies. It is actually sending a part of our souls to another world, populated with its own People who have their own Agenda, which might not include you. Not everyone is welcome in every world, or with every God or Spirit. Just like here in Midgard, some people will have a strong affinity with you and become friends, and some will prefer that you stay away and never come to their house, and many will be in between. For your own safety, it is important to check before every otherworld journey to see if you should go.

Our first journey will be to the world of Vanaheim, the beautiful world of the Vanir tribe of Gods, the deities of agriculture, food, sex, and love. Vanaheim is a green, earthy, pastoral world where every season feels like it will last forever. We are journeying there to meet with Freya, the Goddess of Love, Springtime ... and the patroness of Seiðr. To find out if this journey is safe for you, deal one Futhark or Futhorc rune (or your own personal runic symbols) for each question and consider it:

1) Am I ready to journey to another world?
2) Should I make this journey to Vanaheim?
3) Is Freya willing to speak with me?
4) Is there anything else I should know about this matter?

---

[19] If you do not have a lot of experience doing what most Norse Mystics call trance work, journeying, or faring forth, I recommend reading Diana Paxon's book *Trance-Portation* (Weiser Books, 2008).

Before each journey, you will be asking questions 2, 3, and 4 again. If you are not sure whether the reading is positive, ask your teacher (if you are working with me), or get a second reading from a professional. If the runes pulled are troublesome, don't go. Wait a month and try again. (You can draw a rune to ask, "Should I do this at a later time?" Sometimes the timing isn't right.) Three negative readings, and either you shouldn't be going there at all because the denizens of that world will not get along with you, or something else is wrong and you need to consult a professional diviner about it.

Lesson 2/8: Journey to Vanaheim to Visit Freya.

Before taking a journey to any world (once divination says it is right), you will need to make an offering to the spirits of that world, and to the Gods you want to visit. As an offering to the spirits of Vanaheim, one good suggestion is donating food to a food bank or other organization that feeds the hungry. Traditional offerings for Freya herself might be honey, mead, amber and/or golden jewelry, strawberries (her favorite fruit) or strawberry candy, sweet pastries, or small figures of cats. Her colors are gold, green, white (her warrior aspect) and deep purple-grey (the Sacred Seidkona).

1) Prepare for your journey by creating a sacred space that is hallowed, and by preparing your body and your spirit to fare-forth. You may read this journey outline a few times to put into memory the key points.
2) Set up an altar (if only temporary) for Freya, in Her colors, choose something to offer, and place it on the altar. Ask Her to guide you to Her home and give you what wisdom She thinks is best.
3) Begin by centering yourself on your seat, covering your head with your cloak or eye cover, and beginning to rhythmically tap your Stav.
4) Breathe deeply but naturally in 4 counts in/hold-pause/then out four counts until your mind is cleared and you begin to see the veil of the Otherworld mist form behind your eyes in the darkness. Begin to sing your vardlokkur.
5) As the mist forms, state your intention out loud that you are going to the world of Vanaheim to speak with the Goddess Freya. Call on the

Futhark rune Jera for Vanaheim, and Fehu for Freya. (One of the arts of the Seidkona is that she can speak while still traveling to the otherworlds.)

6) When the mist clears, you should see the starting point, the World Tree Yggdrasil. Greet your Disir (ancient female ancestral guardian spirits) and any other helping spirits who may accompany you. Tell them of your intention to go to the Green World of the Vanir.

7) View Yggdrasil and go to your destination via your map of the World Tree and the Norse Cosmos.

8) When you arrive at your destination, look at all that is around you and take it all in. The sights, the sounds, the smells, the air temperature, etc. Start walking the direction that seems right.

9) Ideally, Freya will appear to you as you move through this world, since you have checked to see if She will speak with you, and made an offering. She may appear in a field, or in a building. When you come to Her, be respectful and listen to what She has to tell you. Do not argue with Her—this is not the time, while standing in Her home. Thank Her for Her wisdom when She is done.

10) After your mission is accomplished (or not) and it's time to return, go in the same manner you got there, re-tracing your steps through the Green World, through Yggdrasil and back to your starting point where the otherworld mist begins to form. Say thanks to all your helpers and your Disir by offering a gift for their service.

11) Be sure to write in your journal all the events as soon as you are awake and grounded in the here and now. Pound your Stav 3-9 times forcefully as you stand up, to place yourself fully back into Midgard.

Lesson 2/9: Reading Material and Exercises.

1) Read and work on the next two chapters of *Neolithic Shamanism*—"The Golden World" and "The Silver World".

2) Read at least five more of the online God-shrines, and ask via Futhark or Futhorc runes (or your own personal rune symbols) whether any of them would be interested in teaching or aiding you. Try not to assume that the ones you like best will decide to deal with you.

3) Read more of the other books on the Required Reading list.

4) Make sure that you are doing some kind of physical practice that combines moving the body with moving the body's energies.

5) Do a daily rune draw. Practice your divination protocol.

Lesson 2/10: Völuspá Continued, Verses 4–10.

4. Before Bur's sons raised up heaven's vault,
they who the noble Midgard shaped.
The sun shone from the south
over the stones of the hall:
then out of the ground grew green leeks.

5. The sun from the south, the moon's companion,
her right hand cast about the edge of heaven;
The sun did not know what halls she possessed.
The stars did not know where they had a station.
The moon did not know what power he possessed.

6. Then went all the powers to their judgment seats,
the all-holy gods, and thereon held council:
to night and waning moon gave names;
morn they named, and mid-day,
afternoon and eve, to reckon years.

7. The Æsir met on Ida's plain;
they built altars and high temples,
furnaces established, precious things forged,
shaped tongs, and made tools.

8. At tables they played at home; joyous they were,
to them was naught want of gold,
until three came, thurs-maidens,
all powerful, from Jötunheim.

9. Then all the powers went to the judgement seats...
Who of the dwarves should create men
from the blood of Brimir and blue bones?

10. There Mótsognir the most esteemed
of all the dwarves, but Durinn the second.
Human forms they made, many
dwarves out of the earth as Durinn commanded.

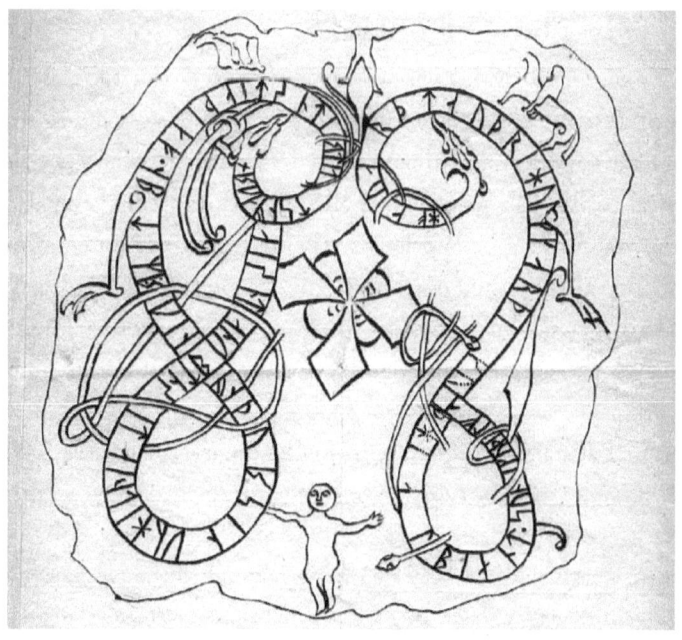

Month 3: Journey to the Well of Urd

Reminder of our working goals: the Self, the Staff, the Song, the Seat, the Spirits, and that we will access these concepts via immersion through the Mind, the Body, Luck, the Runes, and Calling. By this consistent reminder we can remain focused in keeping our minds trained on our work in this reclaiming process. As always throughout the workings of this book, in this chapter we are going to address these individual concepts while visiting one of the Norse Nine Worlds via Yggdrasil. As always, begin the day with your daily rune reading and work with those runes each day.

Lesson 3/1: The Well of Urd

Our next stop in the other worlds is the Well of Urd, also known as the well of destiny, or Well of Wyrd. It's important to keep in mind that the image of Yggdrasil and the Well of Urd should be about going from our physical reality to a place where all reality is created, changed or ended in its "known" form. The World Tree being fed by the waters of potential is the message this mythos portrays to me. I believe that Yggdrasil and the Well of Urd weren't only physical things in a set location. These destiny icons exist at the core of the everyday everywhere, within all time and all space.

As Paul Bauschatz points out in his landmark study *The Well and the Tree: World and Time in Early Germanic Culture*:

> Yggdrasil and the Well of Urd correspond to the two tenses of Germanic languages. Even modern English, a Germanic language, still has only two tenses: 1) the past tense, which includes events that are now over ("It rained") as well as those that began in the past and are still happening ("It has been raining"), and 2) the present tense, which describes events that are currently happening ("It is raining"). Unlike Romance languages such as Spanish or French, for example, Germanic languages have no true future tense. Instead, they use certain verbs in the present tense to express something similar to futurity, such as "will" or "shall" ("I will go to the party" or "It shall rain"). Rather than "futurity," however, what these verbs express could more accurately be called "intention" or "necessity".

To demonstrate the point of non-future tense in correspondence to the Well of Urd and Yggdrasil, blogger Toska[20] explains:

> The Well of Urd corresponds to the past tense. It is the reservoir of completed or ongoing actions that nourish the tree and influence its growth. Yggdrasil, in turn, corresponds to the present tense, that which is being actualized here and now. What of intention and necessity, then? This is the water that permeates the image, flowing up from the well into the tree, dripping from the leaves of the tree as dew, and returning to the well, where it then seeps back up into the tree.
>
> Here, time is cyclical rather than linear. The present returns to the past, where it retroactively changes the past. The new past, in turn, is reabsorbed into a new present, whose originality is an outgrowth of the give-and-take between the waters of the well and the waters of the tree … In contrast to the Greek concept of fate, however, for the Norse; all beings who are subject to destiny have some degree of agency in shaping their own destiny and the destinies of others – this is the dew that falls back into the well from the branches of the tree, accordingly reshaping the past and its influence upon the present. All beings do this passively; those who practice magic do it actively. (In fact, one could accurately say that, in the surviving accounts of the practice of magic in ancient Germanic societies, magic is viewed as being precisely the process of gaining a greater degree of control over destiny.) There is no absolutely free will, just as there is no absolutely unalterable fate; instead, life is lived somewhere between these two extremes."

This month our Utiseta journey will be to the well of Urd in an attempt to understand our Fylgjur, as well as possibly get a glimpse into our own Wyrd.[21]

---

[20] Found in an essay on the "My Little Occult Shop" website, page now vanished.
[21] For other perspectives on the well of Wyrd, I recommend Daniel McCoy's online essay: https://norse-mythology.org/concepts/destiny-wyrd-urd/, and

Lesson 3/2: Soul Part: The Fylgja.

Fylgjur (plural of *Fylgja*) are soul parts described as supernatural guardian spirits, bound to a family line, said to accompany a person throughout life. Like many concepts in Norse mythology, the *Fylgja* is sometimes hard to comprehend or explain.

Sometimes in this modern era, some two thousand years after the fall of our ancestors' pagan ways, we are finding we must rely on fragmented writings gathered by people who were not actually practicing this religion at the time of the accounts being penned. Snorri Sturluson, author of the Eddas, is a prime example. With that knowledge, there are numerous holes and unanswered questions to many of the Ancient Norse spiritual concepts and practices. Add to this the fact that many neighboring countries used to consolidate the scant documentation using similar words with very different meanings, and one can see why many 21st Century Folk might be scratching their heads and arguing over some of the most fundamental concepts left for us to decipher. There seems to be no other Norse Pagan soul part concept which has more discrepancies in its definition than the *Fylgja*, unless it is the Disir and their male counterparts.

Fylgja, translated from Old Norse, means "someone that accompanies" although in some modern Scandinavian languages like Norwegian and Swedish, it is translated as "one who follows". I have come to understand it as a soul part also called "the Fetch", which is a term used by Witches in various traditions to describe a deliberately split-off soul part that is sent out (usually in animal form) to do work that the body of the practitioner cannot do themselves. I have found many writings of modern-day scholars who have used etymology to try to figure out what the Norse actually viewed as roles for each soul part. They usually end up going on tangents which, though they show a great use of research and imagination, for me these accepted hypotheses are not based in solid knowing due to the researchers' lack of actual experience with these mysteries. In other words, they are book-smart but are inexperienced and lack information, due to

---

SjpielseWolf's as well: https://sjpielsewolf.wordpress.com/2016/02/02/yggdrasil-explored-well-of-urd/.

not having actually met with Wights, Ancestors, and beings of the Nine Worlds. Therefore, in my opinion, since they are approaching it from an academic viewpoint, these scholars do not offer any substantial answers other than educated guessing. I do what I am trained to do, and not only do I go to the source for answers, I compare what other traditions offer as the shamanic workings of mankind since shamans first began, thus giving applied knowledge to my conclusions.

To answer these questions myself, I do what all shamans do: I first look to comparisons of similar concepts in surrounding areas as well as worldwide practices. By knowing how shamanic concepts and workings tend to grow up into similar paradigms, I feel assured that through comparing concepts that share striking similarities other than names, I am safe to connect the dots and say, "Aha! So that could be what this means!" (That's why Michael Harner developed "Core" Shamanism in the first place—it's a way of validating a technique or concept in shamanic practices, since it cross-references and gives "proof" that the idea or experience is shared universally by those who do this work.)

So we come to see that many people who have investigated this soul part have come to describing it as an entity of its own volition, a type of guardian spirit, a totem animal, and something that can be passed down to descendants and live on after the death of the owner. In this they are absolutely right; they just are missing some key words here.

A Fylgja *is* an entity of its own volition, once the owner sends it to do their bidding. This brings us back to the concept of the "fetch". A fetch must have a sender that it belongs to so it can "fetch". So this is a type of guardian spirit. As a soul part of the owner's "astral body", of course when we send our Fylgja forth we charge it with our own safety and well-being in mind. This is different from the guardian spirit known as a Dis (plural Disir), who are understood to be female Ancestral spirits allotted to us at birth and if we don't honor her, she has been known to leave her ward without her protection. The Fylgja, on the other hand, is a part of our very souls. (That is not to say if our Fylgja stays on after we, the owner, dies; it won't look after a loved one, as ghosts are known to do.)

I have found in spirit journeys and shapeshifting that our Fylgja can be morphed to take on the appearance of an animal ally we are very familiar with, via our activation of our *Hamr*. (We will learn more about the *Hamr* later.) This is the entire purpose of a Fetch: to do our will as we see fit. Sometimes in spirit walks that means we make it appear to others as we need it to appear. I hate to point out the obvious, but you can't make an actual separate spirit ally appear in what shape you desire. You are only in charge of *you*.

As spiritual people, we sense that a part of us continues after our body dies. The astral double of ourselves (Fylgja) can do that to an extent, as seen by the phenomena of ghosts and shades. If a Fylgja decides it is time to wait in the hall they are destined for after death, when the time is ripe, that soul part has an opportunity to be reborn into their tribe as part of a new person. This would explain the Norse concept that a Fylgja can be passed down, as that is in essence what reincarnation is.

C.G. Jung's take on the Fylgja was presented in an academic paper:

> In Iceland, it is an ancient belief that the child's guardian spirit, or a part of its soul, has its seat in the chorion of the fetal membrane, generally known as the caul, which as a rule forms part of the afterbirth; so the caul is designated as the Fylgja or guardian spirit. Frazer also says that in parts of the world the navel string, or more commonly the afterbirth, is regarded as a living being, the brother or sister of the infant, or as an material object in which the Guardian spirit of the child or a part of its soul resides.
>
> I told you that the amniotic membraine, which is part of the afterbirth, was called the fylgja. This Nordic Fylgja is the same word as the German Folgen "To Follow"; the Greek word is Synopados, meaning the one that follows after, the double of man, the second ego. It is supposed that the fylgja, separates from man and becomes visible shortly before death - that would be the soul leaving the body - and in that case, the soul would get into the skin of an animal and accompany the man everywhere; therefore the soul was called hamingja, which means the one that changes shape. So they thought that Fylgja and hamingja were the same. This is a very primitive concept, and it shows how the soul, which in parts of the world called the bush soul, is the derived from the idea of the double.

A Fylgja is a part one's self, and it can live on after the death of the owner, and we can make it appear as an animal or any other ally we choose. But unlike our Disir, who are female guardian entities separate from the individual and allotted to watch over them from birth to death the Fylgja is actually a part of every individual's soul parts—and it is the Fylgja a Seidkona sends to travel on their behalf into the otherworlds of time and space.

A Fylgja can appear in two ways: as a representation of the human soul it belongs to as their astral double, or as an animal/plant ally. The animal form can be described as an extension of an aspect or characteristic of a particular individual taking the shape of a personal or family totem. The more human form is simply as an astral version of the person it belongs to. The Fylgja embodies the essence of an individual's spirit, which can guide the one they choose, or work deeds for them. Maria Kvilhaug translated and summarized Professor Else Mundal's academic paper on the topic, and states:

> The animal *fylgja* motif is sometimes blended with the *húgr*-motif. *Húgr* (masculine singular) means "intent", "desire", "thought", "soul", "heart" and seems to have been a part of the human soul that could move outside of the body in animal shape. *Manna hugir* ("the intents of men") sometimes replaces the term *manna fylgjor* [the "followers" of men] and usually then appear in the shape of wolves. Wolves, being associated with fierce passion and desire (or greed and hunger) are closely connected to the *húgr*. The other animals appear as *manna fylgjor*.[22]

Unfortunately, the second description from Mundal's article explains (mistakenly, in my opinion) how human Fylgjur are always female entities (does that mean men have no souls?) and this precisely is what sometimes can the Fylgja with the Dis. It may be that the translation of the female pronoun of the Norse Völva used when describing her Fylgja led to the erroneous connection that the Fylgja was strictly a female entity, thereby

---

[22] *Fylgjemotiva i norrøn litteratur"* (Fylgjur Motifs in Norse Literature, Universitetsforlaget, Oslo, 1974)

equating them as one and the same. Fylgjas do act as a guardian for a family if the person it belongs to wishes so after their death, and obviously they can attach themselves to an individual at birth and can act as an Ancestral guardian following through the generations down a certain lineage. But that's where the similarities to a Fylgja and a Dis stop.

Disir are likely to be wise and powerful women from one's ancestral lineage. We know that in ancient times the female spiritual principle was celebrated and revered especially the Mother aspect. These female ancestral spirits who watch over and guide their descendants much as a mother figure would do.

When Disir is described in old Norse, the word means "Ladies". I have found a Disir is unequivocally a female Guardian spirit bound to a family of which they are matriarchal ancestors, and can be both benevolent or malevolent, depending upon the behavior of the descendant they are assigned to watch over. The Dísir will be discussed and explored in their own chapter later in this book.

Author Pollyanna Jones states: "The term Dísir covers a wider spectrum of female spirits and beings within Norse mythology, but the Fylgja is specifically a spirit that guides and protects an *individual* person, and is tied with their fate and luck; called "hamingja".[23] It is widely thought that a Fylgja may abandon their chosen mortal if their behavior is wicked and would bring the name of the family into disrepute," but again, I feel that is a mistaken equation with the Disir once again. In all forms of shamanism, it's agreed that if you lose your astral body you are dead meat.

Side Note: I do, as a Shaman, feel that when "soul loss" is spoken of— meaning a person loses part of their soul due to a particularly traumatic incident—it is the Fylgja soul part we have that flees to the otherworlds to escape whatever the devastation or horror was being faced by the person who houses it. But I feel this "soul-loss" or separation of our soul part called the Fylgja doesn't happen as easily as some modern "shamans" would have us believe, and moreover, it is a temporary separation at best; with or without a Shamanic intervention.

---

[23] https://exemplore.com/magic/Understanding-the-Fylgjur

Lesson 3/3: The Power of Song: Galdr.

This month we will learn about Galdr. *Galdr* (plural *Galdrar*) is one Old Norse word for "spell" or "incantation". A *Galdr* is a magical charm that uses alliteration, and is *not* simply the repeated chanting of a rune's name. Galdralag is usually a piece of specifically metered verse the Vitki or Völvas used to *demand* an action from the otherworldly forces they were working with in tandem with other ritual practices such as a sacrifice (Blót), the charging and wearing of a talisman, or for creating then taking a medical remedy.

Of all the traditional songs used in Norse magic, Galdr is the most easily understood and recreated form of magical singing, since Galdr and Galdralag were still used up to the Christian times of the early medieval era. A good example of a surviving Galdr is the Old English "Charm Against A Dwarf" from the Lacnunga, amongst others.[24] This form of magical spell was either done as a stand-alone incantation for change, or screamed in combination with certain rites. Galdr would have been a form of magic working especially within the wheelhouse of a Vitki, since it was not a form of Seiðr, it was more a form of sorcery or witchcraft. Some scholars have assumed they chanted it in falsetto (*gala*), but as we will learn, besides its metered structure; it was the volume of a Galdr that really mattered.

Let's look at the etymology of the word Galdr to understand more about the importance of a Galdr's volume. The Old English forms included *gealdor* or *galdor*, and the verb *galan* meant "sing or chant". It is contained in the word "nightingale" (from *nӕcti-galӕ*), related to *giellan*, the verb ancestral to Modern English *yell*, and cognate to the Dutch *gillen*, "to yell or scream".

As mentioned at the beginning of this section, today many "experts" decide that Galdr was only used in chanting the Futhark runes, so to do it properly, we are mistakenly told that a Galdr is just Futhark rune names drawn out in a loud call or sung/hummed chant. After all the evidence I have found, I must disagree. In 2017 and 2018, I had the joy and privilege to work with not only a long time Völva from Norway named Inger; I also

---

[24] https://en.wikipedia.org/wiki/Anglo-Saxon_metrical_charms

got to participate in a four-day workshop that included a Völva named Lindy Fey, who was also a singer for the Scandinavian folk-rock group Wardruna. In this workshop they broke down how Scandinavians view Galdr as well as how to do it, which is much different than what I previously thought.

To the Norwegians, *Galdr* literally means to scream. Lindy Fay, who is Norwegian and a professional singer, demonstrated it for us so we could come to a better understanding of this powerful (and loud) way of projecting your intention into the cosmos. By opening her mouth wide and letting her throat open; Lindy screamed three properly alliterated metered lines that was simply incredible to hear. There is a mechanical process to it; opening your throat is crucial so you won't damage your vocal cords, as is unhinging your mouth very wide to let the sound flow. You also must relax your mouth muscles and hold your spine straight; supporting your frame with your abdomen muscles contracted. Think of the power for your Galdr coming from your abdominal wall and your core. Breathe in and look straight ahead, and use your belly muscles to force the sound (and air) out through your throat without straining. Lindy showed us a trick; hold your hands on your waist and visualize your sides are extending outward as your belly compresses. By using the stomach muscles and contracting them hard and consistently, it lets the sound out forcefully and unhindered, unlike simply screaming from the lungs and throat.

For this course I am having you read *Galdrs of the Edda* by Lars Magnar Enoksen for the sake of understanding the formation of a Galdr's structure. His book is invaluable for showing exactly how to use Galdr alliteration. From the *Writing Explained* [25] website, we see the following information:

> Alliteration is the repetition of initial constant sounds of nearby words. It is a literary sound device used for emphasis and effect. Alliteration only occurs when consonant (not vowel) sounds are repeated in words close to each other. These words may be within the same phrase, clause, or sentence, or they may occur on successive lines (as in poetry or lyrics). Tongue twisters are a well-known use

---

[25] https://writingexplained.org/

of alliteration, shown with the example: *Peter Piper picked a peck of pickled peppers.* In this classic example of alliteration, the initial "p" sound creates the alliteration.

Moreover, the sounds that create alliteration need to be the same consonant sound, but not necessarily the same letter. For example: *Gnarly gnats need new necklaces.* Here, the "gn" creates an "n" sound which makes this sentence alliterative.

You may work this alliteration in with runes; the biggest factor is being sure that it is simple and not comprised of too many lines. If it's too complicated, you lose the intention, and you can't scream it out for very long. As you develop your own practice, it is important to experiment and use what works best for you, not to just mimic others because they tell you it's the only "historically" correct usage of any Norse Mystic skillset. (No one is precisely sure how some of these arts were really executed by our ancestors anyway.)

In keeping with cross-referencing alliteration and blending runic magic with the language I speak most readily, the style of Galdr I use has English words infused with intention, followed by runes that match the intention. A very good example of word/rune blended Galdrs can be listened to as performed by modern musical groups like Heilung and Warduna.

I actually use a form of Galdr in my working in the high seat seances. Step 1 is that I set my intention as to why I am visiting the Well of Urd with a Galdr that vocalizes that intention. Simultaneously, my Spá sisters sing a vardlökkur that holds the same intention of the Galdr. When I give the signal I am arriving at the well (usually by my swaying ceasing, or else by becoming very still) the "posse" of Spá singers switch to a vardlökkur of their choice which holds me at the Well of Urd in safety. This second vardlökkur is now a different song than what they sang in the beginning of the journey, which was to keep the intention (and me) headed to the Well of Urd.

Step 2 in the séance makes sure that my body is safe and protected. When I have arrived at my otherworldly destination, the Spá "Posse" (without missing a beat so there is *no* lapse in the singing from the time I sit in the seat till I signal for the singing to stop) changes their vardlökkur from the song of safe journey to the song of arrival, and finally, if necessary; to the song of safe keeping. They sing the vardlökkur of safe-keeping if I am taking a particularly long time to be ready to speak. You see, until Those Who Are Speaking Through Me are indeed ready to speak (which is signaled by a thump of my Stav), the job of the posse is to hold a safe space. Once I thump my Stav, all songs cease instantaneously.

For this month, experiment with both "traditional" rune chanting and with your own "freestyle Galdr."

Lesson 3/4: Our Many Gods II: Altars.

Building altars is an important part of our work, because they act both as a focal point for our worship and meditations, and as a way of showing the Gods honor—having them as "a guest in your house". An altar does not have to be a huge elaborate creation; some altars are simply a square foot of shelf with a piece of cloth in that deity's colors, a cup and dish for offerings, a candle, and an item associated with them. (You would be surprised how many appropriate altar items you can find in thrift stores.) There is now enough art online that it is not too difficult to find and print good votive pictures of nearly all the Norse/Germanic Gods. You can also build an altar to the World Tree, with symbols of the Nine Worlds, or to the spirit of the land you live on, the lake you visit, your animal allies, the deva of your favorite tree species, etc. Altars can be inside or out; perhaps a pile of stones in the yard or a hanging mobile of items. (However, if you are going to put two Gods next to each other, make sure they get along first, or you may find the altars continually upset and broken.) You can find ideas for color or items on the online shrines, or in the appendix of Krasskova and Kaldera's book *Northern Tradition for the Solitary Practitioner* (New Page Press, 2011).

You can also make an altar to your Ancestors—this is called a "harrow" in some circles. An Ancestor harrow can have photos, written names, small inherited items, things from the countries or cultures they came from, or anything else that reminds you of them. Ancestors don't always have to be the people in your bloodlines, either; they can be loved ones who weren't related, like stepparents or former partners, or people who inspired you by their words or deeds, or people from whom you inherited a lineage. The

Völvas and Vitkis of old would fall into this category, and could be symbolized on your Ancestor harrow.

Altars can be in your Seiðrstallr, or scattered around your living space, depending on where you intuitively feel that a spirit might want their altar to be. This month, work on making altars for your favorite Guides. Follow up the altar-making with an offering of some kind.

Lesson 3/5: Odin Staff Posture.

Last month I introduced you to your first ritual body posture, the pose of Freya and the Mead-Horn. Our second posture this month is pictured below; this time, it will be the ritual posture of Odin. Again, feel free to use the ones that work, then leave the rest behind!

Second Pose: Odin Posture.

Odin is the God of inspiration, wisdom and the endless search for Óðr, as well as Seiðr and of the runes. Through his many sacrifices, Odin gained great knowledge, and in this month's posture we will emulate Odin one of his classic postures: that of the Grey Wanderer. This posture is perfect for a Völva or Vitki as it utilizes our Stav; it evokes the energy of manifesting change and it also physically readies us to become a spiritual traveler in any of the Nine Worlds.

To do this posture will require only your Stav. You will actually begin the posture by standing holding your Stav, then planting it in the ground to begin your sacred work, be it ritual or journey work. The understanding is that if one were to position the Stav in the ground, it then becomes Yggdrasil, a doorway to the Nine Realms. When using your Stav to become a mini-axis of the World Tree, it then becomes possible to have access to a portable portal to wherever you want to go.

Once held or stabbed into the ground, energy seems to emit from the Stav; it becomes a sending and receiving station.

By you gripping the planted Stav, you connect with the earth; your body connects and aligns with another level of reality. The Stav also give a sense of balance, supporting our weight if you will, so that we can become portals or doorways to the Cosmos, understanding what it means to having a foot in each world. This pose expresses well the reality of a spirit journey, in which we could learn to leave this physical reality and travel through doorways into other places in the multidimensional universe while still being very much connected to the physical. *(Illustration: Odin the Wanderer, Georg von Rosen, 1886.)*

Use of the Posture: Stand with your feet shoulder-width apart, your head erect, and your spine straight. Position your Stav at either side of your body, and grasp it with your dominant hand at a place just above shoulder level. Your free hand should be held outward at the same height as your gripping hand. Look up and raise both hands overhead, while stepping forward with one foot. Sweep the Stav forward of your body, and while gripping it with both hands; firmly plant it in the soil. With both hands still on your Stav and your knees relaxed, breathe deeply and feel the power of this pose while holding your Stav as a representation of the World tree, your portal to the Nine Worlds. You can now proceed to your ritual work by releasing your grip on the Stav and let it stand "planted" for the duration of your rite, or you may continue to hold it to do your journey work as an anchor point to Midgard.

Lesson 3/6: Journey to the Well of Urd.

This journey, modified from the *Little Red Tarot* website by Abbie Plouff,[26] is to be done on your monthly full moon Utiseta session. Remember, before taking any journey, draw runes to ask the aforementioned questions and make sure that it is right for you.

Be sure to gather any tools required for your out-sitting, and learn the new body posture (next in this book) to incorporate into this journey to the well of Urd to learn your density as it stands right now. Also, you will

---

[26] https://littleredtarot.com/044-nlw-film-04-9/

call on the aid of your Fylgja to assist you on this quest; thereby learning to see, feel, or recognize your sacred "fetch".

Do your best to read through the journey and memorize the steps and procedures, but remember that this is just an outline of the journey—the way it actually transpires might be very different.

Ground and hallow yourself in your space for your Utiseta.

Use your favorite technique for inducing your altered trance state, and as you wait for the veil of the otherworld mist to form, be aware of the astral double of yourself that lives within your flesh. Feel this presence within you. It is part of you, yet you sense you can separate it from your physical body. This is your Fylgja, and it is this soul part of you that actually does the faring forth into the otherworlds. As the mist evaporates and the otherworld's portal opens, picture your astral double of you (your fylgja) stepping out of your physical self into the place of magic.

As you step through the mist you see Yggdrasill in the distance; begin to walk toward it. As you approach the Tree, you study it. What does it look like? What texture is the tree's bark? Are the leaves budding, full, turning autumn colors, or is it a leafless tree?

As you are studying Yggdrasill while approaching its trunk, you hear a flutter of wings. Birds fly overhead—they are curiously silent, determined. The flock swells—you feel their wings beating deep in your heart. It feels as if the whole world flies past you. They draw you in to the tree, swirling around it as they ascend out of sight into the clouds. You know that you too must ascend skywards, via top of the tree.

As you move closer to the tree, it feels as if the ground stretches out further from you, and you realize otherworldly physics are not at all like earthly physics. Finally, you reach the tree's trunk, and seeing that the closest handhold for climbing is out of reach, your inner knowing takes over and you look down at your hands.

Concentrating, you gather up the energy that makes up your *Hamr* (aura) and you will your hands to change shape. You see feathers begin to sprout where fingers were, and see your arms begin to morph into wings. Think of becoming a bird and will your astral body to take that form.

You take a few steps back from the tree, and spot the branch you wish to reach. Running a few steps, you leap into the air, taking flight with your new form. Taking a moment to acclimate to flying, you then land on the branch you originally aimed for.

As you alight on your perch, your attention turns to flock of birds who have returned. The full flock has come, and this time they're flying straight for you. One of the birds clips your shoulder, and you're knocked off balance. You feel a lurch in your stomach, and begin to fall. You reach out for the tree with your arms momentarily forgetting you too are in bird form. With a start, you flap your wings and the air catches you but not before the ground rushes towards you from below. You feel your feet hit the ground, and you look for a sign to find your bearings.

It is all darkness. You shake your feathers and as they do, you turn back into your familiar human form. As you scan the area you realize you have landed in between Yggdrasill's giant roots, and you are now actually below the earth, under the great Tree.

From the darkness comes voices. One moment it sounds like women talking, then shrieking, then whispers. You can make out, flickering there in the darkness, a small fire. As you walk towards the fire, you realize the fire is in a huge clearing, and all around you (as well as this grove of roots the size of subway trains) are millions and millions of threads. As you enter the point where the firelight illumines your presence in this grove of roots, You know you have somehow reached the Norns. You can see them spinning and weaving at the well of Urd, the deep well of destiny they attend—it is just out of reach, but you can hear the cold water lapping in its depths, and it was this sound you thought was voices before.

Blindly, one foot at a time, you walk to the direction of the sound of the water and the flickering light. The well materializes into view in front of you, an ancient stone ring about waist height. As you reach the wells rim you notice the Three are still spinning but they view you intently while their hands fairly fly, and you hear a murmur—"Are you ready?"—but you can't tell where it came from. You state out loud your full name, and you give an oath you are indeed ready to view your destiny at this moment as shown in the waters of all time. You hear nothing more, so you proceed to look within the well. At first you see a mirror like surface and get confused. It is not a mirror, but the well's liquid has an appearance of liquid mercury—still waters that are somehow opaque. You see mist rise from this well, and wonder if the water is warm or cold? You begin to become transfixed and you see something thing moving beneath the surface of the well.

Slowly, the Norns move toward you, still holding someone's Wyrd, pulling it, stretching it, knotting it and cutting it.

The Norns are suddenly in front of you, then—*poof*—they are gone. You feel strangely languid, and slowly turn to look at the Well's water once more. A voice inside your head says that this is how it will be, each and every time you seek answers from Them. They will use you as their fetch, or they will leave you here and be your body's soul for as long as you are visiting this well of destiny. You cannot speak directly to Them, for they are becoming a part of you. The Norns tell you in your mind: "Allow your eyes to soften. See the flickering surface of the well's water. Feel what Fate feels like, as you know we are within you, yet all around you. We are one woman—we are three distinct women, and we sometimes blend together. What do we feel like, housed in your awareness? What do we sound like? What is at our core essence?"

Now The Norns direct your attention to your destiny. They say: "Stare into the well. What appears to you?"

Allow the Vision to wash over you. When you are ready, signal to the Norns. They move away from within you, to once more be three individual beings. The Norns see you, they nod. They know you. The three work together to untangle your strands of Wyrd. Your legs buckle as the world turns right side up. Without speaking, you know that they will take you back to your body, and that you have been here kenning this journey as your fylgja this entire experience since leaving Midgard for the Tree.

But first you must leave something. It must be something precious, but something that is not yours to hold on to. It must be something that has held you back. It must be something near and dear to you, some old habit or belief about your destiny that you need to let go.

What will you leave?

Close your eyes, and make your choice. Take your time. What you leave is never truly gone, but what you leave reveals much about yourself. Whatever it is that you leave, you know the Norns will take and transform into something useful.

Thank the Norns for their assistance. They gently guide your fetch back to your body via up the roots and back at the trunk of Yggdrasil. You step away from the tree, and the mist begins to form. You realize that your fylgja, your guiding allies, and the Norns may be with you in spirit now, only a journey away via your ability to send forth your Fylgja. You now know how the most sacred part of the Spa séance is done.

Time is a never-ending circle. You see that the misty veil between the worlds has cleared. You begin to become aware of your real physical body and breathing, and you like the feeling of your Fylgja within your body. Soon the land you are siting upon feels familiar. You have returned to your familiar sacred space.

Come back to yourself, to your seat, to all your parts. If your body feels stiff, get up, stretch, and come back to yourself. Write in your journal what you saw and what you gave up.

Lesson 3/7: The Power of Concentration.

Sharpening the mind and the powers of concentration requires practice. Like reshaping your body or learning to play a new musical instrument; you must do practice, training, and specific exercises to achieve adeptness. Even as little as five to ten minutes a day of concentration exercises will do you good. It's known that for many people, especially adults, the mind does not like new disciplines and will resist your efforts to train it. Your mind loves its freedom more than anything else, and it will make you forget to do the exercises, or tempt you to postpone performing them. It will find many tricks to occupy your attention with something else, because your mind thinks discipline is punishment

The choice is yours: to be mastered by your mind and its whims, or to be its master. Remember that you are not solely your mind, nor merely the sum of the thoughts that pass through it. Though it might be hard to accept this idea, the mind is neither all of you nor is it the real you, but only a part of you as a tool that you use.

However, you might have heard the notion that you are a product of your mind and the thoughts it contains. Unfortunately, this is true. I have spoken to some "free spirits" who honestly believe that by choosing to control their own minds they will be holding themselves back and denying themselves some sort of freedom to be themselves. They feel that controlling their mind is not natural, and that it is some sort of repression or militant punishment. However, the evidence of their lives shows that these "free-thinkers" usually have a hard time working steady jobs, can't be trusted to come through when the chips are down, and may be given the endearment of "flake" due to being victims of their untrained minds. I don't know about you, but I'd rather be a bit "hard and specialized" then an unreliable space-case. Below you will find another simple concentration exercise. By practicing mental workouts, you *can* train the mind and master it, at any age!

Find a place where you can be alone and undisturbed. If you wish, you may sit cross-legged on the floor, but most people would find it more comfortable to sit on a chair. Sit with your spine erect.

Take a few calm deep breaths and then relax your body. Direct your attention to relaxing each muscle, from head to toe.

Practice for about 10 minutes, and after a few weeks of training, you may lengthen the time to 15 minutes, only after you are convinced that you have practiced it correctly and with good concentration.

Take a book, any book, and count the words in any one paragraph. Then, count them again, to be sure that you have counted them correctly.

After a few times, do so with two paragraphs.

When this becomes easy, count the words of a whole page. Do the counting mentally and only with your eyes, without pointing your finger at each word.

Lesson 3/8: The Power of Silence Seeking Manifestation.

The Way to Enlightenment, according to magician Aleister Crowley, is very simple: "Sit down, shut up, stop thinking, and Get Out!" This should be the mantra of every Völva and Vitki, with the first step being to "shut up", and get silent. We have to invite silence into our heads. This can be achieved, among other techniques, by the "withdrawal of the senses", a stage in which the mind is fully turned inward and in control of the senses. We begin by donning our hoods or veils and "going under the cloak.' The whole point of this practice is to stop the scattering of our energy, of our Önd. We need to seek control over it and harmonize our body-mind with it. This is done through darkening our outward vision and bringing the entire focus of one's attention to a single point in the body via the breath; to unite our Önd and our mind's eye. In having achieved this focus we reach the final stage, which in Hinduism is called *mano pratyahara*—the "withdrawal of mind". We consciously withdraw our attention from any distracting force outside of us and all concentration is directed inwards. The Futhark rune Isa is a perfect representation of this kind of state of consciousness.

Practice "going under the cloak", breathing, and focusing on closing off the senses one at a time, focusing on a single image in the mind. This takes practice and you may need many tries in order to get anywhere. Don't despair; it will come with practice.

Lesson 3/9: Reading Material

This month we will continue the journey of co-creation and begin to learn about the different spirits that are associated with nature and the earth itself. It is crucial to have a working relationship with these wights as they are the doorway to our Earth-home itself. This land is not only the material world, but a magical link to the concepts and powers bequeathed to us by ancestral wisdom. In this way we can reconnect with the Gods and Goddesses via the Alfar and Wights, the landvættir, and of course, our own ancestral Dead. By reawakening them we can call on them to support our work and thus change the tragic wyrd of our peoples. By strengthening our Souls in such a powerful way we can determine our direction and destiny in the world.

1) Read and work on the next chapter of *Neolithic Shamanism*—"The Green World".

2) Read at least five more of the online God-shrines, and ask via Futhark/Futhorc or your own personal runes whether any of them would be interested in teaching or aiding you.

4) Read the "Gods and Wights: Spirit Allies and Spirit Masters" chapter of *Wyrdwalkers*, and also the first section on elemental spirits.

5) Read more of the other books on the Required Reading list.

7) Make sure that you are doing some kind of physical practice that combines moving the body with moving the body's energies.

8) Do a daily rune draw. If you do any other divination, practice your divination protocol.

Lesson 3/10: Immersion into the Voluspa, Verses 11–17

11. Nýi and Nidi, Nordri and Sudri,
Asutri and Vestri, Althiöf, Dvalin
Bivör, Bavör, Bömbur, Nori,
An and Anar, Ai, Miödvitnir,

12. Veig and Gandálf, Vindálf, Thrain,
Thekkr and Thorin, Thror, Vitr, and Litr,
Nýr and Nýrád, Now have I dwarves
Regin and Rádsvid. tallied up right.
13. Fili, Kili, Fundin, Nali,
Hepti, Vili, Hanar, Sviðr,
Frár, Fornbogi, Fræg and Lóni,
Aurvang, Iari, Eikinskialdi.

14. Speak of the dwarves in Dvalin's band,
to the sons of men, up to Lofar to reckon,
those who came forth from the stone halls,
earth's foundation, to Iora's plains.

15. There were Draupnir, and Dólgthrasir,
Hár, Haugspori, Hlævang, Glóin,
Skirvir, Virvir, Skafid, Ai,
Alf and Yngvi, Eikinskialdi,
Fjalar and Frosti, Finr and Ginar

16. That above shall, while mortals live,
be counted, the progeny of Lofar,

17. Until three came out of that company
mighty and benevolent Æsir to the house.
They found on land, with little strength,
Ask and Embla, örlog (destiny)-less.

Month 4: Odin and His Ravens.

Hugin and Munin
fly each day
over the spacious earth.
I fear for Hugin,
that he come not back,
yet more anxious am I for Munin.

– *1866 Benjamin Thorpe in Edda Sæmundar Hinns Frôða "The Lay of Grimnir" 1883 Gudbrand Vigfusson in Corpus Poeticum Boreale "The Sayings of the Hooded One"*

This month, we will learn the importance of Thought and Memory. With this knowledge we can change the direction of our Wyrd and create links to our ancestral past (which is never lost) as thought and memory are profound aspects of our soul. This information can lead to new and deeper understanding as well as clear direction. By participating in rituals that we ourselves invent, then in turn *memorize* (like our monthly Utiseta journeys performed after watching the full moon and *thinking* on it as a link with one's ancestors), we can gain deeper, wider insights (thought) that opens up our soul to become more and more aware of the energies that surrounds us.

Through Thought and Memory we can reconnect with the Gods and Goddesses, Wights, our own ancestral dead, as well as the landvættir. By reawakening them through memory and thoughts, we can call on them to support our work and thus change the wyrd of ourselves, our loved ones, and the world at large.

Thought and Memory strengthen our souls in a powerful way. Those ideas you were made to believe were memories of "superstition" are the very concepts that bring forth the memories of the essence of Heathenry in all its forms, as well as the magic of our ancestors. Our work to recover this magical heritage has much possibility for astounding success; you simply need to accept and use your mind. What we are trying to reclaim is not won by sentimentality and wishful thinking, but by staying focused and effective in this modern world. This soul-work is of paramount importance, and it begins with our thoughts and our memories of understanding.

Lesson 4/1: Odin, Hughr, and Myne.

For this soul, part the best explanation I have found is via the book *Elhaz Ablaze: A Compendium of Chaos Heathenry*, by Henry Lauer. which states:

> The Hughr is in many ways the structuring, analytical, investigative, observing faculty, mostly identified with the intellect. The Myne (minni) represents the imaginative, visionary, intuitive part of the Soul that brings forth images, symbols, symbols, signs, patterns, feelings, and omen-like occurrences. The Hughr and Myne are of course Odin's two ravens Huginn and Muninn. Ian Read calls the Wode, Hughr, and Myne the core-triad. This is so because all three must be developed in a careful and balanced way so that the runic learning can happen in a holistic process without bringing imbalance to the psyche. Too much Wode will simply consume you; your everyday personality won't be able to handle the overwhelming "information", and psychosis or worse would be the result. An overdeveloped Hughr will make you question everything—the typical academic—or you will simply accumulate a lot of knowledge that you can't put into action, like the armchair scholar or the book-learning occultist who knows everything in theory but nothing in reality. If the Myne is overdeveloped and the Hughr is undeveloped one will be confronted with endless images and patterns that will lose coherence. The result in most cases is the occult "master of the astral planes" or the New Age dolphin channeler, who flies off into cuckoo-fairy-tale-land, seeing everywhere coincidences, secret messages, and magic at work without being able to manifest any real results. So, in a nutshell: The core-triad needs to be developed harmoniously for the seeker to have a meaningful learning process.

In this month's work it is important you not only come to understand how you view these crucial soul parts you house within you, but to learn to hon them and use them wisely. If you haven't already begun to do so, being selective about what you fill your mind with in your free time (music, media, literature, news, etc.) ensures you aren't taking up valuable "head space" with useless frivolity, which can be damaging to your thinking/remembering process.[27]

There are varying views to the true meaning of Muninn's name, and as the name can't be clearly defined via old Norse (there are folks who think the name means Memory, and others who think it means Mind) I hold the idea that it means both. In Icelandic, the name *Muninn* actually means "difference" (there is no old Norse reference to that definition), and knowing the Norse held great weight in the naming process, I discovered from the University of Texas in Austin Linguistics Research Center that the old Norse word for "remember" is *muna*. According to UOT, it means "To think or have thoughts; one must remember the data being received, as well as have the abilities to process and analyze the new information; thereby using their mind in conjunction with past informational data to compare it with."

When Odin sent his Two Ravens out to do his bidding, he sent out an extension of himself (his cognitive mind, Hughr) to gain any obscure information that might aid him in his quest for "all knowing". Upon returning, Huginn and Muninn would share all they found via the dual analytical process that make us uniquely human: our thoughts (self-awareness) and our memory (comparing past events for relevance and decision making). Odin's knew that the best tools for the job would be to send the parts of his mind that could discern/recognize any new information (think) as well as retrieve/bring back (remember) whatever new insights were to be found. Our Norse Ancestors were very clever, and the meaning seems obvious to me by the very names Odin used for the bird forms he send forth as his minds representatives, since to be able to

---

[27] Good online references about Odin's ravens Huginn and Muninn, and their symbolism around Thought and Memory include Danial McCoy's website; https://norse-mythology.org/gods-and-creatures/others/hugin-and-munin/, and the discussion of soul parts in Kvedulf Gundarsson's *Teutonic Religion* (Llewellyn Publications, 1993).

remember what was learned would be of paramount importance to fulfilling "all-knowing" aspirations.

As you know by now, Odin has an insatiable thirst for knowledge and would go to great lengths to obtain it. Odin is a profoundly mystical, magical, and mysterious deity that represents Consciousness via Will, Knowing and Ordeal. Only those who are prepared to go through the same trials and ordeals as He did can truly know Him. Many might profess that they worship Odin and call themselves Odinists, but it seems to me that they only worship the archetypal Christian "father figure" Yahweh dressed up in Norse clothing and sporting a missing eye.

When one truly meets Odin, they quickly come to see He is not a God for the sheep, but for the brave (and perhaps foolhardy) few. This is evident in the fact that in ancient Scandinavia, places and things were not abundantly named after Him; whereas Thor and Freyr, who were much more accessible and understandable to the daily lives of most "salt-of-the-earth-people", leave their names all over the landscape. Contrary to what modern people might believe, Odin was never historically a popular God. To assume that today He is suddenly every Heathen's "All-Father" is to deny the deeper Odin who can be cruel, grim, and deceitful. Odin is a God of magicians and Shamans, so to simply place his image over the Christian God is not to know Odin at his very core, which is as a constant hunter for Knowledge, as Knowledge is Power.

Odin's favorite tools for seeking "all knowing" were his two ravens, sent as his intercessors to all the Nine Worlds, which were His very thought and memory given form. Huginn and Muninn would fly all over the world bringing Odin information and news, making Odin the original entity of the Norse Pantheon to recruit familiars. (He was a shaman, after all.) His association with these birds gave him the name (one of many) of "Raven-Lord".

Above I state that Odin was a shaman, and this fact, when understood, is crucial to separate his way of doing things from any other God in the Norse pantheon. (Even Loki.) Accepting the notion that Odin was "the father of Norse shamans" in and of itself explains much about Odin and his personality. Scholars have linked Odin's relationship with (and use of)

Huginn and Muninn to other indigenous peoples' shamanic practices of using animal forms as their "fetch".

The Ravens represent Odin's ability to send forth his "thought" and "mind" out into the world, projecting his will and influence from afar. John Lindow, a professor emeritus specializing in Scandinavian medieval studies and folklore at the University of California, Berkeley,[28] relates Odin's ability to send his "thought" (Huginn) and "mind" (Muninn) to the trance-state journey of shamans. Lindow says: "The *Grímnismál* stanza where Odin worries about the return of Huginn and Muninn would be consistent with the danger that the shaman faces on the trance-state journey when the mind and its thoughts become the vehicle of the shaman's soul."

In Odin's very name we see Wod, or Óðr, which stands for the ecstatic, divine, inspired part of the Soul, and is one of the nine-fold soul parts, eternal and immortal. Most of our life we are unaware of Óðr and normally we only become conscious of it for very short moments, experiencing only glimpses of it, which in most cases are triggered by circumstances we are unable to purposely recreate. Some individuals certainly experience divine inspiration in overwhelming ways through the use of extreme situations like hallucinogenic drugs, sex, or excruciating pain or loss, but I have found, personally, that by cultivating a strong Will, gaining much knowledge, and using thought and memory Óðr can also be accessed when sought out. (One danger for those who use drugs/sex/pain to make the experience happen of Óðr happen is that they may stop looking in more accessible places for inspiration and mystical information, not understanding extreme situations act as cataclysmic gate-openers to those realms of the Soul or Consciousness. These realms exist independently and can in truth be accessed without any of the above-mentioned outer means."

---

[28] *Norse Mythology: A Guide to the Gods, Rituals, and Beliefs*. Oxford University Press, 2002.

Lesson 4/2: Soul Part: Óðr.

This month we now go more in-depth regarding the High Seat, which to me is the gateway to the mind. Let us look first at the description of the High Seat as found in *Eric the Red's Saga*:

> At that time, there was a great dearth in Greenland; those who had been out on fishing expeditions had caught little, and some had not returned. There was in the settlement the woman whose name was Thorbjorg. She was a prophetess (spae-queen), and was called LitilVölva (little sibyl). She had had nine sisters, and they were all spae-queens, and she was the only one now living. It was a custom of Thorbjorg, in the winter time, to make a circuit, and people invited her to their houses, especially those who had any curiosity about the season, or desired to know their fate; and inasmuch as Thorkell was chief franklin thereabouts, he considered that it concerned him to know when the scarcity which overhung the settlement should cease. He invited, therefore, the spae-queen to his house, and prepared for her a hearty welcome, as was the custom where-ever a reception was accorded a woman of this kind. A high seat was prepared for her, and a cushion laid thereon in which were poultry-feathers.

We can see here that the high seat wasn't just a physical special chair; it was also a symbol of the position, power, and privilege earned by the chief or Earl of a clan or village. This seat of leadership was earned due to an individual's ability to guide his people by using his mental adeptness to think out various solutions to any threats or problems effecting his people at any given time. To the Norse, a quick and cunning mind was a highly esteemed quality, so it shows that to offer up "the High Seat" to a travelling witch meant it was recognized she had an exceptional power of discernment and problem solving, as well as the cunning to change perceptions and thoughts in the minds of men.

Nordic witches were also known as *spákona* in Old Norse, or *spækona* or *spæ-wife* in Old English; *spae*, or "truth-speaking", was associated with prophecy.

In her paper "Traditions of the Nordic Völva"[29], Samantha Catalina Sinclair quotes the paper "Wise Women, Witches and Intergalactic Crones" by Dr. Randy P. Conner, which defines the spækona as having "...all the supernatural wisdom, some of the supernatural power, without any of the malevolent spirit of witches." He goes on to say that the spækona was "skilled in medicinal and surgery, in dreams, in foresight and second-sight, and in forestalling the evil influence of witchcraft. Such women were looked upon with a kind of holy respect."

We must remember that the magical arts were practical, not fanciful, and were the precursor to science. Magic evinced a desire to exert power over a perceived cause to produce an effect. It was and is a way to understand and have a willful outcome on the random-seeming circumstances of life. Whether we are using magic to learn the gender of a child, to affect the fertility of ourselves, our fields or our livestock, Völvas have been using Spá since we learned to walk upright to affect the outcomes of life. Be it to heal disease, to control the weather, to predict the future, or to consult deceased ancestors, Spá is the language of magic and the otherworlds.

In addition, magic was also a way to enact retribution, to exact justice, and to impose some sense of order. We see from other accounts of the Völva that not only was she cherished for the ability to grant much benevolence to a village or tribe she visited; she was also feared and reviled as she could curse just as easily, bringing malevolence upon the town if it was necessary. We see in the primary sources some examples of the spákona changing the weather for ill, bringing blights upon crops and livestock; she could also change, cloud, or poison the mind through the images and thoughts sent into a person's perception.

As we are learning the power of the mind, it is essential that we understand the concept of divine inspiration and the ability to push that desire through our Will. Our ancestors, as well as our Celtic cousins the Druids, knew fully the power of magic changing destiny via surrender into our divine ecstatic inspiration. Empires were built from being divinely

---

[29] https://www.academia.edu/1617364/Traditions_of_the_Nordic_V%C3%B6lva

inspired and it is no less effectual today. We can change the world by applying a focused will toward a divinely-inspired thought. For me, it's simply a matter of using a combination of well-honed magical instincts and divine messages that show me that it is correct and right to assert my will into the cosmos.

I would now like to introduce you to the concept of *óðr*, as it is through this divine inspiration we actually learn to wield intention and will. The Old Norse word *óðr* has been used to mean many things, including "mind", "soul", "spirit", "song", "poetry", "inspiration", or even "divine possession". It is cognate to the Anglo-Saxon *wód* meaning "fury" and *wóð* meaning poetry, eloquence, or voice. It may be the root of the name of Óðinn.

As we delve deeper into the immersion process, we are beginning to realize that to the Norse, certain abilities and qualities of the human condition were revered and held in high regard, because these qualities aided in the furtherment of our species Human traits that were spectacular to our ancestors became divine qualities, making some humans seem as if they were descendants of the Gods themselves. Moreover, human attributes such as the mind, breath and (visited in next month's lesson) the will, were all given the status of divine attributes and considered to be gifts of specific Gods—for example Vili for the will, Vé for the psychic powers, and Odin for the breath and the *óðr*, the inspiration.

Why? I think it might be because it is these very human qualities, of Mind/Will/Thought/Breath/Inspiration, which are truly what makes us "god-like". It is the human ability to think out solutions and to will those thoughts into existence on a multi-level process that gives us a glimpse of the sacred science and order that makes up this universe. We are an example of "divine intelligence".

Intelligence and cunning, along with inspiration, will, and breath, are the cornerstones of the Arts of a Völva/Vitki, and therefore are the keys to opening the door fully into the practice of Seiðr.

Lesson 4/3: Óðr, Odin, and Asatru.

Controlling the thoughts and honing the memory is the work of this year's immersion. Once you can control your ravens, you are much like Odin, as you come to understand your Óðr, via Önd.

You will see me speak a great deal about Óðr throughout this book. Why? Because to truly be a Völva and seiðkona, we must come to know, recognize, and access Óðr to be successful in our magical endeavors. The aim must obviously be to cultivate this part of the Soul and to be able to stay aware of it, so that it can lead oneself towards higher truths and deeper mysteries, as well as power and adeptness.

Óðr means Divine Consciousness, and in the literature of mysticism, it is "a state of being is described which lies beyond even the perfected personality." Diana Paxson says of Óðr:

> It is this which Hinduism calls atman, the immortal soul. In sophisticated spiritual traditions, including those which are polytheistic, one finds the concept of a godhead which is not personified, an ultimate divinity which cannot be described but only experienced. In the ultimate form of spiritual union the mystic contacts this aspect of divinity, and in the process loses awareness of selfhood. In Eastern traditions, it is this Divinity, which is not so much a Being as a state of being, with which the soul that has gone beyond the need for incarnation unites. Can we find any traces of such a concept in Germanic tradition?
>
> In the Norse creation myth, Hoenir's gift is *ödhr*, translated as consciousness, sense, and the like. However the word is the root from which we get the name Óðinn, usually translated as "ecstasy". This concept, like the nature of the god, is more complex than it might appear. Dr. Martin Schwartz of the University of California has traced the etymology of Óðr and its older cognate, wodh, back to their Indo-European root, and demonstrated their relationship to concepts having to do with the activity of the mind.
>
> His analysis makes it clear that for the ancient Germanic peoples, consciousness was not an intellectual process, but rather an ecstatic experience of connection and creativity. This aspect of existence is beyond all temporal relationships, and is neither born nor can it die. This ultimate experience of consciousness sounds a

great deal like the mystic rapture, and the part of our soul that can connect with it. In the Feri tradition, this part of our soul is known as Ori as that soul part defines the capacity of the human psyche which is capable of identifying with and losing itself in the Divine.[30]

This is the soul part we must access most when doing our trance work, and especially with our work at the well of Urd. But we must fully understand Óðr for the moving force it is, as it is neither benign nor subtle, and it hinges on Önd to manifest. Asatru and Heathenry as a Religious practice can be confusing at times, since not every Heathen is involved with the sort of activity we deem "magic" or "mysticism". I am discovering that in general, neither active Asatru practitioners nor the serious Scandinavian academic students ever touch on, nor give validation to, the ecstatic aspect of Norse Paganism, and I must wonder as to why. I believe some of the reasoning comes from the idea that Norse Paganism was revived at the turn of this century, when many people were becoming dissatisfied by the emptiness that Christianity and other monotheist religions offered them. Monotheist faiths have been the ruling spirituality worldwide for over a thousand years, and that means their dogma and deep ideologies have been ingrained into countless generations of people for a long time, unconsciously creating a rift within the newly developing Heathen community. It has also influenced the interpretations teachings we have discovered within ancient lore and mythology.

What this means to me is though instinctually people know there is more to our spiritual lives than "one truth", it's hard for some to supersede that stunted mindset that unfortunately accompanies many of us when we leave the spiritual teachings of our childhood. For centuries most folks believed that esoteric practices and the occult were dangerous waters best left unchartered, and that its participants were delusional. Unfortunately, this mindset still follows some who come to Asatru today.

For many Heathens right now, understanding of the mystic veneration of the Old Norse cosmology is limited. Moreover, most modern-day

---

[30] https://hrafnar.org/articles/dpaxson/norse/hyge-craeft/

Heathens keep to acknowledging and revering a scant few Gods and Goddesses of Norse mythology, and it seems many 21st century Asatru followers (perhaps unknowingly) have chosen to view Odin as a substitute for the Judeo-Christian omniscient and omnipotent Father God, keeping alive the mindset that Divinity is one-dimensional and un-knowable. I have begun to realize because of the generational conditioning of today's people by "only one truth" religions, Odin is seen only as the wise, untouchable All-Father, and that this very humanized Divine Being is removed from people, human happenings, and the goings on here in Midgard. Sadly, many Asatru followers don't know or acknowledge Odin's primary role as a magician and ecstatic shaman, nor do they realize or accept that a Norse mystic's abilities and base spirituality hinges on the ability to actually work with Odin in this aspect.

Another side effect of the lack of participation in the ecstatic/occult side of this religion is the pervasive idea that Odin and the Other Gods do not care about us; they are simply there doing whatever it is Gods do, and we mere mortals simply struggle along in Midgard, doing whatever it is we do, abandoned by the Gods who made us ... because that's what it appears like if you don't believe that the Gods can be very interested in the affairs of men. When discussing their practices of esoteric work with non-mystical Heathens, sometimes a Völva or a Vitki or other seiðr practitioners can fall into a firestorm of ridicule. In doing this, we all create a dividing rift within this reclaiming process. The Völvas who practice seiðr are discovering through their ecstatic occult work that Odin is much more than the limiting "Jehovah" replacement; and everything about Odin is esoteric, occult and ecstatic.

How do I know this? By the very things that help us create "magic" in the first place: Önd and Óðr, the very essence of Odin. There have always been arguments in the study of Norse religion between those who feel that veneration of the Gods in a cerebral fashion (via reading and study with occasional Blóts and seasonal rites) and the mystic practices are incompatible, thereby causing discord within the Asatru community. Another source of discord is due to Norse mystics' use of practices like trance work, which relies very much on each practitioners' ability to interrupt images and messages via personal gnosis. The cerebral Heathen gets angry because they feel the person who is doing mystic Asatru is somehow disrespecting the Gods, claiming fraudulent ideas for their personal status and gain, and generally making a mockery of Norse mythology. Most Heathen Völvas and Vitkis I know use primarily the information found in the lore combined with personal gnosis; this lore tells us how a Völva has the ability to interact with Odin and that he actually sought one out for knowledge.

However, any remaining information is very vague, so the Völva or Vitki must then take a leap of faith to know more, and surrender to the idea of becoming an open vessel for the Önd and Óðr Odin might bestow upon them after much diligence, dedication and work. It requires the Völva/Vitki to become intimate with the beings of the Norse cosmology. The metaphysical side of Asatru can only be understood by those who are actual practitioners, and most do not have the ability to be a Völva or Vitki, and not every Völva/Vitki can do seiðr. I have found that to understand this path of mystic religion, one must have the ability to be open to Óðr, and in being open to Óðr, everything from simple rune-casting to healing work is accessible.

I feel that Óðr is Odin's gift to us to reach higher planes of existence, via visions, dreams and spá. Many people can't—and shouldn't—aspire to immerse themselves into the Norse mystical arts if they don't have the ability to surrender to Óðr. Mysticism exists because the Divine exists within and around us, and a human being is capable of touching the limitless via Önd. One can be an ecstatic being, but one will never fulfill one's complete potential until one experiences states of higher consciousness. Transformation and ecstasy, illumination and inspiration, creativity and self-exploration, meditation and world(s)-expeditions; these are at the core of Norse mysticism, which—according to the myths of our forefathers and foremothers—is a Gift of the God who Himself represents these qualities.

Lesson 4/4: The Kvad.

To picture how a seiðr High Seat session might unfold in the Viking era, we can turn to the most famous seiðr account, that of Thorbjörg in *Eric the Red's Saga*. Thorbjörg—an experienced, professional wise woman and seiðkona—is sitting on the seiðr seat (seiðhiall) with her staff. The people who have summoned her to help solve the problems of illness and bad hunting luck in their settlement surround her singing the seiðr song (vardlökkur). Thorbjörg's spirit allies gather around her, called to her by her magical chanting, and the song she is singing transports her into an altered state of consciousness, into the spirit world. There she meets with spirits, divine beings or nature forces, asking for help on behalf of the suffering community by singing another magical chanted formula, but the saga doesn't expand on this intimate part of the ritual. Her task completed, she signals the song to end by a thump of her Staff. The saga then tells that she chants a *kuað* (or in Norwegian *kvad*, which roughly means "ballad") which is a spell to do the work so that both health and fertility shall speedily return to the settlement. She says this magical chant in the silent "space" following the vardlökkur song, out loud, while she is still between the worlds. From there she gives divinatory answers (Spá) to the questions put to her about health, the crops and the future.

This month we will examine the seldom mentioned but (I feel) very important *kuað/kvad*, which by all accounts means the "incantational ballad of intent", a song of magical formula used by the Völva to wield her Will into manifestation.

Since ancient times, many cultures recognized the power of a ballad sung in its entirety with its power of energy/consciousness manipulation when spoken with unwavering intention in structured metered flow, and charged with emotion. It then becomes a sort of "magic formula", which is also referred to with the word "kunna", meaning knowledge.

Ballads, no matter which category they fall into, mostly rely on simple and easy-to-understand language or dialect from its culture of origin. Stories about hardships, tragedies, love, and romance are standard ingredients of the ballad, irrespective of its geographical origins. Another element of any ballad is the recurrence of certain lines at regular intervals. Ballads can also be in a questioning form, with the appropriate answers to every question asked contained within it. Ballads don't usually give a *direct* message about a certain event, character, or situation, as part of the magick is in the deciphering of the ballad's message.

So as you can see, the Kvad (*kuað*) becomes the vehicle with which we infuse our power, and see to it that the strands of Wyrd are altered in the way we see as best for the situation. Though seldom mentioned in modern-day seiðr, kuað/kvad to me is an essentially powerful song to use as a Völva or a Vitki when either in the high seat, or working spa for one's self or others.[31]

This month, I would like you to create your own *kuað/kvad* to use in a spell you will create for a more divine connection with your Hughr and Myne. It should be short and to the point of your work this month, and it should also rhyme in a way you can easily infuse it with power.

If you ever get a chance to perform a seiðr séance ritual; *kuað/kvad* would be used by the Völva/Vitki on the high seat to state, upon her arrival at her Otherworld destination, why she is at the well of Urd, why she has come to weave Wyrd, and what she intends to do with the information. This might be to read Spá for the surrounding listeners, or affect the outcome of communal events and Wyrd. The *kuað/kvad* song is also the outward signal to others involved in the seance that she has arrived at her destination, and the experience has truly begun. Up until now the Völva on the high seat is being kept in the otherworlds by the song being still being sung (the vardlökkur) by her attending spa sisters, aiding her in this magical mission, but as soon as the kuað begins, all other sounds abruptly cease.

One example of a kuað said as a magic ballad-type formula is used by Imma, a young Northumbrian warrior, captured by his Mercian foes after the battle of Trent in 679.[32] Imma was said to have used "loosening runes" carved on willow staves, and instead of just using Galdr (the runes screamed in a loud voice) to make chains fall from him, he sang a ballad-

---

[31] For information on ballad construction, see the English Broadside ballad Archive at: https://ebba.english.ucsb.edu/page/ballad-measure-in-print.

[32] The story of Imma is preserved in *Book IV, Chapter XX of Bede's Historia ecclesiastica gentis Anglorum*, a work completed in AD 731. There are also two other, later versions of the story in Old English, both largely dependent on Bede's Latin version, one in the Old English Bede, the other in a homily by Ælfric.

type incantation of intention to be free via his knowledge (kunna) of a magic and metered song to break the chains instead.[33]

Here I share the actual words in modern English, but remember that Imma was speaking Northumbrian dialect, which is difficult to translate today, and it would have a more ballad-like quality in the original language.

> Though I be weak, Let my spirit be free.
> Though I be strong, Let my spirit be free.
> Though I be sick, Let my spirit be free.
> Though I be well, Let my spirit be free.
> Though I be poor, Let my spirit be free.
> Though I be rich, Let my spirit be free.
> Though I be sad, Let my spirit be free.
> Though I be happy, Let my spirit be free.
> Though I be bound, Let my spirit be free.
> Though I be free, Let my spirit be free.
> Whatever my trial, Let me die unto me.
> Whatever my trial, Let my spirit be free.

Practice: Create a *kuað* of your own choosing, using a metered ballad form, for doing high seat oracle work.

Lesson 4/5: The Empowerment Posture.

Again we will visit the concept of the power of ritual postures and poses, taken from images found in Norse history, used in conjunction with our Utiseta. This month's pose mimics a 9th-10th century Middle Saxon

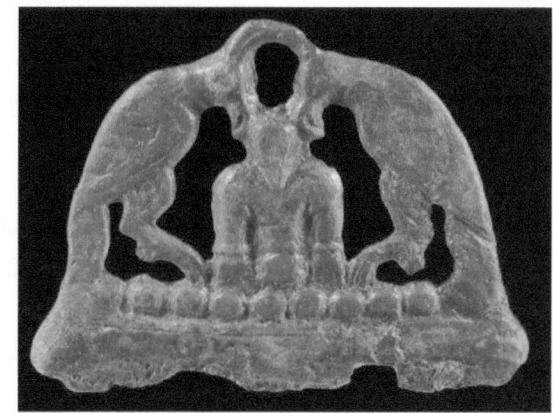

---

[33] http://www.odins-gift.com/mp3/others/untyingwords.mp3 and http://www.odins-gift.com/mp3/others/untyingwords_vocals.mp3.

bronze artifact depicting Odin with Hugunin and Muninn on his shoulders.[34] For our ritual pose this month, we will also pantomime this image, by placing our body in this posture.

Kneel on the ground or floor with your heels together and your knees apart, rest your buttocks on your heels. Keep your spine hunched and your body weight resting on fisted knuckles. Imagine two huge ravens perched on each shoulder. Inhale for three breath cycles while you uncurl your spine and lean your head back, taking in a big breath of air.

Pause for a moment, turn your head to the right, and blow out your air to the "raven" on your right shoulder. Tuck your head down while inhaling through your nose, and repeat the process to the left. On the third movement blow the breath straight up, keeping your mouth slightly open as you return to your starting "tucked" position.

Lesson 4/6: Journey to Asgard to Meet Odin.

As Odin is the other patron of Völvas and Vitkis, it is important that we have some kind of relationship with Him. He is the Seeker of Wisdom and the Hunter for Power, the Mage-King, the first Runemal. This month, we will be journeying to meet him and ask for his wisdom. Remember, before taking any journey, draw Futhark/Futhorc or your own personal runes to ask the aforementioned questions and make sure that it is right for you. In this case, ask a further question: Does Odin wish you to come to Asgard, or does He wish to meet you elsewhere? (He has been known to meet with people in all sorts of places.) You can pull two runes to gauge each possible option, and see which one is more positive.

1) Prepare for your journey the way you normally do: by creating a sacred space that is hallowed, and by preparing your body and your spirit to fare-forth. You may read this journey outline a few times to put into memory the key points.

2) Set up an altar (if only temporary) for Odin, in His colors (grey, black and cobalt blue), choose something to offer (he likes good-quality

---

[34] Hammond, B. *British Artefacts Vol. 2*. Greenlight Publishing 2009.

alcohol), and place it on the altar. Ask Him to guide you to the right place and give you what wisdom He thinks is best.

3) Begin by centering yourself on your seat, covering your head with your cloak or eye cover, and beginning to rhythmically tap your Stav.

4) Breathe deeply but naturally in 4 counts in/hold-pause/then out four counts until your mind is cleared and you begin to see the veil of the Otherworld mist form behind your eyes in the darkness. Begin to sing your vardlokkur.

5) As the mist forms, state your intention out loud that you are going to the world of Asgard to speak with Odin, and call on the Futhark rune Ansuz for Asgard. If divination has shown that you are not going to meet Him in Asgard, voice your intention to go to where He wishes to meet with you and call on the Futhark rune Raido to take you there.

6) When the mist clears, you should see the starting point, the World Tree Yggdrasil. Greet your Disir (ancient female ancestral guardian spirits) and any other helping spirits who may accompany you. Tell them of your intention to meet with Odin, wherever He wishes.

7) View Yggdrasil and go to your destination via your map of the World Tree and the Norse Cosmos.

8) When you arrive at your destination, look at all that is around you and take it all in. The sights, the sounds, the smells, the air temperature, etc. Start walking the direction that seems right.

9) Ideally, Odin will appear to you as you move through this world, since you have checked to see if He will speak with you, and made an offering. He will choose the place, and it will be meaningful. Try not to make assumptions about where you will see him, even in Asgard. Be respectful and listen to what He has to tell you, and thank Him for His wisdom when He is done.

10) After your mission is accomplished (or not) and it's time to return, go in the same manner you got there, re-tracing your steps through Yggdrasil and back to your starting point where the otherworld mist begins to form. Say thanks to all your helpers and your Disir by offering a gift for their service.

11) Be sure to write in your journal all the events as soon as you are awake and grounded in the here and now. Pound your Stav 3-9 times forcefully as you stand up, to place yourself fully back into Midgard.

Lesson 4/7: Intention.

We hear the word "intention" in all forms of self-work; be it for inspiration, goal setting, or effective ceremonial magic. I drive home to my students that all *forms of change, magical or not, lie within your intention*. It must be clear (to you and anyone listening) and it must be focused.

For example: Upon waking, the average person groggily exits their bed and then make coffee or tea to help wake up. Next comes a shower. Then check their phone/computer while eating breakfast on autopilot. They then get dressed, and head out the door amongst the ever-growing crowds of pedestrians, traffic, etc. or they make their way to their home office to get down to the grind of the day.

In this ritualistic morning routine, can you find a use for an intention? What if our ordinary Joe/Jane tried fitting an intention in this routine as to how they intend to have it proceed—from what they produce at work, to how they react to others they meet via the trek to work that day? What if the worker-from-home set the intention for the day to be a wise, strong, empowered, Völva/Vitki in this day of walking/working through Midgard? What if everyone set an intention of connectedness to all as the first thing they do upon awaking?

By acknowledging how you desire to feel and what interactions or outcomes you intend for your day, you can enter any situation with a whole new sense of being—even as you're simply drinking your cup of joe, enduring being stuck in traffic, or focusing on productivity.

Taken in our immersion context: It is personal intent, and how that intent manifests into action and form in the outside world, that colors the purpose of our work in the High Seat, as well as in our Seiðr and runic work. Intention is a way of focusing the mind and making the universe aware of what we are intending to do with our journey, our spá, our Wyrd-weaving, and our power. The energy within us is neutral. The energy that comes from The Void is, by nature, also neutral, but if directed toward our own greatest good (if that is our intention), we can perform miracles! We can use our own intention to accentuate the existing flow of energy that comes from Ginnungagap, and *intend* it to take us toward our greatest good at a much faster, cleaner progression. Likewise, we can use our own intentions to fight against the flow toward our greatest good if we have a vague and unclear intention, as we then argue with the Norns about how our lives should be, and slow down the process of getting there. It is up to us how we use our own personal energy and intentions, and it is this very specific and directed power of our free will via specific intentions (or lack thereof) that makes or breaks our proficiency as Norse Mystics.

Remember the idea that the energy you receive and wield is power—and power, much like electricity as energy, can be used to harm or to illuminate a dark space. Again, the intent is vital to the outcome.[35]

Lesson 4/8: The Power of Concentration.

In our ongoing mind training, we will use Huginn and Muninn as our vehicle for this month's mind exercise. Numbers are used as a form of symbolic language much like music and letters are. They represent a calculated and measurable way of coming to answers (equations) that relay expressly on memory and thinking. To hone our minds, we must learn to exercise them from every angle—and unfortunately for all you haters of math, that includes numbers!

Practice:
1) Count backwards in your mind, from one hundred to one.
2) Count in your mind from one hundred to one, skipping each three numbers, that is 100, 97, 94, etc.
3) Count in your mind from one hundred to one, skipping each six numbers, that is 100, 94, 88, etc.
4) Count in your mind from one hundred to one, skipping each nine numbers, that is 100, 91, 81, etc.

Do each of these until you can do them quickly and without much thought.

---

[35] For a deeper look at this concept, I recommend Hale Makua's *Shared Wisdom* site: http://www.sharedwisdom.com/page/shamanic-personal-transformation.

Lesson 4/9: Reading Material and Exercises.

1) Read and work on the next chapter of *Neolithic Shamanism*—"The Brown World".

2) Read at least five more of the online God-shrines, and ask via Futhark/Futhorc or your own personal runes whether any of them would be interested in teaching or aiding you.

3) Read more of the other books on the Required Reading list.

4) Make sure that you are doing some kind of physical practice that combines moving the body with moving the body's energies.

5) Do a daily rune draw. If you do any other divination, practice your divination protocol.

Lesson 4/10: Immersion into the Völuspá, Verses 18–24

18. Önd (spirit/breath) they did not possess,
óðr (mind, inspiration) they did not have,
blood nor motive powers, nor good colour.
Önd gave Odin, óðr gave Hoenir,
blood gave Lodur, and good color.

19. I know an ash standing named Yggdrasil,
a high tree, laved with white mud:
thence come the dews that fall into dales
stands ever green Urd's fountain.

20. Thence come maidens,
much knowing, three from the sea,
which under tree stands;
Urd hight one, the second Verdandi,
on a tablet they graved, Skuld the third.
They laid down laws, they allotted life
human born; örlog (destiny) pronounced.

21. She remembers that folk-war, the first in the world,

The Deeper Arts of the Volva

when Gullveig was studded with spears,
and in the High One's hall burnt her,
thrice burnt, thrice born,
often not seldom; yet she still lives.

22. Heid they called her, to whatever house she came,
the well-foreseeing Vala: she enchanted gandr
sorcery she knew, sorcery she played;
she was ever the joy of evil people.

23. Then all the powers went to their judgment-seats,
the high-holy gods, and thereon held counsel;
whether the Æsir should pay a fine,
or all the gods pay tribute.

24. Odin cast (his spear), and shot into the people
that was the folk-war first in the world.
Broken was the board wall of the Æsir's burgh.
The Vanir, prophetic in war, tramp the plains.

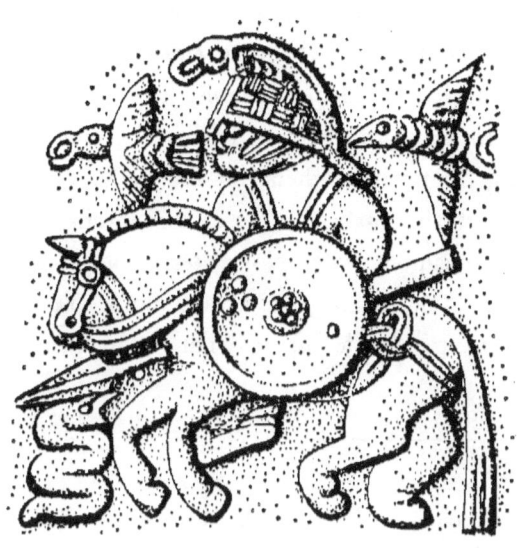

Month 5: A Walker With Many Skins

Lesson 5/1: Soul Part: *Hamr*.

The *Hamr* is a soul part best explained as the subtle force surrounding our human form. This energy shapes our magical and physical forms and has been compared to the "astral body" or "aura" in Western occult lore, or "anam" in Druidry. As a mundane example, many actors can make good use of their *Hamr*, since it is their job to appear as multiple faces or personalities to the audience. The face is still that of the actor, but they assume within their "aura" a different face, appearance, and mannerism which they have adopted though their thoughts and memories of the chosen character. When a person dies, Önd and *Hamr* immediately disappear. Dead people's faces lose all expression and familiar characteristics, as if they were not the same person.

Daniel McCoy's blog Norse *Mythology for Smart People*[36] describes the *Hamr* as literally translating to "shape" or "skin"—the *Hamr*, in this definition, being one's form or appearance; that which others perceive through sensory observation. Unlike in our modern worldview, however, that which is perceived by the senses is not absolutely and unalterably static and fixed. In fact, *Hamr* is the most crucial word in the Old Norse lexicon of shapeshifting. The Old Norse phrase that denotes the process of shapeshifting is *skipta hömum*, "changing *Hamr*," and the quality of being able to perform this feat is called *Hamramr*, "of strong *Hamr*".

I view our *Hamr* as the field of energy that surrounds every living thing, stemming from within their physical body, yet created from the ethereal energy stuff that makes up the entire universe. Often when I first was becoming acquainted with Norse terminology for concepts that seemed strange, I would investigate surrounding people's concepts on very similar constructs to decide upon what each term meant for me personally.[37]

---

[36] https://norse-mythology.org/concepts/the-parts-of-the-self/
[37] For more about the Hamr, see Nicholas Haney's website at: https://fireiceandsteel.wordpress.com/2015/05/27/Hamr-the-northern-spirit-part-4/

To clarify my ideas of the *Hamr* being our surrounding astral energy field that activates our other souls parts (especially the Fylgja), I looked to our Celtic cousins in Druidry, and there I found they indeed have an individual soul part of called the Nemeton[38]. According to Joanna Van Der Hoeven[39]:

> ...That physical space around us, where we feel uncomfortable if someone we do not trust enters, is a valuable space. It is our personal nemeton, a space where our energy exists outside of our bodies. Many liken it to your aura. Some nemetons are strong and radiant, some wounded with gaping holes, others barricaded with steel. What we have to learn, or relearn, is how to open this space in love and trust—that is what Nemetona provides, often in a world wherein we feel no other human is able to provide this for us.

I then discovered through cross-referencing various spellings on the word *Hamr* that it also is written as *Hama* or *Hame* in Anglo-Saxon. (One can find the last vestige of that word in older poetry about werewolves where it says that the individual "went out in wolf's hame".) The etymology of Old Norse, Old Anglo-Saxon, Gothic and other Germanic-speaking peoples can leave us a bit confused with multiple meanings for the words used to describe spiritual concepts of ancient peoples. But I cannot stress enough that we must always take comparisons of what surrounding cultures conceptualize for esoteric and mystic teachings. I know Norse Mysticism is unique; but its not so unique that a common theme or thread of thought-processing wouldn't have been prevalent in the Ancient world back when these concepts were being formed. I feel that all ancient peoples were connected much more to their Akashic Records (Orlog) and those of each other, so even if the words were pronounced

---

[38] For another look at the Druidic concept of shapeshifting, read the Druid Network website: https://druidnetwork.org/what-is-druidry/learning-resources/polytheist/lesson-seventeen/

[39] Van Der Heoven, Joanna. *Pagan Portals: Dancing with Nemetona.* Moon Books 2014.

differently, it's only logical that they would share very similar concepts and ideas. [40]

On the website "Wind In the World Tree"[41], the anonymous author discusses the word Hama (*Hamr*) and so beautifully says:

> The Hama is a bit tougher to get into and somewhat contentious. Hama means a natural covering, a membrane, like the skin shed off of a snake ... The Norse connection would be with the cognate *Hamr*. Within Norse literature we see examples of this concept through the *Hamför* or a journey outside of oneself and in the Havamal Odin claims to know spells to keep witches from returning to their *heim hama* or home skin. Essentially, the Hama is that which is spiritually surrounding us in a covering.

So with these concepts firmly planted, I will define the *Hamr* as the energy found around the outside of our bodies—think "aura" but more than that—and that we can use this energy to project our will into the universe through conscious intention. Doing this, we find that via activation of our *Hamr,* we can then use our *Hamr* to then command our Fylgja to either fare forth into the Otherworlds for us (as our body's spiritual double or as a animal, plant, or other shape) or we can communicate with it directly through Utiseta (meditation) and receive answers from our beloved Dead and our Orlog (which I see as the Akashic Records, the record of your soul's journey from the time you first arise from Source until you eventually return home). To create Orlog can take millennia. But no matter how new or ancient of a Soul you are, the Wyrd holds all your thoughts, feelings, actions and deeds from each lifetime.

I did a journey to follow up a New Moon ritual I did recently. In the journey I was seeking manifestation, as prescribed by Odin, for access to Huginn and Muninn. I used my Fylgja to travel there. During my otherworld access, I used my *Hamr* via my intention to change my Fylgja

---

https://fireiceandsteel.wordpress.com/2015/05/27/Hamr-the-northern-spirit-part-4/

[41] https://windintheworldtree.wordpress.com/2018/01/24/the-multi-part-soul/

form into that of an owl, as that is how I saw an opportunity to move about Yggdrasill and get the answers I was seeking.

Below is a simple exercise to get to know, feel, and flex your *Hamr*. Our *Hamr* is the part of us we use to cast sacred space, so if you can learn to feel it and control it, your magical work will grow in power and effectiveness. Remember, your personal *Hamr* is that space within and around you where you would not allow anyone but those beings with which you are most intimately acquainted with. You know your *Hamr* has been breached while on a bus or in a checkout line and someone sits or stands to close to you without your consent. Just as our physical bodies differ, everyone's *Hamr* is unique since it can vary in size, color, and shape at any given time, and more interestingly, each individual has the capacity to consciously control their *Hamr*'s composition at will. It is this conscious control that allows us to delineate sacred space, also known to Witches as "Casting a Circle."

Practice: Flexing your *Hamr*.

When you extend your *Hamr* to merge with another's, you are engaging in a process known in Druidry as "defining your edge". When you are aware and can control your *Hamr*'s edge, you can more skillfully broadcast a circle (create sacred space), as you are extending out from your sacred body space (*Hamr*) and co-mingling it with the outside world's space to form an encompassing sphere which is a temporary space to contain your sacred rite. In this next exercise, you are going to practice the art of moving your body's *Hamr* out far enough outward from your body's physical space that it will actually form an orb about nine feet from your being in all directions. Most importantly, with practice, you will be aware of your *Hamr* and actually feel its existence, as well as possibly seeing it as a color or perhaps (as I do) colorless waves.

Begin with grounding and centering. Look down at your hands and bring them together in prayer position. Slowly bring your palms about three inches apart and place the tip of your tongue gently against the roof of your mouth. Become aware of the heat that is transferring between your palms. Look to see if any sort of color or visual changes are happening in this space between your hands. Don't obsess too much on trying to see something, just be aware of the energies that are there by feeling them in the form of heat or tingling; the visual aspect might come later.

When you feel your own natural body's energy become activated, begin to pull your hands farther apart, stopping your progress if you lose the sensation of energy flowing between your hands. To regain the connection, simply bring your palms closer together. Continue this exercise until your hands are extended fully out at arm's length from your sides.

Breathing deeply and slowly (be careful not to hyperventilate), use your breath to begin pushing your *Hamr*'s energy about a foot away from your body. Move both hands down towards the ground, visualizing that you are building a sphere of energy into a space that will surround your entire lower body, pushing your arms in the front of you, then sweeping behind you in a graceful arcing motion. (This should take about two sweeps of your arms, one sweep to the front, one sweep to the rear.)

At the end of the sweep to the rear, your palms will be facing upward at shoulder level. Sweep your arms upward over your head, pushing the sphere you are creating with your *Hamr* above your head via your breath and will. Finish creating this *Hamr* sphere as you lower your hands to about face level, palms facing outward from the front of your upper body.

Now try to "see" your *Hamr* as a sphere encasing your body. Take a moment now to try to sense if you can feel a change of any kind; for example, is it warmer or cooler, is the air heavy, or do you perceive any color changes or some sort of vibration, sounds or smells? Most importantly, are you aware of the edge of your *Hamr* being extended a bit farther, touching the edge of a boundary you have created consciously?

When you are ready, bring your *Hamr* back to its natural size as it covers your body normally without conscious thought on your part; by retracing these steps in reverse. Always be sure not to allow your *Hamr*'s boundary to reach out farther than you can maintain, as this opens us up to unwanted invasions by other beings' *Hamr*s. (Remember the bus analogy above!) In a natural, relaxed state your *Hamr* usually is only reaching a few inches outward from your physical body. With practice and awareness, this exercise can be done in moments by simply focusing your mind on your *Hamr* and with each breath pushing it outwards as far as you wish to go.

All Shamans use the *Hamr* for shapeshifting (whether they call it by that name, or by a word known as simply "soul"). Having a strong *Hamr* means you can not only pass undetected through the Nine Worlds, you also could appear as any creature you desired, as long as your will and knowledge of the chosen subject you wish to shape-shift into was good enough. With practice, you can transform yourself to appear to become another entity or object in a split second, via thinking of your chosen object, then remembering its form, and then passing that information via your *Hamr* to your Fylgja. (See how the parts are all coming together?)

The Norse people attributed the power of shapeshifting to their *Hamr*, and how well the *Hamr* was developed. Loki, the God of chaos and mischief, was particularly fond of (and skilled in) shapeshifting and could take any shape that he wanted, even mothering a few monsters while he was in a female shape! Freyja, the goddess of love and fertility, had a cloak of feather falcons which allowed her to transform into a falcon at will. Likewise, Odin was fond of transforming into various shapes, humanlike and otherwise.

All collective mythology and folklore are full of stories of the Gods, animals, and humans shapeshifting into other forms or spiritual entities, as well as the opposite gender, and animals both mystical and real. Throughout the mythos, otherworldly travelers or spirit-walkers do this by combining their own will, intention, thoughts and memories with magical artifacts, songs and ritual gestures.

Shapeshifting using our *Hamr* to change our fetch's appearance can also occur in the personal and collective consciousness—in politics, in business, and in society at large. If a group of Shamans or Witches decide to collectively turn their Fylgja in to wolves to devour a social "monster" by doing a group ritual accessing in unison each *Hamr* to become a wolf pack, that magical action can change the immediate collective consciousness as well as each practitioner's personal world.

Sometimes Norse people other than Völvas and seiðkonas were inspired to attempt to "shapeshift" their outward appearance as well. The best example, of course, are the "berserkers" and "ulfhednar" who believed that they could take the shape of a bear or wolf in battle by wearing the animal's attributes and skin over their own. By altering their appearance to that of a fierce beast, they struck terror into the opposing warriors, thereby giving them the upper hand at the start of the battle. Of course, they weren't traveling to another world; they were very much in the moment!

The sacred traditions of the Norse were passed down from the Völva's and Oldest Shamans; The Sami People. Like all the aboriginal peoples of a region, the Finnish Sami use ceremony and believe there is a spirit in all things of nature. They shapeshift into animals, and even rocks or trees, to do their Shamanic work, as well as change their *Hamr* by wearing animal spirit masks or even real animal heads, like the animal skins that Norse warriors used in shapeshifting during battle.[42]

Shapeshifting is an ancient practice, and it can be liberating because you are tapping into a great power. A word of caution about disrespecting great power, however, as it can lash out at you: At all times, remain extremely respectful of all the magical energies and the animal allies you are working with, and always remember to offer something to the earth, spirits of place, your ancestors, and the animal spirits in return.

Another rule is to never abuse shapeshifter talents, and always remain open to all the magic that surrounds you everywhere. There is truth to the saying, with great power comes great responsibility. If you harm another soul with this power, it will come back to you, and it can even make you very sick or kill you. There are plenty of legends about spirit-workers who made this mistake and were "set up" by the spirits to fail badly. Shamans who abuse strong magic rarely live to be old. Do not take this caution lightly. All magic is very powerful and can turn against you if you use it wrongly.

Lesson 5/2: Shapeshifting.

For this lesson, you will consciously try to change the shape, form and density of your *Hamr,* which is best pictured as a "spirit-skin" or "aura",

---

[42] For more information on Nordic totemism, see Daniel McCoy's essay at https://norse-mythology.org/concepts/totemism/. For a good look at how shapeshifting can help with internal emotional work, see Ravenari's site at: http://www.wildspeak.com/other/shapeshiftingintro.html.

resembling yourself in appearance most of the time.[43] *(Note: Some people with specific conditions, such as gender dysphoria, primary vampirism, or very active nonhuman blood, may have a Hamr that does not, and possible never did, resemble their physical bodies. Don't be alarmed if this is the case for you; it's just something that happens.)*

1. Close your eyes and allow yourself to become deeply relaxed. As a suggestion, you may wish to drum a very steady continuous beat. (This is a traditional method of shapeshifting for the Sami.) You may play music designed for relaxation which can help you enter into an altered state of consciousness; just be sure it is free of lyrics!

2. Picture what animal you are choosing to become. Recall its appearance; its habits. Now imagine that animal's essence slipping over your body via your *Hamr*. Feel that your body is metamorphosing into another form in its *appearance*. It can be anything you choose. Take time to experience fully how that other being feels.

3. With your eyes closed, allow your body to move subtly, almost imperceptively, while feeling your outer-self changing into another shape.

4. Visualize that you've become in looks that animal, plant, mineral, or even another person. Involve all your senses. Imagine what you would smell, taste, hear, and feel like to someone else viewing you. For example, if you become a wolf, imagine having an acute ability to smell. If you become an eagle, imagine your eyesight to be very sharp and far-seeing.

5. Afterward, while it's still fresh in your memory, make notes about your experience. Later in this lesson we will use the idea of ritual postures and dance to integrate our animal power into our skin-walking.

Lesson 5/4: Dancing With Our Animal Spirits.

In the next segment we will be working on shapeshifting into our chosen ally for skin-walking. Instead of a ritual posture, this month we will utilize the art of sacred pantomime, experiencing our spirt work

---

[43] For information on shapeshifting with the direct intervention of an animal spirit, see Wyrdwalkers (Raven Kaldera, Asphodel Press, 2006), pp. 314-334.

through our body, which is after all the vehicle we must use to access all of our profound spiritual work.

Finding Your Animal Totem.

For this ritual, you are going to want to go outside and be in Nature. I understand that are many who live in the city and are disabled (or are in prison), and have no access to the great outdoors. In those emergency cases, you can do this ritual inside, but if you are at all able-bodied and can get yourself to a piece of Nature, do that. Animals and animal spirits are part of Nature and you can't walk this path without deeply understanding how much a part of Nature you are as well, and you can't do that while insulating yourself against Nature.

Understand, also, that if you make contact with an animal spirit, that is a two-sided relationship, not one of convenience. You will be expected to maintain that relationship in some way—regular offerings, regular loving contact, or perhaps some favor that the animal spirit might want. (Since you are going to be leaving offerings, don't do this ritual in a place where signs tell you not to feed the animals or toss scraps into the woods.)

In addition, try very hard not to assume what the animal spirit who approaches will be. in more New Age circles, it seems like everyone wants to connect with the "glamorous" animal spirits like Wolf, Bear, Lion, Eagle, etc. You might get Chipmunk or Squirrel. You might get a fish, or an insect. Be open to whatever comes, because every species can teach us something. Small, unobtrusive animals can sneak in where larger ones would be seen, for example.

Also, this may not be the only, or the last, animal spirit that you work with. Records about Seiðr workers mentioned them having more than one "faring forth" shape, and records from witch trials mention witches having multiple "familiars" whose shapes they could take on. In Northern Tradition Shamanism, shamans and shamanic practitioners eventually collect, over their lifetime, one animal spirit ally who helps them shape into a flying form, one a swimming form, one a running form, one a digging/burrowing form, one a predatory form, and one animal form from your ancestral lineage. In addition, shamans who specialize in plant spirits may have dozens more.

Bring the following items with you in a pack:
- ❖ Your drum.
- ❖ A small bowl of water.
- ❖ Some kind of offering for the animals—if you aren't sure what sort you might get, bring a little raw meat, some grains or seeds, some fresh greens.[44]
- ❖ Recels (incense/smudge) and a fireproof bowl or slab to burn it on. (Since by now you will have read "The Green World" chapter in Neolithic Shamanism, you will know what works best for you. You'll also have read "The Brown World" and so you'll have a idea of how to call animal spirits.) Don't forget a lighter.[45]

Find a secluded place, lay out the offerings, light the recels. Smoke the area and around yourself while Galdring the Futhark runes Ansuz (for the divine message) and Uruz (for the strength of wildness). You can also sing a Galdr for your purpose and intention, or just speak those words aloud.

Put down the recels (on your fireproof surface), pick up your drum, start a slow heartbeat rhythm, and just sing a wordless call. Let the call drift on and off. Into it, put your intention: that the spirit of the right animal will come to you and teach you how shift your energy body into that form, that you will be able to form a relationship with that spirit, and learn from them.

As you sing, very slowly speed up the rhythm. At some point, if the spirit approaching is an animal with a heart, the rhythm will reach the heartbeat of that animal. (You probably won't know what that rate of speed is; don't worry about it. Just wait until your intuition says "Hold it at this rate!" and then do that. (And, of course, animals, like us, have different heart rates depending on activity and emotions.) If it is an animal without a heart (there are some) or a plant (rare, if you're asking for

---

[44] If you are in an area where loose domestic animals come through, don't leave raw meat where they could get it—many modern domestic animals are intolerant of raw meat and milk. When you leave, put it in a tree where domestic animals are unlikely to get it.

[45] If you are in a drought-stricken area, don't use flame. Instead, put energy into an electric votive candle, mark it with a Kenaz, and use that instead.

animals, but still possible—the spirits do what they think is best), then that point will not come, so just slow it back down.

If an animal spirit approaches, stop drumming and get down on the ground, at least sitting or kneeling, ideally on fours if they are quadrupedal. It's a way of saying, I am here with you on the earth. Give them the appropriate offering. Thank them for taking the time to come to you, and ask them what their advice to you might be. At that point, it's between you and them, and it will go as it goes. Listen to them and take their advice.

If they want you to go into an altered state and follow them in that shape, you can start drumming again to put yourself there (or singing/chanting, whatever works best for you) and journey with them. You can also start dancing while you drum and sing, if moving your body feels like the right thing to do. Ask them to show you  how to shift your energy body around to take their shape, if possible. You may feel your energy body shifting shape as you dance with the animal spirit, or they may want you to get down again and move like them on the ground, depending on the nature of the animal spirit involved.

Afterwards, thank the animal spirit and go, leaving the woods as close to how you found them as possible—but leave the food offering for real animals to come and eat, ideally in an out-of-the-way place where people won't step on it. Pour out the water on the earth.

When you get home, you can research the ancient traditions and symbolism surrounding that animal, but remember that the animal spirit knows best. If it doesn't like that symbolism for whatever reason—and keep in mind that symbolism is a human thing, not an animal thing—then that symbolism isn't for you personally to use, although someone else might be able to do so. Lastly, if the animal spirit tells you to change something in your life ... well, if you want to keep working with them, you'd better change it. These relationships are reciprocal. Value them like the good friends they can become.

Lesson 5/5: The Well of Mimir.

We are conceived and born, and our existence begins. As we move through the worlds, we spin our own meaning from the slender fibers with which we have been provided. We may ply with others' threads, braid with them, weave, plait, wear, fray ... and try to cut. Necessarily, our perspective narrows: we know of our thoughts accumulated though our unique life experience and our memories of its unfolding thus far, but will we know more? In this and similar ways do each of us trade breadth for depth of perspective, and half our sight for a narrow sort of wisdom.

For this month's Utiseta, let us travel to Mimir and see if we may receive deeper kennings. After reading this suggested journey, your goal is to create your own visionary experience with the purpose of Knowing more and uniting with your own Huginn and Muninn. Keep what works and change what you need. Remember to do divination before making this journey—you will be going to Jotunheim, which may not be as friendly a place as Vanaheim or Asgard (unless you already have a strong relationship with some Jotun Gods). If the divination says that you should not go, skip this section and try again another month.

Prepare for your journey the way you normally do, by creating a sacred space that is hallowed, and by preparing your body and your spirit to fare forth. Begin by centering yourself on your seat, and cover your head with your cloak or eye cover, and begin rhythmically tapping your Stav. Breathe deeply but naturally in four counts—in/hold-pause—then out four counts until you your mind is cleared and you begin to see the veil of the otherworld mist form behind your eyes in the darkness. Begin to intone or hum the vardlokkur of your making, and as the mist forms, state your intention out loud via your own Galdr as to where you are going.[46]

Mímisbrunnr is the Old Norse word for "Mímir's well". Mimir (pronounced "MEE-meer") was a hostage for the Aesir, beheaded when the Vanir thought they got a raw deal in their exchange of hostages.

---

[46] If you prefer a more modernized and technological context to your journey, please check out Lorrie Wood's account of her journey to Mimir's Well: https://hrafnar.org/articles/lwood/well-and-web/.

Mimir means "the rememberer" or "the wise one". After Mimir was beheaded, Odin embalmed his head with special herbs and chanted magical songs over it to preserve it, and then dropped it in a well in Jotunheim for safekeeping. He consulted the head in times of need, as it continued to dispense incomparable advice, even when separated from its body.

Mímisbrunnr is the well containing the head of Mimir, which will give advice when asked. This well is located next to a root of Yggdrasil that passes into Jotunheim. In addition, the water of the well contains so much of Mimir's wisdom that Odin sacrificed one of his eyes to the well (and Mimir) in exchange for a drink. Mimir is an exceptionally wise being and a counselor of the gods. More than any other being in Norse mythology, he seems to be regarded as the divine force behind the wisdom (knowing/remembering) of past tradition and its indispensable value as a guide for present actions. For this month's Utiseta, we will journey to Mimir's well to experience our thoughts and memories.

Practice: Journey to Mimir.

Once you are in trance, take the form best suited for journeying. Move into Yggdrasil in the way that you normally would—by now you should have a method down—and go down the Tree until you come to the branch that is Jotunheim. You don't have to go in very far—you will see the huge root that extends into the world; just follow it closely. It looms above you like a hill of rough bark; great tangled vines and greenery cascade over it. You see ahead a dark cave opening into the ground under the root, almost entirely camouflaged by shrubs and vines. Go down into the cave, into the dark. As you pass out of the light, you see another light ahead of you, faint and blue-green.

Stop here and ask for permission to enter. wait until you hear the high, thin voice whispering from the well. When Mimir says that you may approach, come closer and see the great well of black water with the ring of stones around it. Bones float in the water—those whom Mimir slew magically for their disrespect to Him. A disembodied head floats in the center of the well, eyes dark in the shrunken face, white hair and beard floating around it like a halo. Before Him in the water, like the floating pendant of a necklace, is something gleaming and blue that lights the cave with an eerie glow. You realize that this is Odin's eye.

The dark eyes find yours with a penetrating gaze that freezes you in your tracks and makes you feel as if Mimir is looking right through you, to your soul. He sums you up and His eyes narrow. "Why have you come here?" he asks. Do not lie or exaggerate right now—He can smell that. Just reply, "To learn." It is the safest answer, for a beginner.

He looks at you for a time, and then tells you something about your Hugr (cognition) and Mynd (memory), meant only for you. Take the precious knowledge and go home with it—out of the cave, out of Jotunheim, all the way home. When you are back in your body, find a pond, lake, river, or wellspring and pour out some liquor as an offering to Mimir the Wise.

Lesson 5/6: Oathmaking.

Oathmaking is one of the most important ceremonies in Asatru. In ancient times an Oathbreaker was as viewed as heinously as was a murderer; this reminds us that the power of our words are the strongest magics we can wield. To swear an Oath or profess one's belief in and kinship to the Gods, Wights and Ancestors should be recognized as an irrevocable act, as well as an important turning point in one's life. It is the beginning of a new understanding of the self and all the beings of the Nine Worlds we choose to work with.

Oathmaking (or Profession in modern mainstream religious terms), with all its power and weightiness, is surprisingly a very simple and rather short ceremony. It can be done as its own stand-alone Utiseta, or either before or after the Blót offering. It is not an occult or initiatory ceremony. It is nothing less than its name; one professes (declares, affirms) his wish to become one of those who is true to the Asa/Van/Jötnar. The oath below, for example, is usually taken by the Kindred-Gothi on the oath ring or some other holy object as follows:

The Godi (priest) or Gythia (priestess) stands in front of the altar and says "Will [insert name here] please come forward." After he or she does so, the questions are asked; "Are you here of your own free will? Is it your intention to solemnly swear allegiance and kinship to (the Gods of Asgard, the Aesir and Vanir, The Alfs, etc.)?" If the answer to these questions is in the affirmative, the presiding Godi/Gythia takes up the oath ring (or some other holy object upon which oaths are sworn), holds it out to the person professing, and says "Repeat after me. I swear to ever uphold the (gods, wights elves, etc.), to follow the way of the North, to always act with honor and bravery, and to be ever true to the (Aesir, Vanir, Jötunn, Elves, Dwarves, wights of the Nine Worlds, etc.), and to (Asatru, Heathenry, Vanatru, Rokkatru, the Northern Way. etc.). By the Gods, my ancestors, my descendants and all my soul parts I so swear. By my honor I so swear. On this Holy Ring I so swear. Hail the Gods." The kindred then replies "Hail the Gods!" and the Godi/Gythia finishes "Then be welcome to the service of the Gods and our community."

The essence of Oathmaking is professing allegiance as well as a commitment to the Norse Cosmology and all that give a Völva/Vitki their power. It should not be undertaken without thought and prayer. When one Professes, one is leaving behind all doubts, hesitation and fear. If one isn't yet comfortable in doing this, then Oathmaking should be put off, perhaps indefinitely. It should be reiterated here that there should be absolutely no pressure put on people to Profess. False or coerced oaths merely cheapen the ritual and the commitment that it represents. It should also be said that all seiðr work, and ritual is open to anyone; however, to earn the kinship and working relationship with certain entities, one must prove they are worthy, as well as able and ready for a relationship which is co-creational and mutual. This is done by the simple act of giving your word and professing your willingness to do your part when asked.

Lesson 5/7: Vanquishing Doubt.

Our thoughts are creative, yes, but only to the point they define concepts and create within us a specific emotional state. The emotional state has a far greater effect on successful application of the principle of attraction than mere analytical thought. The emotion is the vibration or the underlying energy and power of attraction. Even in a state of no-thought (which is not easily attainable without years of practice and teaching), how you feel would still affect your reality, if not your actions.

With conscious thought and feeling, you can create powerfully. However, each serves a different function.

Doubt is an emotion, and if you allow doubt or second-guessing to begin to creep in while doing energy work, Wyrd manipulation, spell casting, or journeying, it can kill your connection and success almost immediately. Emotion provides the need; or more correctly the catalyst, but emotion without thought (intention) is also ineffectual as it leads to chaotic outcomes. If you consistently sabotage the outcome of your rituals or spiritual work by letting your emotions overwhelm your intention, that will only naturally increase doubts when performing your Work as Völvas/Vitkis. So since we now understand the results of doing your seiðr with just emotion and no strong intent becomes completely unpredictable, we need to know how to avoid this waste of time and energy. Successful spiritual work manifests *where thought meets emotions in a trained manner*, and it's called FOCUS.

Focused thought shapes the energy and directs it to a specific result, much like the lens of a magnifying glass focuses light. The more focused and controlled the thought, the more certain will be the outcome, so long as the energy that is created from emotion matches the intent of the thought. Therefore, the secret of vanquishing doubt is first to focus.

Visualization is the first element of Focusing for manipulating energies. The second element is trust. It's very simple: Once you have visualized your energy—for example moving it toward your hand—you need to know (trust) that this energy has been "transferred" into your hand. Don't just visualize, trust in your skills that you have done it.

Nearly everything in a metaphysical practice is related, more or less, to energy manipulation—moving, transferring and sculpting different types of energies. In order to manipulate energy, you don't just need to know what this energy is, or what type of energy you're manipulating. You have to be able to feel it, then focus it toward your intended goal via focused manipulation.

So how to actually do this "focused manipulation"? Well, everyone has a different technique. In my technique there are basically two elements: visualization and trust. The first element: visualization, is pretty simple—you need to visualize (or feel) this psychic energy for yourself, then you must trust beyond the shadow of a doubt you can focus your intention of will as to where that energy will be going. There is energy all around your body all the time you're alive. This is known as your *Hamr* (or aura/auric body). This energy which surrounds your physical self hovers for about an inch above your body. So basically, all you need to know to do some "manipulation" is to visualize your own psychic energy gathering in your hand, as taken from your own bodies energy field [*Hamr*], and trust you have the ability to do so.

Using your own energy field for hands-on healing. or for moving energy some other way, is just a simple example, but what you need to remember is that by visualizing this energy moving from your entire body to your hand, you're really moving this energy via **focus**. This "energy transfer" will make your hand full of energy, and feeling the results of your focused will, you have full trust that your skills work. So this month, work on training your focus and trust as your Seat work for the month.

Lesson 5/9: Reading Material.

1) Read and work on the next two chapters of *Neolithic Shamanism*—"The Blue World" and "The Red World". Water and Fire balance each other.

2) Read at least five more of the online God-shrines, and ask via Futhark/Futhorc or your own personal runes whether any of them would be interested in teaching or aiding you.

3) Read more of the other books on the Required Reading list.

4) Make sure that you are doing some kind of physical practice that combines moving the body with moving the body's energies.

Do a daily rune draw. If you do any other divination, practice your divination protocol.

Lesson 5/10: Immersion into the Völuspá, Verses 25–35

25. Then all the powers went to their judgment-seats,
the high-holy gods, and thereon held council:
who had mingled all the air with evil?

or to the Jötun race had given Od's maid [Freyja]?

26. Thor was there alone swollen with anger.
He seldom sits, when he hears of the like.
Oaths are not held sacred; nor words, nor swearing,
nor binding compacts reciprocally made.

31. I saw Baldr, the bloody god's,
Odin's son, hidden fate,
stand grown high on the plain,
slender and very fair, mistletoe.

32. Of that shrub became, it seems to me, a deadly dart.
Hödr took the shot; Baldur's brother was
born quickly so Odin's son
one night old began to fight.

33. He never washed hands nor combed head
till he bore to the bale Baldur's adversary—
When Frigg cried in Fensalir for Valhall's woe.
Know ye yet, or what?

34. Bound she saw lying, under Hvera-lund (Kettle-grove),
a monstrous form, like unto Loki.
There sits Sigyn, for her husband's sake, not right glad.
Know ye yet, or what?

35. A river east, through venom dales,
with knives and swords, Slith is its name.

Month 6: Wyrd Weaver, Spinner of Fate

Lesson 6/1: Weaving Wyrd.

This chapter marks the point where we will delve into the procedures and methods used to preform Wyrd-working. The most fundamental concept in heathenry is Wyrd. It is also one of the most difficult to explain and hence one of the most often misunderstood. Here's the best explanation I have found: an excerpt from the article "What Is Wyrd?" by Arlea Æðelwyrd Hunt-Anschütz, published in Cup Of Wonder Issue #5, October 2001[47], used with permission.[48]

> The Anglo-Saxon noun *wyrd* is derived from a verb, *weorþan*, "to become", which, in turn, is derived from an Indo-European root **uert-* meaning "to turn". If you noticed the redundant use of "turn" in the previous sentence, good. The use of the modern English phrase "in turn", illustrates wyrd in action. Watch for it throughout these slides. Wyrd literally means "that which has turned" or "that which has become". It carries the idea of "turned into" in both the sense of becoming something new and the sense of turning back to an original starting point. In a metaphysical terms, wyrd embodies the concept that everything is turning into something else while both being drawn in toward and moving out from its own origins. Thus, we can think of wyrd as a process that continually works the patterns of the past into the patterns of the present.
>
> A good metaphor for wyrd is spinning with a drop spindle. As the fibres turn round and round, they twist together and become thread. In Norse mythology three female entities called the Norn's are responsible for shaping lives out of *ørlög*, the layers of the past. Their names are Urðr (Wyrd) "that which has become"; Verðandi

---

[47] http://www.wyrdwords.vispa.com/heathenry/whatwyrd.html
[48] For other useful views on Wyrd, please see WyrdDesign's Patheos article at: http://www.patheos.com/blogs/pantheon/2011/06/wyrd-designs-understanding-the-words-wyrd-and-orlog/ and Dr. Karl Siegfried of Cherry Hill's article at: http://www.norsemyth.org/2016/11/wyrd-will-weave-us-together.html.

(related to the Anglo-Saxon *weorþan*, see above) "that which is in the process of becoming"; and Skuld (Should) "that which should necessarily be". In the Eddic poem Helgakviða Hundingsbana 1, the Norns twist the strands of the infant prince's *ørlög* (which in this case can be seen as his heritage, since he has no personal past to speak of) to create a golden cord representing his life.

Another way of understanding wyrd is through a weaving analogy. In the Anglo-Saxon Riming Poem, the narrator says of his life circumstances *Me þæt wyrd gewæf*, "Wyrd wove this for me". In the Icelandic Njal's Saga, valkyries weave out the course of a battle on a loom made of weapons and threaded with human entrails. Imagine a patterned piece of cloth being woven on a loom. The horizontal threads (the woof) are woven in in layers along the vertical threads (the warp). The horizontal threads represent layers of past actions. The vertical threads represent a timeline. The color of each horizontal thread as it is woven in will add to the pattern that is already established and influence the pattern that emerges. The threads already woven in cannot be changed, but the overall pattern is never fixed. Existing designs can be expanded into new forms. New designs can be added. Everything we do adds one more layer to the pattern.

One ramification of Wyrd in personal human terms is that our past (both our ancestry and our personal history) affects us continually. Who we are, where we are, and what we are doing today is dependent on actions we have taken in the past and actions others have taken in the past which have affected us in some way. Every choice we make in the present builds upon choices we have previously made.

The philosopher Schopenhauer voiced the notion that "our lives are somehow irresistibly shaped into a coherent whole by forces beyond our conscious will". He believed that neither chance events nor inborn character were enough to explain the consistency and direction in the life course of an individual, and so he postulated "the intention of Fate" to explain this controlling force in our lives. Many people have equated the notion of Wyrd with this sort of "fate" concept, and the Norns with the Moerae or Parcae, the Greek and Roman Fates. However, to do so is to ignore the constant interplay between personal wyrd and universal wyrd and the role we each play in creating our own destiny.

The key Schopenhauer seems to have missed is that what he calls "the intention of Fate" is itself created by an interplay between the events that happen to us and our inborn character. We interact with wyrd (that which has become) to create certain personal patterns which affect and are reflected in universal patterns. Those universal patterns, in turn, exert forces which shape our lives.

For example, say I happen to find myself in a situation where someone insults me. I can "freely" choose any one of a number of immediate reactions, from ignoring the person to slapping them. But my choice at that moment is obviously going to be constrained by a number of patterns of wyrd already in place, including my inborn personality characteristics, my social conditioning, my past experiences with being insulted, my relationship with the person who has insulted me, even my hormone levels.

To the extent that my reaction is determined by these patterns, wyrd is shaping my life at that moment, and my reaction may feel to me as though it were predestined (if I want to deny responsibility) or the only "right" choice (if I want to claim responsibility for it). To the extent that I am aware of certain recurring patterns in my life, I might feel as though the person was fated to insult me at that moment. But no matter which way I chose to react to the insult, my reaction will add to the patterns in place and constrain my future actions (if I'm insulted a second time, my reaction will be determined in part by how I behaved when I was insulted the first time.) So, at the same time I am caught up in experiencing certain patterns of wyrd, I am creating them.

Moving from the personal to the universal, my reaction will also add to the patterns affecting the behavior of the person who insulted me. As a result of my response, she may change her behavior towards others which will, in turn, change their personal *ørlög*, and so on. Ultimately, each little choice we make affects universal forces which can come back to affect us in weird ways. The larger patterns of wyrd created by individuals in a particular time and place is the source of the zeitgeist (spirit of the age) which informs the beliefs and behavior of everyone in a society. Thus, "that which has become", wyrd, both creates and is created by individual actions, states, and choices.

The metaphor of the "Web of Wyrd" is often used in modern popular sources to illustrate how the actions of individuals can have widespread effects. If we imagine the universe as a big spider's web and imagine that each node where two strands meet represents an event (or a person or a life) we can visualize the interconnectedness of things. We can see how some things are directly connected whereas others are more distantly connected through a series of links. We can also see how nodes which are closely connected from one perspective (following a single strand from the center outwards) can be distantly connected from another perspective (following the spiral that continually expands its radius as it moves from the center). Furthermore, we can see that if we were to disturb any part of the web --say by blowing on it or shaking it, the entire thing would reverberate --through the parts closest to the disturbance would react the most strongly.

With an understanding of wyrd comes a great responsibility. If we know that every action we take (or fail to take, for that matter) will have implications for our own future choices and for the future choices of others, we have an ethical obligation to think carefully about the possible consequences of everything we do. But even if we manage to make all the right choices, we are bound to find ourselves facing difficult circumstances or tough decisions at various times in our lives as a result of the past choices of those connected to us through the web. Since we can't control everyone else's actions, nor can we change the past, sometimes we just have to live with what's been woven for us. In such a case we still have choices. We can ignore our problems in the hope that they will go away, we can burden other people with them, or we can boldly face up to them and do our best to overcome them. A verse from the Anglo-Saxon poem "The Wanderer" observes:

Ne mæg werigmod wyrde wiðstondan,
ne se hreo hyge helpe gefremman.
For ðon domgeorne dreorigne oft
in hyra breostcofan bindað fæste;
"A weary mood won't withstand wyrd,
nor may the troubled mind find help.
Often, therefore, the fame-yearners
bind dreariness fast in their breast-coffins."

Through the Web of Wyrd may force us into circumstances we would never have freely chosen for ourselves, we always have some choice about how we react in those situations. And how we choose to react will always make a difference, if not to the world at large, then at least to our own *ørlög*."

Lesson 6/2: Wyrd Working.

In this chapter I will truly and unabashedly use the words and experiences of trusted other Spá workers, as for me, the paramount importance is for you, the reader, to fully understand Wyrd, what it is, and what you can and cannot do with it. By showing you in their own words what other esteemed Wyrd-workers have found, I (and you) know you aren't just taking *one* Völva's word on the subject, and that gives you the best possibilities. Again, the most important thing you will want to remember is that when working with Wyrd, you will be going directly to the well of Urd, and by the Norns' leave you will attempt to straighten, twist, knot or sever your own, or someone else's strands of Wyrd. I highly recommend learning actual fiber arts techniques such as spinning or weaving, so that when it comes time to do it astrally, you will have a visceral sensation to hold onto.[49]

Also: To make any of this work successful, but especially in the realm of Wyrd weaving, you must have these three factors working in your favor: *intention*, *trust*, and *will*. All three concepts coincide with each other and must all be done with unwavering focus. If doubt or hesitation creep in, you will be ineffectual in your otherworldly endeavors.

For this lesson, you need to read the chapter on Wyrd Working in Raven Kaldera's book *Wyrdwalkers*, which sums up the nature of this practice in a better way than I ever could. Read it and take notes on it in your journal. What does it bring up for you? What hard ethical decisions can you imagine having to make? Write out your answers as you ponder this.

---

[49] Here I will also recommend Janet Allen-Coombe's interview with Brian Bates in *Shaman's Drum* magazine, found online at https://library.wisn.org/wp-content/uploads/2016/02/130121-Weaving-the-Way-of-Wyrd.pdf.

Lesson 6/3: Ritual to Change Hamingja.

This month your Utiseta will be to sit in trance while holding some homespun yarn and to try to get a glimpse into what your own personal strand of Wyrd looks like, as well as how to interpret what its knots, tangles and interconnection of other stands means. You will attempt to draw what you see in your out sitting-session, then you will divine in any form you like (or multiple forms) what the Wyrd meaning holds for you. In this month's out-sitting you will have to focus on your freedom to allow Öðr to connect you with the Norns. In other words, you will be working on this process of ecstatic and inspired workings long after your monthly out-sitting is over.

Remember, when working our intentions into the web of wyrd, it needn't be a impossible task. If you simply work in both the real world to better yourself as well as with the Norns, miracles can happen! Below is a simple exercise in Wyrd weaving, done simultaneously in Midgard and at the well of Urd.

To rid ourselves of bad Hamingja, we will do this simple knot magic and use our will, intention, and an altered state (trance). We are the sum of a thousand lifetimes and loves, so it's well worth it to persevere and try to change your "luck" or bad Wyrd, as it becomes someone else's Orlog one day. Do not let the simple appearance of this ritual fool you as to the potency of this working. Do keep in mind, however, that the ritual must be followed in its stated order. Skipping or altering a step may get undesirable results.

1) Take a fearless inventory of yourself and your reoccurring bad behaviors that get you into undesirable situations. Manifest an unwavering intention to fix them.
2) Dig deep and look for these patterns within your family line, in the event that this is Hamingja you have inherited, which will (if unchanged) pass down to your descendants.
3) Write down all the qualities you wish to change on a piece of paper, and gather a thick strand of the finest wool you can find. (If you could spin your own strand, all the better, but purchasing one is fine.)
4) Go to your Hof or Vé and prepare to do a Blót of change.

5) Begin your Blót as you normally do, and ask for the Norns to be present, as well as your Disir. Be sure to pour out offerings of welcome and gratitude.
6) Go into your trance state, and begin a Galdr for the change of your Hamingja. State clearly that this is a rite of Wyrd change as your intention, and be sure to scream that intention to the Norse Nine Worlds.
7) Once you have attained a good trance state, pick up your wool string and begin to sing your Wyrd into change! While holding the string, sing the Futhark runes Nauthiz, Hagalaz, Thurisaz, Algiz, Ingwaz (in that order) while tying knots for each bad behavior manifestation that is in your life. Be sure to sing and name each bad inherited trait while tying each knot.
8) As soon as the knots are tied, hold the string over a fire. Using your *Hamr* with full concentration, untie each knot as you sing the Futhark runes Jera, Dagaz, Berkana, and Wunjo. You can end your song by singing: "This bad Hamingja I inherited from my family's line, no longer is mine, nor will my descendants be maligned! By Fire, need, and solid will, a better hamingja is now fulfilled!"
9) Throw the string in the fire-and send the changed Wyrd to the Norns. Be sure to thank them, and make an Oath that you will live very differently from this point onward, proving you are worthy of good Hamingja.

Lesson 6/4: Spinner Posture.

Here's a new posture to add to your routine: Freya as spinner.

In this Iron Age figure from Tisso, Denmark, we see Freya actually spinning her own hair on distaffs. In ancient times a woman's hair was viewed as a part of her where her power resided, so as traditional Witchcraft practices all across Europe attest that a witch's power is most often strong when her hair was unbound and free.

In keeping with this month's work of spinning, we go further in deducing that in this representation of Freya, she is spinning the power of her own hair onto distaffs to use for either her own future work, or to perhaps pass the power to someone else.

1) Stand with your feet shoulder width apart, with your head high, and eyes fixed forward.
2) Grasp your hair and begin to twine it nine times between your fingers, revolving the entire hand on your wrists in a circular clock wise motion.
3) When the hair is tight, look up and take a deep breath in, holding it for four counts.
4) Then look up, and exhale forcefully while spinning your hands counter-clockwise, unraveling your "spun" hair.
5) Shake both hands in front of you, and then clap them together saying a forceful "Ha!"

Lesson 6/5: Our Many Gods III: Ritual to Find your Patron Deity.

(This rite is excerpted with permission from **Candles In The Cave: Northern Religion for Prisoners.***)*

First, I want to make it clear that not everyone has a patron deity by any means. Many people have relationships with a wide variety of Gods, and perhaps a handful who are rather special to them, but not one who is the center of their world. This is just as acceptable as having one special patron. In fact, it has been said that those who insist that everyone should have a patron deity are actually just indulging in a holdover from monotheistic religions, and are secretly uncomfortable with the abundant multiplicity of polytheistic Gods. In addition, you don't choose a patron. They choose you, because they have decided that you have an affinity of some sort with them. In short: Some have Gods choose them in patronage. Some don't. Both are equally fine.

Some folks in Northern religion use the old Norse word *fulltrui* to describe their patron deity. The word means "fully trusted one".

Any of the deities in this book (except for the Norns who are beyond such relationships) might claim someone for a close relationship. As far as we can tell from primary sources, in ancient times only priests had fulltrui, but these are different times and the Gods are reaching out in different ways. If you do this rite in order to invite (and the key word is invite, not command; if it's not meant to happen for you, it won't happen) a deity to take a personal interest in your life, you must go into it with no preconceptions. If you go in hoping that it will be Odin, you might ignore signs from Frey, for example. Of course, nothing is stopping you from going ahead and actively dedicating yourself to a God or Goddess that you love, as they are generally never offended by sincere devotion. Keep in mind also that the Gods are not gender-separated in this tradition; a man may dedicate himself to a Goddess or a woman to a male God. Sometimes one's fulltrui comes as someone to emulate; in occasional cases they come as a Beloved, wanting a relationship of semi-romantic love and devotion. Sometimes they come as a parent – Father or Mother; sometimes as a wise elder to give advice to their Younger Kin. The Gods are older and wiser than us, and they can look at someone and know—better than we can know ourselves – whose attention would do them the most good, and what sort of relationship with be right for them.

It is also important to understand that once you have been chosen by a God or Goddess, there is no going back. You have a bond with them that will last until you are dead, and possibly afterwards. To renounce them—for example, if you decide to convert to a monotheistic religion—will offend them, and your luck may not be worth much after that. In addition, it is also important to understand that just because a deity is in relationship with you does not mean that they will coddle you or do whatever you want; they, not you, are in charge of the relationship. They may help you in your need, or push you to find ways to help yourself. They may push you to evolve as a human being and reach greater potential, or clear some obstacles out of you way, but what they will not be is a wish-fulfillment center. You will have to keep up your end of the bargain, too, and do things to show your love for them, for the rest of your life. Consider this before you get involved.

For the ritual: First, ground and center. Visualize a candle before you, enveloped in a cloud of mist. You can barely make out its outlines, and you cannot see what color it is. Try not to make assumptions about what it might look like. While it is hard not to let your mind fill in details with wishful thinking, try to do this in a spirit of "I wonder what will happen?" rather than "I hope X or Y happens!"

Now place your hand on your heart and visualize a flame burning there, a fire of the love and respect you have for the Gods. Say:

O Mighty Ones who watch us with love and pride,
I ask that you look upon me here tonight
And hear my prayer, in my love for you all.
By heart and mind, by hand and eye,
May it be so, may it be so.

With your finger, draw a Gebo Futhark rune (which looks like an X) over your heart, and say:

Here is my heart, burning with love,
With pride, with respect, with longing for your flame.
This heart is offered to hand outstretched
Who is right to hold this heart and this soul.
I await your signs, O Mighty Ones.
Send me thrice three signs,
Clear as day so that I will believe them.
If I receive these signs, I will devote myself
To my Fulltrui forever,
But I will not forget the names of other Gods,
Nor fail to honor them for their blessings.
If I receive no signs, O Mighty Ones,
I will wait until a sign comes to try yet again,
And in the meantime I will make of myself
A worthy gift to offer to the Holy Powers.
Help me to do this, O Gods.
Help me to make myself worthy
And be the gift I would wish to give you.

Press your index finger into your chest. Now visualize that the fire burning inside you lights the end of your finger, and reach out to light the invisible candle with it. As it is "lit", the clouds and mist should clear, and the color of the candle, and any markings on it, will be visible to you. Take note of any colors or runes or other symbols marked on it. These will be your first omen, pointing you to a deity. Over the next several days, weeks, or months, you may be given eight more omens, as you have asked – nine is a sacred number in our faith. If the candle's colors or markings do not make sense to you, wait and see what comes up as omens; they may clarify things.

If the mist does not clear, you will not be shown your fulltrui at this time. Work further on becoming a worthy gift, and perhaps one will be revealed to you ... or perhaps it is your job, for now, to honor many Gods but belong to none.

Lesson 6/6: More Mind Training.

This month I am sharing this free website that gives (seemingly) simple memory exercises. When we hone our vision memory of what we take in as visual information; we learn to process patterns, as well as routes and paths we have taken. Try it, and report your performance in your journal. See: https://www.neuronation.com.

Lesson 6/7: Reading Material.

1) Read and work on the next chapter of *Neolithic Shamanism*—"The Grey World".
2) Read at least five more of the online God-shrines, and ask via Futhark/Futhorc or your own personal runes whether any of them would be interested in teaching or aiding you.
3) Read "Wyrdworking: Combing the Threads" in *Wyrdwalkers*.
3) Read more of the other books on the Required Reading list.
4) Make sure that you are doing some kind of physical practice that combines moving the body with moving the body's energies.
5) Do a daily rune draw. If you do any other divination, practice your divination protocol.

Lesson 6/8: Immersion into the Völuspá, Verses 36–42.

36. Stood facing north on Niðiʼs plains
halls of gold, Sindriʼs clansʼ;
And another stood on Okolnir (Not-Cold),
the giantʼs beer-hall and so called Brimir.

37. She saw a hall standing, far from the sun,
on Náströnd (Corpse-beach); its doors face northward,
venom-drops fall in through apertures:
So that hall is woven of serpent's backs.

38. There she saw wade sluggish streams
bloodthirsty men and perjurers,
and him who begiles the ear of another's wife.
There Nidhögg sucks the corpses of the dead;
the wolf tears men. Know ye yet, or what?

39. East sat the crone in Iron Wood,
and bore there Fenrir's progeny:
of them all one especially shall be
the moon's devourer, in a troll's guise.

40. Sated with the last fated breath;
the gods' seat he defiles with red blood:
swart was the sunshine then for summers after;
weather all wicked. Know ye yet, or what?

41. Sat there on a mound and striking a harp,
the giantess's herder, the joyous Egthir;
over him crowed, in the gosling-wood,
the bright red cock, so named Fjalar.

42. Crows over the Æsir Gullinkambi (Gold-comb),
which wakens heroes at Host-father's;
but another crows down below earth,
a soot-red cock, in the halls of Hel.

Month 7: Movement into the Ecstatic.

Lesson 7/1: Soul Part: The Lich.

The word *Lich* (or *Lyke*) refers to the actual physical body. the Old Norse *Lyke* is pronounced *lee-keh*, where the Old English name *Lich* is pronounced *leekh*. When we get involved with higher spiritual pursuits, it's very easy to overlook this crucial soul part, and this month's lesson is to remind you without it, we wouldn't be! Your Lich *is* your sacred vehicle. It should go without saying that our bodies are extremely necessary to do *any* work, spiritual or otherwise.

As a Feri initiate of Victor Anderson, one of the first things we are taught is to revere our physical selves, and that its functions are holy. So, for our total selves in the Norse tradition, I choose to honor the component parts of a living person as follows:

1) *Lich:* The physical body (lich).
2) *Hugr:* The mind.
3) *Hamr:* The etheric energy field (aura) that surrounds our physical body
4) *Ek:* Personal awareness of consciousness or identification of self.
5) *Fylgja:* Our astral "double".
6) *Dis:* The higher "god" self.
7) *Önd:* The breath of life or spirit.
8) *Oðr:* Divine consciousness and inspiration.
9) *Hamingja:* Our inherited traits, behaviors, and "luck".

Each of these parts creates a working and cohesive whole, and if one is overlooked we can't know our full power in my opinion. That means much time and insight are needed via getting in touch with all your parts! This month it's our bodies, and this outward manifestation of ourselves is the essential part of our being that has its own intelligence and provides us our interface with life and all things mystical.

The physical body, whose parts appear and function in the same way regardless where we hail from or what we believe, has its own kennings and instinctual ways of performing which allows us understanding of the world around us; both seen and unseen. As we have discovered thus far, the parts of the soul can be divided up in a number of ways, depending on cultural or (as in this case) personal preference, but as physical proof of our existence, the body itself must be approached as a scared and holy soul part.

In 1985, I read a book called "The Body Electric" Robert O. Becker[50], a pioneer in the field of regeneration and its relationship to electrical currents in living things. He tells the fascinating story of our bioelectric selves which in many ways challenges the established mechanistic understanding of the body. In his iconic book, Robert explores new pathways in our understanding of evolution, acupuncture, psychic phenomena, and healing. It is through understanding the body (Lyke) as an organism that houses its own intelligence, and muscle memories; that can repair itself, fight off microbial invasion, and generate its own biomechanical energy and heat; we come to see our bodies as miraculous self-sustaining entities in their own right.

This month we will celebrate the body as our ally and its own soul part, full of its own intelligence, wisdom, and connectiveness. Let us revel in the body, and learn ways to actually experience our faith more deeply though this beautiful and wondrous soul part.

Practice: Does your body sometimes get in the way of your signal clarity? If so, are there things you could be pursuing or disciplines you could be maintaining in order to take better care of it, so that this wouldn't be happening? How about making a commitment to do those things? If you're not sure where to start, there's no harm in talking to experts (both medical and alternative-health) to find out what is possible and right for you. You may have to experiment with a few different practices to find the right things, but now is the time to start looking at an actual physical discipline of some sort. This month, work on finding and slowly implementing that discipline.

---

[50] Avon Books, 1989.

Lesson 7/2: The Joik.

This month we are going to introduce sacred dance and drumming into our practice. By now we have gotten familiar with looking to other Norse/Germanic ways of mystical practice to help fill in the wide gaps in bringing all these elements together, making it a viable, vibrant, living path. I was heavily influenced by the Sami people, as my mentor was a man named Ailo Gaup. He was actually a Core-shamanic teacher as taught by Michael Harner, and during his lifetime he tried to bring together the old Sami ways of doing sacred shamanic work (almost wiped out by Christian conversion) with the "new" ways of approaching core shamanism. Ailo was much maligned for his innovation, but in many ways I feel he led the way to a renewed interest and awaking of the Sami peoples' shamanic heritage. In keeping with the mindset of fearless experimentation to assist ancient reclamation, this month we will utilize the most powerful tools of the Sami to connect with the spirit world; joiking and drumming.

By already seeing the use of the Stav as a percussion instrument to aid us in "traditional" Völva singing (Galdr and vardlökkur) and trance work in previous months, we can now appreciate the power of the oldest of tools which is the sacred drum, as well as the purest form of soul singing which is the Sami joik.

The *joik* (pronounced "yoyk") is a unique form of cultural expression for the Sami people, and can be understood as a style of singing that represents the Sami traditional culture itself. Like the Sami people, the *joik* has been misunderstood, ridiculed, appropriated, and even threatened to be lost in annuls of antiquity when the Sami way of life was almost wiped off the map due to the Lutheran faith and modern resettling of nomadic peoples. Joiking is a form of song which uses a type of scale and vocalization which is probably unfamiliar to most people. Thankfully, although threatened by Christianity and modernization, the Sami traditional way of life has survived along with the powerful soul song known as the *joik*. The resilient Sami have adjusted to new global and local circumstances and continue to endure. However, there is still much work to be done to ensure preservation of the *joik* in its traditional form. As a key element of the Sami culture, the *joik* is growing in recognition as well as cultural acceptance by the world as a valuable, unique, viable form of music.

Ursula Länsman of the Sami group *Angelit* defines the joik thusly:

> A *joik* is not merely a description; it attempts to capture its subject in its entirety. It's like a holographic, multi-dimensional living image, a replica, not just a flat photograph or simple visual memory. It is not about something, it *is* that something. It does not begin and it does not end. A *joik* does not need to have words—its narrative is in its power, it can tell a life story in song. The singer can tell the story through words, melody, rhythm, expressions or gestures.

This description provides a good starting point for understanding the *joik*. The concepts of "music" and "song" in Western culture are not completely applicable to the *joik*. First and foremost, a *joik* is not a song in the sense that it is about something. Gaski explains the research of Ola Graff:[51]

> The reference to the object of a *joik* is not something which someone may add to or leave out from the melody ... the melody is closely connected to the referential object in an indissoluble relationship. Linguistically this is expressed through the fact that one does not joik about somebody or something, there is a direct connection; one *joiks* something or someone.

What I have found to be the significant differences between Western and Sami music relates to Sami songs sound and structure. The *joik* is almost exclusively vocal. A drum will accompany the voice, and occasionally a *joiker* will gradually increase the pitch of the melodic pattern as the *joik* continued. Those familiar with Western music may expect the heavy use of musical instruments, which are not expected in the traditional

---

[51] Gaski, Harald. *The Secretive Text: Yoik Lyrics as Literature and Tradition.* Nordlit No.5.,7 Nov 2000. http://www.hum.uit.no/nordlit/5/gaski.html.

joik. In fact, "the advent of accompanying instruments has made the gradual pitch changes impossible."[52]

Another important distinction between the *joik* and the Western song, according to acclaimed multimedia Sami artist Nils-Aslak Valkeapää, is that "the *joik* was never intended to be performed as art" (Valkeapää, cited in Krumhansl et al. 6). It is a song used for spiritual and religious reasons, not to entertain other listeners.

The *joik* both historically and today has a sacred purpose: it can serve as a tool for community-building and sharing memories (for a single family or within a tribe as a whole), and "for personal self-expression, to calm the reindeer or frighten the wolves, or even to transport one between worlds" (Krumhansl et al. 6).

The third notable distinction between Western song and the *joik* involves form. Ánde Somby, a noted Sami and scholar and joiker, describes the differences in form between Western song and the Sami joik tradition:

> The regular concept of a western European song is that it has a start, a middle and an ending. In that sense, a song will have a linear structure. A *joik* seems to start and stop suddenly. It hasn't a start or an ending. *Joik* is definitively not a line, but it is perhaps a kind of circle. *Joik* is not a circle that would have Euclidian symmetry although it has maybe a depth-symmetry. That emphasizes that if you were asking for the start or the ending of a *joik*, your question would be a moot point.

In ending, the structure of a *joik* thus follows the Sami worldview of "no beginning, no end". The Sami see the world as following the circular patterns of nature, and this is reflected in the depth-symmetry of this prominent form of cultural expression via song.

For this month's work you will listen to many examples of how *joiking* is done,[53] and then create your own joik. Your joik will be of the body, as this is the soul part of us we wish to honor and came to know this month.

---

[52] Laitinen, Heikki—1994.

Lesson 7/3: Drum and Dance.

In keeping with the physical interfacing with the spiritual, this next lesson introduces the importance of drums. We will also learn the art of ritual Dance and by doing so incorporate these two ancient methods of melding the physical self with the spiritual self.

I feel that learning to drum and dance in ritual will deepen your practice, as well as aid you in achieving deeper trance states. To *joik* our body into our awareness with a drum and ecstatic dance movements is the traditional Sami way to do it.

I have found many staunch "pure" practitioners in this art of reclaiming the arts of the Völva/Vitki are adamant we are not to use drums or dancing in our practice of seiðr, and I must ask why? The Finnish Sami were healing right alongside the Norsemen, so why wouldn't a Völva had utilized a drum if given the opportunity? Moreover, dance *was* a part of sacred movements for the Sami, even though for many years there was a misconception that the Sami were the only indigenous people in the world without a dance tradition. Of late, Sami dance companies have emerged, such as Kompani Nomad.

Moreover, a book about the "lost" Sami dance tradition, called *Jakten på den försvunna samiska dansen,* was recently published by Umeå University's Centre for Sami Research (CeSam.)[54] In the eastern areas of Sápmi, the dance tradition has been more continuous and is continued by groups such as Johtti Kompani.

---

[53] Because it's important to hear joiking in order to understand it, here are some Internet links to work with:
Teach Indigenous Knowledge: https://teachik.com/heavy-joik/
Bryan Hemming's "Pedersen's Last Dream" website:
https://pedersenslastdream.wordpress.com/2013/03/25/joiking-songs-of-the-sami/
One can also search out the recordings of Mari Boine, Wimme Saari, and other performers, or do a web search or youtube search on the subject.

[54] Ola Stinnerbom and Birgitta Stålnert. *Jakten på den försvunna samiska dansen.* Umeå University, 2013.

In closing, Icelandic sagas did mention dance usage by the Völva Thorbjörg in Erik the Red's Saga: "The völva was to sleep at the farm during the night and the next day was reserved for her dance." As we read, we may not be clear on the specifics of how to dance, but we see they most certainly did, by the evidence of the still-extant European folk dancing styles that still exists today as a cultural heritage art.

Part 1: The Drum.

In Sami shamanism, the *noaidi*—the Sami shaman—used the drum to get into a trance, or to obtain information from the future or about other places. It also was a map to the spirit world, as many *noaidi* drew a literal map of the Otherworld locations right on the head of their drum.

The Sami drum (called a *runebom*) was traditionally held in one hand and beaten with the other. While the *noaidi* was in trance, his Fylgja left his body to visit the spiritual world or other places. Moreover, the Drum could be used for divination purposes. Used alongside with a drum hammer and a *vuorbi* (index or pointer) made of brass or horn; any answers could be interpreted from where the *vuorbi* stopped on the membrane, and at which symbols.

Besides functioning as a Otherworld map, the patterns on the drum head could reflect the worldview of the owner and his family, both in religious and worldly matters. Pertinent information, such as reindeer herding, hunting, householding and neighborly and community relations S were often drawn on the *runebom*. Many drums were taken from the Sami during the 18th century, due to Lutheran conversions. A large number were confiscated by missionaries and other officials as a part of an intensified Christian mission towards stamping out the Sami indigenous way of life. Serendipitously, some drums were bought by collectors, thereby saving artifacts that depicted the importance of the *runebom* to the Sami. Between seventy and eighty drums are preserved; the largest collection of drums is at the Nordic Museum, Stockholm. In the next paragraph we will see how to actually use your drum!

Practice: How to Drum. Shamanic drumming helps not only to induce trance states, but to create a mainline connection to our ancestors, as drumming for shamanic work is shared by all indigenous shamans. The techniques are simple and effective.

However; Before exploring the drum methods outlined in this section, it must be said that seiðkonas did not appear to use drums in their Spá work, so in the earlier chapters you have been encouraged to experience thumping the Stav to show you how the body responds to different rhythms. Whether you thump your Stav or merely tap your fingers, you have begun to learn to "feel the beat" by allowing it to sink into your body and consciousness. Notice how your body responds to tapping each pattern. Keep in mind that the manner in which you play or shape a rhythm will affect your response. One of the paradoxes of rhythm is that it has both the capacity to move your awareness out of your body into realms beyond time and space, or to ground you firmly in the present moment.

So grab your drum and begin by playing a steady, metronome-like rhythm with uniform time intervals. A clockwork drumbeat generates a dynamic energy that is creative, and expansive in nature. Dynamic energies are ascending forces that carry consciousness into higher realms. At a rapid tempo of three to four beats per second, a steady, rhythmic pattern (or "eagle-beat" as it is referred to in neo-shamanic drumming circles) will arouse and vitalize you. It creates the sensation of inner movement, which, if you allow it, will carry you along.

As you continue to drum, you will notice that your mood lifts and your mundane thoughts begin to fall away. You and your drum will seem to merge. You may speed up or slow down; that is perfectly normal. Shamanic trance is characterized by its range and flexibility, so don't get hung up on trying to maintain a certain speed. It can be distracting and your hands may get tired. Follow your inner sense of timing as to both tempo and duration.

After drumming the eagle-beat, simply relax and take note of the sonic-induced residual "afterglow" of physical and spiritual well-being. When the final drumbeat fades into silence, an inaudible, yet perceptible pulsation persists for a brief period. This silent pulse is ever-present within each of us, but our awareness is rarely in sync with it. Listen to this silent pulse resonating within your body. You may experience the sensation of every particle in your body pulsing in sync with the rhythm you just played.

This inner pulse entrains to the rhythmic pattern as soon as you begin to drum.

For the next exercise, try playing the steady pulse of what shamanic drummers term a "heartbeat rhythm". This rhythm has a two-beat rhythm that produces a different sonic experience. The soft, steady *lub-dub, lub-dub* of a heartbeat rhythm has a calming and centering affect. It reconnects us to the warmth and safety of the first sound we ever heard—the nurturing pulse of our mother's heartbeat melding with our own.

According to Ted Andrews, author of *Animal Speak* (Llewellyn Publications 2002), "a rhythm of two is a rhythm that helps connect you to the feminine energies of creative imagination, birth, and intuition." At a more rapid tempo, the heartbeat rhythm stimulates a downward flow of energy within the body. It generates a magnetic energy that is yin, intuitive, and receptive in nature. Magnetic energies are descending forces conducive to great healing, mind, and regenerative powers. These two simple drum patterns form the rhythmic basis of all drum patterns. They are the healing rhythms I use most often in my shamanic work.

Part 2: The Dance.

The spiral dance is a central ritual dance to Reclaiming Witches. The first spiral dance was performed in Berkeley, CA, in the 1970's by Starhawk's famous "Compost Coven" in a ritual intended to meld art, music, and energy raising during sacred ceremonies of feminist witchcraft. The spiral dance, also called the grapevine dance and the weaver's dance, is a traditional group dance taken from various cultures around the world. The steps are done with one heavy step in the direction you want to go, follow by two lighter steps to adjust your feet, what tap dancers call a "step-ball-change". It feels like weaving with your feet!

I have always danced my sacred rites, and have experienced deep ecstatic trance states by doing so. If we stick to the limiting mindset that dancing wasn't done in our Northern traditions simply because Snorri forgot to write it down, we would be limiting ourselves, and very incorrect to boot. I sent out a questionnaire on all the webpages I belong to (or write for), asking if there was any historical evidence of the Völva using dance as other witches throughout history did, and Kari Tauring shared with me her thoughts on Dance and movement to share with you. Please see: http://karitauring.com/nordic-movement/.

For this month's lesson we will begin to experiment with various forms of ecstatic dance and add them to your Utiseta along with your drumming and joiking. (I hope your sacred area is private; you are going to be making quite a ruckus this month!)[55]

Lesson 7/4: Ulf Dance Posture

Since our ritual work this month will involve doing everything standing and moving, the ritual pose we will learn will work for this. We will use this posture after we center and ground ourselves, right before our journey to Muspelheim, which follows in the next few pages.

The below image depicts Odin **dancing** with a Berserker warrior while taking on the guise as a wolf (Ulf) before a battle. Berserkers were of a elite warrior class whose secret weapon was fighting in an ecstatic altered state. Berserkers may have taken part in a sort of shapeshifting ritual in which the movements of the wolf were mimicked. By performing such rites as a "wolf-dance", the warrior would gain "sympathy" with the wolf-spirit. Giving credence to this idea is the famous plate from a 6th-century helmet from Bjornhouda, Torslunda parish, Oland. In this we see a *dancing* figure with a horned ceremonial helmet (most likely a priest of Odin or perhaps the god himself) and a warrior in the guise of a wolf. It has been speculated by historian, Michael P. Speidel, of the evidence of a

---

[55] For some examples of Nordic dancing, please see these Internet sites:
https://www.youtube.com/watch?v=DhWp828ig_Y
https://www.youtube.com/watch?v=KvjdBelNFZM&feature=youtu.be

warrior wolf cult, associated with Odin. These *Ulfhednar* wore the skins of wolves when they charged into battle, like the *Berserker* who wore the skin of a bear.

Again we will use our Stav as a prop. Standing with your feet about hip distance apart, grip your Stav in front of you and point it out in front of you like a sword.

Begin to stomp with each foot in a deep lunge for about four steps. As you step forward with purpose and poise, swing the Stav from side to side using your waist to execute the movement, in large graceful arcs. Breath out with force the word "Ha", then "Ho" with each alternating footstep.

After four steps bring the Stav down into the ground and plant it finishing up with a "Hey!" You are now ready to do your drumming/dancing ritual work.

Lesson 7/5: Journeying to New Worlds.

Not everyone is welcome in every one of the Nine Worlds, at least not necessarily as a beginner, and sometimes even when experienced. To do this work, we need to remember that these spirits—divine or otherwise—are actually People. They are not metaphors or pieces of the human collective unconscious. They are actual entities with their own agenda, and like all People, they are going to be drawn to some, neutral about others, and not overly fond of some. Don't take it personally if you can't visit a given world at this time, just as you shouldn't take it personally if you don't get a relationship with the spirit animal that seems the most glamorous to you. You might be able to get there later, when you have achieved some understanding that the People of that world find valuable, or it might just not be your place to go, and that's all right.

For this chapter, we will be suggesting journeys to three separate worlds, and you will find out via runic divination which one of them you will be allowed to visit. While no world is completely safe, these three can be dangerous, and getting permission to visit them will depend on the Gods and spirits who inhabit them and whether they feel an affinity toward you personally. You will need to make offerings to them before asking and divining.

So your first task is to read about all three worlds in the text below, then to acquire a two-part offering for each one. Since the denizens of Muspellheim prefer their offerings burned in a fare and those of Niflheim prefer theirs flung to the wind and the wilderness, you may want to go out in Nature to do this divination. (It is acceptable to feed the Dead in Helheim inside; you can leave food at home before going out if you like.)

Then go through your divination protocol, make an offering to the spirits of one world, ask formally for Them to let you know if you may be allowed to visit, and draw three Futhark/Futhorc or your own personal runes to hear their answer. Then repeat the process for the other two worlds. If none of the three divinations looks good, it may not be time for you to venture into dangerous areas quite yet. Instead, ask Freya or Odin (or some other deity) if you may visit them again instead. If more than one option divines well, you may journey more than once, but no less than a week apart so that your Lich will be able to recover.

For visiting any of these worlds, here is the basic outline of the trance: Begin as you normally do, by gathering your horn and mead, ale, or milk as an offering. Hallow your space and stating your intentions, as well as giving an offering to your helping spirits and Landvaettir. We will assume that you have already made offerings to the Gods and spirits of the world you will be visiting.

Center and ground using Ulf Dance posture. Start to drum a slow steady beat, while moving your feet in time with your drum's tempo. Concentrate on your intention of traveling to the Realm that has invited you. Let your voice vocalize this intention, and freely allow sounds to emerge.

As you drum, dance, and joik, feel the veil between the worlds form, and begin to sense that world materializing. Call upon your Hamr, and choose your Fylgja form for this journey, asking your Disir to help guide you through dangers to where you need to go.

Dancing in Niflheim, let your Lyke (body) feel the clear cold winds that blow away confusion and pain. Revel in the feeling of the wind flying past you, and go fearlessly to the secrets of the Well. Dancing in Muspellheim, let your Lyke feel the fires of transformation, burning away any blocks, or illness that physically keeps your Lyke limited and removed from your soul's awareness. Give your body back its power and adoration as you fearlessly journey to world of fire. Walking the Hel Road, let your Lyke feel the silence and peace calling from the Land of the Dead; breathe in the scent of a beautiful autumn as you come up to the Gate. Let go of any fear you may still have of death, decay, and the end of all natural cycles. Continue this way until you feel your journey has accomplished all you need to know, feel, see, and integrate.

When your journey is complete, begin to slow your beat and steps, and begin to sing a joik of gratitude and thanksgiving for this body and life you have been given. When you are finished moving, put down your Drum and get your horn. Be sure to thank any entity that helped you this session.

Niflheim

In Norse mythology, the incarnation of this life as we know it all started with the first *elemental* worlds that existed before the existence of any other matter, and the mythical story of antiquity follows closely to what modern-day scientists know to be a very plausible theory.

The two Worlds that bore the building blocks of life are called Niflheim and Muspelheim, which are depicted as the primordial realms of ice and fire. They were separated by Ginnungagap, the yawning black void of the abyss, from which all things issued. When the fire of Muspelheim and the ice of Niflheim collided, huge energy shocks and reverberations occurred, and the ice began to melt. The result was a steaming soup of creation (the primordial ooze) and the first being, the giant Ymir, was formed and appeared.

Eventually as the story goes, the icy realm of Niflheim was populated with Frost Giants (Thurses), while the fiery land of Muspelheim was populated with the Fire Giants (Etins). These "giants", in my understanding, underlie all the natural world's processes, along with its wild feral inhabitants. and Giants (or Jötunn) are the "grandfather spirits" of Primal Nature.

Niflheim is the first of the Nine Worlds, and the eldest of the three sacred wells is located there—Hvergelmir, which means "boiling cauldron", protected by the huge female ice-dragon called Níðhöggr. It is said that all cold rivers come from Hvergelmir, and it is said to be the source of the eleven rivers in Norse mythology. The well Hvergelmir is the origin of all living thing and the place where every living being will go back to. This is the place of primal chaos and original creativity, where everything is a possibility, and nothing is static. Hvergelmir manifests the *first* access point to self and our Hamingja. In the Celtic tradition of shamanism as taught by Orion Foxwood, there is the ancestral life river of connection and return known as the "River of Blood", and this "River of Blood" is described similarly to Hvergelmir.

For a Völva or Vitki, the foremost reason to make a first journey to Niflheim is to gaze into the Well of Hvergelmir. This is the place of Primal Chaos and Creativity. Creation is, by its nature, wild and confusing as well as inspiring, and to look within it is to get in touch with the primal chaotic creativity in one's self, including—and perhaps especially—the scary parts. However, it is wise to make an offering to the frost-giants, and especially their chieftain Kari the North Wind. They particularly enjoy warm soup, ideally hurled into the wind in some wild place. if you give them liquor, it should be high-proof, but hot tea or coffee is just as good. Their world is very cold and they rarely get anything warm, so that is a luxury. Since the Well is guarded by Níðhöggr the dragon, you might want to throw some meat to her as well. (If this journey chooses you, it would be worth your while to read the online shrines for Kari and Níðhöggr on the www.northernpaganism.org site.)

The frost-giants love to sing, and will appreciate it if you create a special song—galdr or joik—for them, another reason to bring your drum along. Trust your intuition when you create such a song; visualize the powers of Ice, Mist, Frost, Snow, Wind, and Cold, all parts of Niflheim, and sing to the beauty to be found in that aspect of Nature.

Use your map to find where Niflheim lies, and after you begin your journey, state your intention out loud that you are going to the well of Hvergelmir in the world of Niflheim to attempt to look within the well. Call on the rune Isa. When you arrive at your destination, look at all that is around you and take it all in. The sights, the sounds, the smells, the air temperature, etc. Look for the Well of Hvergelmir, and when you find it, attempt to approach it to look within. What do you see? Hear, smell, feel? What is around you and the well? Look within, and see what there is to see. Later, when you have retraced your steps and come back, write in your journal what you saw, and what it inspired in you. This is a place of great power, and even if it inspires fear, it is likely that the fear is covering something important that you should be looking at.[56]

Muspellheim

In Nordic mythology, Muspelheim is named as one of the Nine Worlds, a realm of fire, ash, lava, and the home of the Fire Giants. Muspelheim is ruled by the giant Surtr and his consort Sinmara, and according to Snorri Sturluson (whom, I will remind you, was a devout Christian) the Fire Giants are thought to be the sworn enemies of the Aesir, and Surtr is prophesized to ride out with his flaming sword at Ragnarok to attack Asgard, and turn it into a flaming inferno. The truth is far more complicated than that, but that is for another book entirely!

Muspelheim was named as one of the two primordial realms in the Gylfaginning and also has the energy of creation as well as destruction. So why in the Nine Worlds would we desire to go *there*?

Faring forth to Muspelheim is a journey that can test our limits of human experience; and generally speaking, we are very limited by our human awareness. Going to the primordial land of Fire will allow us a chance to feel what "primordial Fire" is truly like. Muspelheim can seem a dangerous and daunting journey. However, it is when we realize that we are not separate from the realms, but are a part of them, that we can connect with the primordial forces within ourselves. This month's lessons are all about pushing boundaries of how we view our Lich or Lyke, as well as how we connect to our very intelligent bodies as a sacred and powerful entity via the language our Lich understands best: movement! And movement equates to heat, and heat equates to fire.

As Völvas and Vitkis reclaiming this path, we are foremost pioneers dancing into uncharted territories, but as modern people we have come to the limiting view of our bodies as "tools" that we use, unconsciously, to do

---

[56] For more information on Niflheim, check *The Pathwalker's Guide* chapter at: http://www.northernshamanism.org/niflheim.html.

our souls' (or egos') bidding, thereby ignoring its beauty, wisdom and power. This goes for Fire too. Our Ancestors discovered how to harness and use it, and saw it as very sacred, but we tend to forget just what a integral element Fire is to our lives. We are going to attempt to utilize those things which might help us deepen our connection with our bodies within our pathworking, which might include ideas that are stunted by the idea our Lich is simply a vehicle to transport us around Midgard, and that fire is only used when we go camping.

Via drumming, dancing, and a trip to Muspelheim, we will attempt to understand the fire of the primal life force that inhabits our very real and sacred Lich animated by the fuel of passions, desires, needs, and energy exchange from other sources of the building blocks of creation. As we gather whatever power of adeptness we can, with whatever tools are at our disposal, we will continue the ancient dance of physical existence. We *can* journey to Muspelheim and become the flame, and become the ash, and learn to understand the true nature of it all. We can see the beauty and necessity of creation and destruction within the fire of life emerging, which also exists within the hidden parts of our physical selves, and thereby we begin to better understand the thin line between the two. Knowledge from the Fire Giants may be hard-won, and take time and effort, but the journey will be all the more rewarding as a result.

Fire-giants require that offerings be burned in a fire, even if that is a small one. They enjoy any food that can be burned to ash, although they are particularly fond of sweet things like fruit or sweet pastry. If you give them alcohol, it should be very high proof, and ideally flavored with hot spices like cayenne. They love to dance, and if you are allowed to go there, they may expect you to dance with them around a fire. (If this journey chooses you, it would be worth your while to read the online shrine for Surt on the www.northernpaganism.org site.)

When attempting this journey, you will want to use all the skills et you have learned thus far. You will want to shapeshift your *Hamr* into a creature of fire, or else choose to be invisible. You will also want to invoke your Guardian Disir (as well as your Fylgja or fetch) to be at your back from the moment the mist clears and you set foot in this fiery primordial land.

Use your map to find where Muspelheim is located, and set out with the intention to connect with your own inner spark of Muspelheim. You intend to ignite that primal fire that is a leftover ember from before our recorded time began, and you intend to bring it back for use in Midgard, to fuel your body and to lend you the passion, drive, and transformation needed to be one with your life's work as well as physical existence. after you come back, make an oath to Surt and/or Sinmara that you will take more care and awareness with your body and use His Fire of creation to further yourself and others on this path of ecstatic living called Seid.

I suggest using your drum and your *joik* to create a fire and flame dance to begin this adventure—just trust the process and your intuition. Call on the rune Kenaz if you work with the Futhark, or Cweorth (the rune of Surtr Himself) if you work with the Futhorc. This is very powerful stuff indeed; be sure to record your experience in your journal when done.[57]

Helheim

Nordic religion had a very strong tradition of honoring the Dead and the Ancestors, and Seid-workers often took journeys to the Deathrealm to consult with the wise Dead. Traditionally, one does not go deep into Helheim, because it is ruled by Hela, the Goddess of Death, and She is very protective of Her Dead souls. The best place for beginners to go is to walk down the Hel Road to the great Hel Gate, and ask to speak with any ancestors or wise Dead who are willing to come to the Gate. If a trip to the Land of the Dead divines well—which means that Hela is willing to allow it—then food and drink may be placed on or near your Ancestor altar. Hela appreciates it when you feed Her people. She is not usually offered alcohol by those who work with Her, but She likes a good cup of tea, especially unusual or gourmet tea, and perhaps some small cakes. Anything given to Her must be left on an altar until it withers, rots, or molds.

---

[57] For more information on Muspellheim, check *The Pathwalker's Guide* chapter at: http://www.northernshamanism.org/muspellheim.html.

The Hel Gate separates Niflheim from Helheim. To find the Hel Road when using your Yggdrasil map, point yourself at Niflheim, but instead of invoking the Futhark rune Isa, invoke the Futhark rune Raido (the Road) and, if you work with the Futhorc, invoke Ear, the rune of the Grave and Hela's own rune. Don't worry if your divination about Niflheim told you to stay away for now—the Hel Road is its own place, and none of the denizens of Niflheim will touch any soul walking on it, alive or dead.

As you walk the Hel Road in your journey, do not be afraid of the ghosts who walk alongside you. They will not harm you, although they may be weeping or in shock from their recent death. If you want to be helpful, reassure them that they are going to a place of peace and rest and healing for the soul. At some point, you will come to a rushing river with a bridge across it. This is the River Gjoll, and the Bridge of Knives. Cross the bridge without looking down; if you look down, you will see knives laid edge-up all the way across, but if you keep your head up, you will feel nothing.

At the end of the bridge is Mordgud's Tower. Mordgud is an armored giantess who is Hela's gate-guardian (and if this journey chooses you, it would be worth your while to read the online shrines for Hela and Mordgud both) but if you have gained permission in advance; She will let you by. When you come to the great black Hel Gate, let the ghosts go on by; you should stop and declare your intention to seek wisdom from the Dead. Then wait and see who comes. The Dead like singing almost as much as the frost-giants, because music soothes them and reminds them of their lives before. If you can sing to them as an offering, all the better.

Through the Hel Gate, you will see that while Niflheim is in a state of cold winter, Helheim looks like a beautiful autumn day, and you can smell the scent of its land as you stand there. Waves of peace radiate through the Hel Gate; take note of what you see, hear, smell, and feel, but take care not to fall asleep here! One of the dangers of this world is falling asleep among the Dead and losing a piece of your soul. Stay alert and wait for the willing souls to come forth and speak with you. Listen to them, take their wisdom, and thank them. When you come back, you should put their names—or if you don't know the names, something written about them—on your ancestor altar to honor them. [58]

Lesson 7/6: Reading Material.

1) Read and work on the next chapter of *Neolithic Shamanism*—"The White World".

2) Read at least five more of the online God-shrines, and ask via Futhark/Futhorc or your own personal runes whether any of them would be interested in teaching or aiding you.

3) Read more of the other books on the Required Reading list.

4) Make sure that you are doing some kind of physical practice that combines moving the body with moving the body's energies.

5) Do a daily rune draw. If you do any other divination, practice your divination protocol.

Lesson 7/7: Immersion into the Völuspá, Verses 43–49.

43. Loud bays Garm before the Gnipa-cave,
his bonds he rends asunder; and the wolf runs.
Further forward I see, much can I say
of Ragnarök and the gods' conflict.

44. Brothers shall fight,
and slay each other;
sisters' children
shall violate kinship;
Hard is the world
much whoredom
an axe age, a sword age
Shields are cloven.
A wind age, a wolf age,
before the world sinks.

---

[58] For more information on Helheim, check *The Pathwalker's Guide* chapter at: http://www.northernshamanism.org/helheim.html

no man will
spare another.

45. Mim's sons play, and the fate-tree kindles
at the resounding Gjallar-horn.
Hard blows Heimdall, his horn is aloft;
Odin speaks with Mim's head.

46. Groans that aged tree, and the Jötun is loosed.
Trembles Yggdrasil's ash yet standing;
47. Bays Garm now.

48. Hrym steers from the east, his shield raised in front,
Jormungandr is coiled in Jötun-rage.
The worm beats the waves, and the eagle screams:
pale-beak tears carcasses; Naglfar is loosed.

49. The ship fares from the east:
Muspell's men will come over the waves,
and Loki steers. Fifel's kin fares all with Freki;
in their company is the brother of Byleist.

Month 8: Mastering the Self

Lesson 8/1: Soul Part: Ek.

The most obvious of all the soul parts a Völva/Vitki can come to know (as well as master) is the concept of self—that part we refer to as "me" or "I". In Jungian teachings this part is known as the personality or Ego, which in some western and eastern philosophies is a soul part we are encouraged to "conquer", supersede, or even destroy.

The Norwegian word for I is called Ek. In the book *Elhaz Ablaze: A Compendium of Chaos Heathenry,* Henry L. describes the Ek as "...one's everyday personality, which needs to function well so that it can deal intelligently with, and make meaningful use of, the other Soul parts." I tend to agree with Henry that the understanding of our own workings within our unique personalities is critical to furthering ourselves as Norse mystics, and it falls into the ancient Oracle of Delphi's only warning before approaching the Limitless: "Know Thyself."

Our northern ancestors required that each person be a self-sovereign, independent soul, but they equally held sacred the idea of being a attributing member of the collective tribe. A healthy person certainly can fully know themselves (all their strengths and weakness) and at the same time turn this knowledge into useful traits that benefit their survival along with the furtherment of the tribe. This concept is no different when we are a Völva or Vitki, and conversely, it is of more importance. As a Pathwalker, Witch, or Shaman, our "tribe" becomes much bigger; we meet and co-create with a plethora of other beings, many of which are not human-like in the least. If we approach these other entities without having a handle on our triggers, our blind spots, our weaknesses, or our points of vulnerability, we become at worst a very easy target to dismantle and destroy, and at best ineffectual in our esoteric work.

I believe that we are who we are for good reason, and to be the most powerful individuals we can be, we must learn to master those parts of selves that might inhibit our successful dealings with the world outside ourselves. Moreover, when we understand those things within our self-identity that can be a weakness, we then can examine them and manipulate them so they constantly work in our favor.

In my previous book, I have an exercise for turning our "shadow selves" into an ally. I liken our shadows to the monster under the bed, and I suggest an exercise to take this monster out of the darkness of our rooms and bring them into the light of day, taking the shadow out on the playground and coming to know it by exploring it in a friendly and lighthearted way, much as we would do with a childhood companion.

This approach of knowing the Ek goes for the parts of ourselves that give us much pride and joy. When we excel at something, it benefits us and the cosmos around us as a whole. We evolve successfully, and in doing so the world evolves with us. However (and this is where the whole idea of being "ego-less" in more ascetic traditions stems from), if we let that pride of self-accomplishment turn into a type of enamored-with-myself-ness, we then run the risk of becoming "egotistical"; self-centered, self-righteous, and blind to the important workings of others in the world around us. We develop a overinflated sense of Ek (I) thinking we are the only God-selves in the room. This can be very dangerous and limiting, as we will fail to acknowledge our weak points, bulling through those things we really can't (and shouldn't) be attempting in comparison to our skill sets, thereby setting ourselves (and others) up for a world of hurt.

So how do we really learn to "know" ourselves and have a healthy well-functioning Ek? I have a three-way approach to this very vexing quandary of knowing ourselves; i.e. the notion that we learn our parts and every aspect of our motivations:

- ❖ Observation. By simply observing with an open mind and unbiased attachment to what is igniting our reactions to any given situation, we can begin to decipher what makes us tick. We learn to see what triggers us, where we are the most beneficial, and where we are own worst enemy. We can then make comparisons to the environment outside of our Ek and judge by collective experiences what behaviors and thought patterns best serve the Cosmos as a whole, and those who repeatedly seem to be unbeneficial and destructive. The most powerful times of observation is when we sit with ourselves alone, in deep meditation.

- ❖ Experimentation. After simply observing the complexities of our individual Ek's reactions to others, we then begin to experiment with change, for better or worse. We begin to play with the notion that we can change our reactions or thought process, and in doing so we experiment with habitual experiences by approaching it differently through experimentation of handling the situation differently. Empathy plays a huge role here; by placing our awareness in the shoes of another being, we begin to see our view isn't the only one in the Nine Worlds. Having the power of empathy actually allows us to observe how things might be perceived when it isn't viewed by our own personal Ek. This takes a lot of openness and willingness to be vulnerable, as well as wrong on how we instinctually have lived our daily lives until now.

- ❖ Application. All the observing and experimenting is for naught if we can't learn how to apply these new insights and kennings. Once we have had that "Aha!" moment of a part of our Ek we wish to change, we simply must work at doing so, every minute of every day, until it becomes a true change. Habits are a settled, regular tendency or practice, especially ones that are comfortable and hard to give up, and this goes for habitually being and reacting from the Ek. For example, it can be daunting and scary to give up our knee-jerk rage, as that gives us a feeling of power and righteous entitlement. However, to truly know power, we must know how the antagonist provokes us. Therefore, that rage must be understood—why and where it comes from—as well as what its most productive use can be for Ek and the world if wielded properly. So we must apply our observations and experiments to show us what triggers our power of rage and why we allow it to be unleashed. For most people, it is simply because Ek says it feels good, powerful, or righteous to unleash a blind fury, yet it almost always causes more harm than the situation demands. Through experimentation, we begin to see a controlled rage funneled through empathetic understanding gets us father and gets more things accomplished. Through application of this insight we begin to have less stress, more friends, and less injuries due to explosive, selfish, tantrums.

Lesson 8/2: The High Seat.

As we work toward self-mastery, we may be challenged by temptations to use our growing skills as a way to feed our egos and/or gain status in a community. As an example, many find that the High Seat ritual is the most alluring skillset for a Völva to master. It is not only a representation of us reclaiming our individual power, it also represents the Völva's ability to be a representative and spokesperson for the otherworlds. It was a Völva's ancient duty to serve all the tribesfolk she visited with prophecy, magics, and healing. With this sort of weighty sacred responsibility, we need to be very humble and diligent in how we handle such awe-inspiring power. One of the most difficult lessons we learn is that our authentic self is not our ego nor our self-serving drives. To accept the task of sitting upon the High Seat of Seiðr especially requires full awareness of who we are and why we are doing it. Acknowledging/embracing your complete self in its full spectrum means that you must tirelessly work to recognize, understand, and control your self-centered ego.

As many psychologists point out, the "me" of the ego has only one drive and desire: be self-realized, and therefore the center of the universe! This overwhelming drive of "self"-ishness can blind you to what is really going on around you, as well as the goal of evolution of yourself and your "Tribe". You must make sure your work as a Völva and Seiðkona it is not a hunger for self-acclaimed power. It should be a service and a joy, and nothing more. Anyone can choose to sit in the High Seat and attempt to be a mouthpiece between the worlds, but it is important to understand that when a person decides to do seið they are altering the Web of Wyrd and all its strands. It takes thorough knowledge of the Norns' weaving, and spinning, and of what wyrd really is, before ever attempting to alter its strands.

The High Seat séance especially has a high appeal and draw to the egocentric who wishes to experience public otherworldly contact, whereas it inspires awe and dread in a non-ego driven Völva. The High Seat is first described to us in *Erik the Red's Saga* as a place of prominence in the physical area the Völva was visiting to do her work, like the throne of a noble, and we also learn it was specifically set up in a certain way to aid her in her task of either healing (blessing) the settlement, or destroying (cursing) an enemy of the settlement, where anyone present could witness this awe-inspiring form of Norse magic.

Energetically, what takes place when we decide to sit in the High Seat is that the Völva is forming an agreement with the surrounding spirits—i.e. the spirits of place (landvættir), the spirit of her Disir (guardian spirit), the ancestors of the people gathered (as well as her own), and the Norns (whom even the Gods answer to), with the Völva hoping that all agreements made will grant her the ability to dip into the well of Wyrd and hear the spirits speaking to her with messages, or through her with messages. The High Seat isn't just a physical place to do oracle work; it is a symbol of self-sovereignty, self-awareness, and self-control. Ego running rampant is not self-mastery.

In looking at the etymology of the word *seiðhjall*, we find it is often translated to simply mean "high seat". A Völva who does the High Seat "seances" must remember the one and only warning above the "High Seat" for the Oracle of Delphi: Know Thyself. Why *that* saying, we must ask? It is because whenever performing oracle work as an intercessor between the Wolds of Gods and man, we must thoroughly know and understand *why* we are doing this work; and *where* the power (as well as answers) comes from. We must know *how* this information is possible, as well as the difference between our egos driving the bus, or something greater speaking to/through us.

To prove my point, let us go back to the Lore and look again at the case of Thorbjörg, the Völva documented in a visit by Erik the Red's Saga. The night she arrives, she is led to the *hásæti* and asked to greet all who invited her there. That word *hásæti* means "high seat", but it means in this example a seat of social prominence, like a throne. The next day when doing the seiðr seance, the Völva climbs onto what is called the *seiðhjall*. So what is the difference? The public high seat (*hásæti*) is a seat of social honor in the hall, and the folk want everyone who will gather to witness the ritual to understand the importance of the Völva's visit.

A *hásæti* is a seat of Midgard, a place of one human's rank or station as viewed by other people, and it can easily lead someone to be taken over totally by the dreaded ego. In contrast, the high seat of spiritual contact (*seiðhjall*) is only used for the most sacred form of Spá in seiðr, and a Völva doing her "great work" knows it is a seat built expressly for the occasion of communing with the Otherworlds. This seiðhjall is holy, and is blessed by the Norns, who have no room for ego.

As Annette Høst states so aptly in *A Journal of Contemporary Shamanism*: "The seiðr practitioner—like all shamans—is, while on the job (and the seat!), the servant of the people and at the same time a servant of the spirits, a mediator sitting between the worlds. It can be very seductive to sit on the seiðr seat if the distinction between the two seats is not made clear and well understood. The danger is in forgetting that the authority of the words coming out of your mouth does not belong to you, but to the spirits."

So this month we want to begin to master the art of self-sovereignty via understanding and self-control. This will be an ongoing project for as long as you're a Völva/Vitki, but if we begin to do the inner work, the outer work will naturally fall into place.

Practice: For the rest of this month, each time you decide to assert yourself, be it in ritual for a manifested intention, or to state (prove!) your opinion to someone who has a differing view from yours (either real time, or online), *before* you make your opinion heard, stop and evaluate your need for control/dominance of the situation. Look to the reason *behind* your thought process. Is it coming from your ego with the drive to be heard and recognized? If so, go deeper as to why. Or is it because you genuinely know this intention or conflicting opinion has a purpose for good or ill? If so, go deeper and ask yourself about your core factor or need.

It is only when we become clear in our inner realms about why we do, say, think, believe or feel—then act, as we do—that we truly gain power. When we understand our motives, as well as embracing all our inner truth, we then truly "know ourselves".

Lesson 8/3: Example of a High Seat Séance

Our chosen spot to perform the high seat at the NERF festival was in a secluded temple space with a permanently erected ancestral altar. It had enough room for the twenty-two participants, myself, and my watcher, Seiðr sister River. (As you will come to see, the Watcher is just as pivotal for a successful High Seat rite as the Völva on the high seat, since it is She who holds the space, guards the traveling Völva while she fares forth, and is the intercession between Midgard and the Otherworlds. The Völva faring forth is simply the mouthpiece!)

All twenty-two people were tutored earlier that day by me on what the steps of this ritual would entail, as well as the process and what to expect:

- ❖ We had to agree upon a communal intention. Why were we going to the Well of Urd? The intention was to seek answers to specific questions that affected each participant as a Tribe of Folk. If we were in a severe weather situation, the group intention might have been to get answers on how to slack a drought, or if we were at war, perhaps how to deflect invading troops; but that day, it was questions of how each individual might further their Heathen path personally for the betterment of the community at large.
- ❖ Next, each participant was told to create a worthy question that would be asked of the Norns in accordance with the group intention. What that means is any self-serving frivolous question was discouraged; for example, "My wife is pregnant, will she have a boy or girl?" or "Should I buy that new car?" or even (and yes, I have seen this asked) "How do I make so-and-so fall in love with me?" For this High seat only questions of community were encouraged by each individual.
- ❖ The group then heard the song of the Völva; also known as a Vardlökkur. We learn from the Sagas it was so beautiful a sound that the spirits found the song irresistible, and it could only be made up on the spot. As the vardlökkur was being discussed in a meeting before the actual High Seat séance, the song we sang together was just a practice song, but as we sang it I could feel the wights listening intently.

- Finally, the group was told the ground rules for the ritual. No one can touch the Völva on the seat, nor could they break the circle once the rite began, and once the vardlökkur was sung each participant must continue the singing until the Völva on the high seat gave a signal she had arrived at the well. (I do this by stopping my movements as I tend to sway in my chair, and I grow silent.) Most times I will chant a galdr or joik to induce my trance state as I too am "singing" my intention around seeking the Well of Urd while the group is singing the vardlökkur.) I also thump my Stav one time to signal I am there.
- River, my Spa sister and fellow Völva seeing I was at the well would signal for silence. That night she knew I could only stay in trance just so long; so only nine questions could be asked. She opened her Hamr and her awareness, choosing the nine she was guided to pick. Earlier that day she had gathered nine natural tokens from the Land, and we carried them around for the rest of the day infusing the organic items without intention of community cohesion. During the rite, River handed each person chosen a item, they then held it tightly while asking their question out loud, blowing their Önd on the token, activating their essence with the object. Then River came to me, and whispered their question in my ear, while pressing the object into my hand. The Norns would then answer through my mouth. After receiving the answer, River took the item from my hand and repeated the answer to the querent giving them back the stone, shell, twig or leaf.
- After all the questions were asked, I then was signaled it was time to leave the Well, and (this is always the worst part for me) my Fylgja was sucked back from the Norns' Well into my fleshly form on the chair with dizzying speed. After getting my bearings and grounding myself fully in Midgard, we discussed briefly what was said, and then we opened the space thanking the spirits with offerings and gratitude and saying our farewells until next we met. As in creating the space, each Landvættir, Ancestor, guardian spirit, element, and God was thanked and honored before we broke the boundary of the sacred Vé we had created.

So that, in a nutshell, is one way a modern-day High Seat séance is done in our 21st century. The training needed to accomplish this most sacred of duties is complex: one must have both good trance skills and a working relationship with the Wyrd sisters. The ability to create sacred space and to coalesce a group in unity is crucial, and again, the assisting Watcher is as important as the Völva who acts as an oracle for the session.

The high seat séance must always be approached with these two questions in mind: Why are we seeking answers? Are all involved prepared to accept and hear them as they come? One's intention for going to the Well is of utmost importance, since the Norns suffer no fools or charlatans. Those seeking glory by showing off their Spá skills are in for a unpleasant awakening if this is their intention for traveling to the Wyrd Sisters' abode.

The High Seat, for me, is one of the most terrifying yet rewarding acts of sacred work I do as a Völva. I only do it when necessary and when it benefits my Tribe. But not every Völva is called to do this form of Spá, so don't feel lacking somehow because you can't or won't perform it.

Here is another view of the High Seat séance from the inside, recounted by Susannah Ravenswing, Northern Tradition shaman and spaekona. Her experience is similar to mine, but varies in specific ways because her tradition and training is different. I include her account as a contrast, and to give other perspectives.

> When I first became a Northern Tradition shaman's apprentice, my teacher provided me with a basic chant and protocol as part of my training to serve as a Spaekona. I subsequently "got my coat" and became a working shaman in my own right and my Patron, Freya, advised me that I needed a different protocol and chant, one which would afford me greater protection. I was told that I needed to undergo deeper preparation prior to trance and should be seated within a sacred *vé*, a small square defined by four hazel rods with their ends painted red. She also instructed me that querents need privacy and that there should be an offering cloth near my left foot where each querent could leave something of value in exchange for the service, thus fulfilling sacred Gebo, a gift for a gift.
>
> I begin my preparations with divination to determine whether to proceed with the spae. When the runes indicate I should go

forward, I spend some time prior to serving just resting and clearing my being. The vé is established at some distance from the gathered folk, with a high-backed oak chair and a reindeer hide before the chair for querents to kneel upon. A harrow to Freya is also set up before the folk, holding an image of Her, beeswax candles, amber, a horn of mead, loaf of bread and dish of salt, and my horse bone wand. An assistant strikes a sacred fire and from it lights the candles and *recels*, the smoke of which is then used to hallow the space and gathered folk. Meanwhile, my attendant bathes and then anoints me with fragrant oils beloved by My Lady. I am then dressed in a slate-grey gown and voluminous dark blue veil, along with specific sacred jewelry. When I return, the participants surround me and pray in unison:

> *Oh Divine Powers and Patient Dead,*
> *We hail you with our heartfelt prayers.*
> *Protect and preserve our Spaekona who serves.*
> *Hold her safe from harm, banish baneful forces.*
> *Aid our asking, true be our tales and our intent.*
> *Keep all answers clear and clean,*
> *Lend our longing minds relief.*
> *Fair Freya, from Thy throne*
> *Look fine upon this legacy*
> *And accept our loving thanks*
> *For this ancestral mystery.*

I face the harrow and pray softly that my intent and service be true, then take a small piece of the bread, sprinkle it with salt, dip it in honey and raise it in offering before consuming it. I raise the horn of mead, drink a sip and return it to the altar. (This constitutes confirmation of a contractual agreement between the person serving as spaekona and The Gods, and serves as the opening act of the spae process.) I take my wand in my right hand and with my arms raised, I sing the chant Vanadis gave me, and then am led to the spae seat by my attendant, who closes the *vé* around me. I draw my veil over my face and continue to sing the song until my consciousness steps aside and I cease singing. At first my head drops back, I continue to sing, and then my head falls forward and I experiencing a sense of the crown of my head opening and light swirling down to fill me, then I am conscious of nothing.

As the querents stand well apart from the *vé* to afford privacy, my attendant brings them one by one, while the other assistant remains with the folk, available to assist anyone needing care or grounding. Each querent places their offering on the cloth and kneels. Questions are asked and answers given. I have no awareness of what I say or do but am given to understand that my voice changes, depending on Whom is speaking through me. The process continues until all who seek guidance have approached.

The attendant advises when the final querent has come and helps me begin my callback chant, which is very difficult initially, like struggling to awaken or swimming up from deep underwater. I repeat the callback chant as necessary until my personal consciousness in present.

Since I'm often unsteady on my feet at first, my attendant opens the vé and assists me in rising, then escorts me back to the gathered folk, who encircle me and repeat the opening prayer. I acclaim, "All hail the Gods in Their wisdom!" and the folk reply in kind. This marks the ending of the rite. I find I'm often overly sensitive and need to go somewhere quiet afterwards, remove my veil and all ritual jewelry and have some food and drink to help me ground completely. Later, the attendant carries the mead, salt, bread and honey out to a tree which has agreed to accept these offerings on Freya's behalf.

Lesson 8/4: Music Theory.

Throughout this book I have tried to demonstrate the styles of song used in this reclaimed practice as based on historical classifications of various singing techniques. This month, however, I wish to address the importance of music theory.

As mentioned throughout this book, when a Völva or Vitki weaves their magic, one of the deeper magicks we begin to learn is that of Song. But it isn't simply a matter of us choosing what style of song to be used; we must understand the very construction of these melodies.

As we learned, the song of a Völva is known as a Vardlökkur, and it can sometimes take the entire community to create this very sacred and special melody. We also have discovered the chanting power of Galdr and

Galdralag, and the *kvad*. We even touched upon the wordless *joik* used by the Sami people. To create such sacred and powerful music, it is the job of the Völva/Vitki to recognize and identify each of these varying songs components, and that comes when one begins to really listen to the various parts of a melody necessary to coalesce a powerful and effective tune.

Does this mean we need to become a serious student in music theory? (I can hear you groaning from here.) Not necessarily; but by being able to understand as well as hear all the parts of a song, we can then choose to sing the musical parts in a way that suits each of us best for our magical Wyrd-weaving work, whether alone or with others in group work.

For example: To sing any song, one must know the melody, as this is the most recognizable component to identifying any song we learn to know and love. Let's use the example of "Twinkle, Twinkle, Little Star". It is the melody of this childhood song which when heard is immediately recognizable, so it is through the Melody that you can name a song and mimic it. Melody is also the part of a song most people will begin to sing along with, but it isn't the only part that makes a tune beautiful and powerful. We also have the harmony, the tempo, the volume, and more.

Melody is what results from playing notes at different pitches one after the other in an "organized" way. However, the mere succession of pitches doesn't make a melody. Each note played has a duration, and the relation between durations refers to rhythm.

But before we go into rhythm, let's talk about *pulse*. Like every living organism, music has a pulse—beats like that of the heart, and although we not always hear it, it is always there. Do you remember when children learn to clap their hands to follow songs? There is a constant implicit beat, in some cases played by instruments. For example, in Australian aboriginal music the pulse is often played by clap-sticks.

Rhythm is not just a constant beat. The beat or pulse is a piece of the music's core, and rhythm is how you inhabit the pulse. Rhythm is what results from combining notes of different durations, sometimes coinciding with the beat and sometimes not. For example, we notice that in Reggae or Ska music, the guitar or keyboards at times plays exactly opposite to the beat.

And, last but not least: harmony. Usually melodies are not just played alone by a solo instrument or a group of instruments playing the same thing. Very frequently there are "lead" instruments which play melodies (such as the voice, wind instruments, etc.) and, others that accompany them doing something else. The relationship between different notes played at the same time is what we call harmony. Sometimes this can be done by one instrument such as guitar or piano, but other times it is done by several instruments, like flutes or a string ensemble. (Most Völvas, however, learn to harmonize solely with the voice.) There are many types of relations between two or more notes played at the same time, but they can be classified into two main divisions: consonance and dissonance.

Consonance refers to a sense of stability and "relaxation" experienced when listening to some harmonic relations. Opposite to this, dissonance (like loud chants that sound odd/harsh in Galdr work) refers to the sensation of "tension" or the feeling that something is "unstable". Depending on the "distance" between one note and another, we can classify their relations into consonant and dissonant.

Remember, even though I think it is beneficial to understand music theory and how music is created, when we actually sing, the most crucial thing to know is we are simply using our voice as a vehicle to unite us with nature, the Nine Worlds, and our ancestral wisdom. Don't refrain from singing because you don't think you have a "good" voice! Sing anyway. It is the first tool of our practice.

Lesson 8/4: The Pose of Receiving.

Since Chapter 2, you have been introduced to ritual body postures. Our new posture this month is below. Feel free to use the ones that work, then leave the rest behind.

Practice: The Pose of Receiving.

Identified simply as "a Freyja Amulet," this small bronze pendant now lives in the Danish National Museum. Looking at the image, we see that the figure of Freyja wears a shawl which she is opening as if to receive a welcoming of some kind, be it power in her Seiðr, or perhaps even to simply remove her shawl covering from her shoulders in preparedness to cover her head and "go under the cloak". The figure seems to me as if she is in the position of receiving, whether it be otherworldly messages or blessings from the powers she serves.

When I personally prepare for Seiðr journey work, I always place my cloak over my head and face, as that is the final signal that I am about to start a trance journey. By covering my head, I then become open to receive kennings and insight. Receiving is the second component to success in Spá, since to obtain the skill of a seer, one must be open to receive the messages. The ability to be receptive also comes with the assumption that the Seiðr worker is not afraid, nor selective of the messages or wights that may come to them. We may not choose to stay in the presence of a Wight who isn't in our best interest to work with, but we can meet them on the otherworldly plane without fear or pre-conceived human ideas, simply because we are open to receive unbiased information.

Most people report significant swaying, rocking, pulsating, vibrating, or twitching, indicating the level of energy being built up to within this posture to accomplish a spirit journey.

Performing the Posture: Stand with your feet parallel, about six inches apart and with your toes pointing straight ahead. Bend your knees slightly. Hold both arms close to your body and bend them at the elbow so that you have the appearance of removing a article of clothing from your shoulders.

Take a deep breath inward, and using an opening gesture extend your arms outward and then overhead, while arching your back slightly backwards, and breathing in a deep receiving breath. Allow your mouth to open like a big yawn. Keep your eyes closed as you face upward.

Lesson 8/5: Journeying to More Worlds.

Again this month we will be offering three separate choices of journey, and as in the past month, you will be expected to study them and divine on them to see where you will be allowed to fare. Instead of last month's elemental-state worlds—Fire, Ice, and Death—this month we contrast three separate "races" of spiritual beings: Elves, Dwarves, and the wild Giants of the Iron Wood. These tribes of beings are choosy about who they will work with; if they decide that you have an affinity with them, you will have gained powerful allies in your life and work. You will have to remember to pay attention to them and make offerings on a regular basis to show your regard, but it will be well worth the work.

When you do the divination for each world, ask an extra question: *If you are willing to allow me to come to you, and form an alliance, will you want my oath to you?* That will not always be a "yes" answer, at least not right away. However, you should not take it personally if not every spiritual tribe of entities wants to adopt you. In most cases, a rejection is not done with contempt, but more of a "You're not for us, but you'll get along better with those folks over there." Understand that while some can make strong alliances with more than one of these ally groups, more commonly, if you are chosen by one of them, you may have to sacrifice alliances with the others. Sometimes they can be territorial about your kinship agreements.

Because these are journeys to one of the Nine Realms to actually meet another entity, we are going to perform this Utiseta within a formal "Trance Blöt". I use these when first going to a place in the world of Yggdrasil where I have never been before, thereby ensuring the most successful outcome possible. I find it beneficial because the ritual keeps one focused on one's goal, which is to make contact with a being from that world. Do it as directed; however, with time spent in any of the other worlds inhabited by hommorphic entities, you can later just access the world simply by entering a trance state and directing your intention.

Lesson 8/6: Alfheim and the Alfarblót.

The Norse otherworldly beings known as Elves are most often described as beautiful beyond imagination, and are often equated with the Celtic Tuatha de Danann. (Think J.R.R.Tolkien-style Elves here.) They are said to have nearly divine qualities that other beings of the Norse Cosmology don't share with the Elven Race. However, some factions of Elves, we will come to learn, are more elemental and primal, and we must remember when dealing with any race - especially the Elves - that they are not human, and do not have human ideas and agendas. If the Völva or Vitki is lucky enough to gain their favor, and wise enough to keep it, the Alfar can be consulted for healing (or harm!).

Elves are generally classified as "light" or "dark" Alfar, but we will be dealing primary with the Ljóssalfar, or Light-Elves. (The Ljóssalfar are allied with the Gods of civilization and agriculture, the Aesir and the Vanir. Due to their love of Nature, they are also allied with many of the nature-spirits in our world, and make friends with them.

The term "Light-Elves" doesn't mean Ljóssálfar were always good, accessible and benevolent, nor does the term "Dark-Elves" mean that the Dokkalfar were always dangerous, ever eager to stay-in-the-shadows, and malevolent. The distinction is that the Dark Elves lived in a lower world (Svartalfheim), and the Light Elves dwell above Midgard in higher realms. The Dokkalfar share a world with the Duergar, or Dwarves, who live underground in Svartalfheim in an area called Nidavellir, and they have a fair amount of interaction with humans, but we will be looking at them in the next section. The Dokkalfar themselves are more elusive and have less to do with humanity. Dealing with the Dokkalfar is a challenge not to be taken on by the beginner.

The Light Alfar are typically found in airy high places, wanting nothing better to do than pretend we lower forms of life don't exist. (I know, sad but true!) Don't get me wrong; they have remarkable magics and healing abilities, but it's a matter of IF (and that's a big IF) one can spark their interest enough to get to get them involved with our meager human lives.

Elves, like their Celtic cousins the Fey, are very complicated and tricky beings. For instance, you could be very polite and offer them gifts, do their bidding, and kiss their ugly grandma's lips (believe me, not all Elves are beautiful and full of splendor as Tolkien would have you think; some of the wild faeries actually smell really bad and are as scary as Hela) but one wrong move or slight on your part while venturing forth in their world and you're cursed for life, or worse. You might end up dead or disappearing from human records. Elves are known to sometimes be happily and unapologetically douche-baggish to humans, causing illnesses or death. But if they take a liking to you, with the right approach and understanding of their customs and ways, they can do miracles for humans by healing great wounds, sicknesses, fertility, and other Midgard maladies when they can be enticed to help a poor earth-bound person out.

The secret in getting them to be benevolent or kind (or to actually just *not* take any notice of us at all; sometimes anonymity is *the* best call with an Alf) is like any other being of the Nine Worlds. Give them stuff, make nice with stinky Granny who rocks a mean set of claws and pupil-less eyes, and meekly ask to be spared their wrath. Because unfortunately you can provoke the wrath of the Alfar just by being a careless, stupid twit. We don't want that; we want to **live** to tell our tales of the Otherworlds. So this leads us back to Utiseta and what it really meant to our ancestors. In knowing the concepts behind out-sitting on a burial mound, you will come to understand its magical and shamanic seiðkona significance. It's the most direct way to the Alfar.

The skald Sigvatr Þórðarson (also known as Sigvat the Skald) records coming across a town in the middle of a sacrifice ceremony for the Elves and was turned away no matter where he went. Sigvat was confused and put off by this community-wide turning away, and in his refusal to be allowed to take part in any of the "private" rites the entire village was collectively involved in, he gave us a little information about why he was being turned away so abruptly. But there was one thing he forgot to mention: he was an Icelandic Christian in still very Pagan territory, so he wasn't allowed to know what was really going on.

In Sigvat's search for answers and hospitality, he approached the home of the man who was reported to be the most hospitable in all the village and was surprisingly refused welcome quite rudely, leading him to reflect that he was glad he didn't go to the home of the person reputed as being the meanest man in the village!

Although we aren't specifically told in his written account the town was specifically doing the kind of AlfarBlót we describe here, by comparing the time of year Sigvat was in the village, and by looking at other stories, (especially of Elves and their connection with the dead and the Underworld, as well as how to appease them or win their favors) we can connect the dots and piece together a clearer picture of what was really happening. Utiseta would be combined with rites of honor, song, and dance, all done to give sacrifice and appeasement to the Elves.

Stories found in the Sagas tell of wounded heroes and sick folk who were often told to make sacrifices to the elves on their very own, special elf mounds. These mounds were almost always graves. Most who died in the "Viking era" and before were not treated to a classic "Viking funeral" and burned in a boat with all they possessed. The Norse most often buried their dead semi-mausoleums under the dirt, making big mounds on top. The mounds are sometimes called a "barrow", a "howe", or a "tumulus". That is why Völvas did out-sitting on graves; so they could access otherworldly information via the most direct route to the otherworldly knowledge: Death, which included Dead Ancestors. This is also why in the Völuspá Odin roused the Völva; he wanted answers to his biggest questions, and who better to answer him then a dead witch.

> There is another part to the equation besides just meditating on the burial mound; we must give some form of sacrifice to the Elves. Sacrifice can be given in many forms: from killing a live being and

offering up its life force to simply giving the greatest performance of your life in a way only you can uniquely offer. Singing, dancing, storytelling and oath-swearing your unending services are very popular with the Alf Folk, as H. A. Guerber says in *Myths of the Norsemen*[59]: "In Scandinavia and Germany sacrifices were offered to the elves to make them propitious. These sacrifices consisted of some small animal, or of a bowl of honey and milk, and were known as Alf-Blót." And on Dancing: These elves, [who in England were called fairies or fays] were also enthusiastic musicians, and delighted especially in a certain air known as the elf-dance, which was so irresistible that no one who heard it could refrain from dancing. If a mortal, overhearing the air, ventured to reproduce it, he suddenly found himself incapable of stopping and was forced to play on and on until he died of exhaustion, unless he were deft enough to play the tune backwards, or someone charitably cut the strings of his violin. His hearers, who were forced to dance as long as the tones continued, could only stop when they ceased.

The Elves **can** be accessed and reached to work with and alongside of. The Key is that we must do it with reverence, with awareness, and with our eyes wide open. We are human, but with enough interaction, discernment, wisdom and tact, a relationship can be forged. We just need to understand that Elves are elemental beings by nature, and their thought processes are very far from being held to "human standards" and "human sensibilities" (read "human expectations").[60]

For this month's Utiseta, you will do a two-part ritual. First you will design an Oath to go with an AlfaBlót you will perform. You will then enter a trance state, and as the mist begins to form as the boundary between the Otherworlds, you will attempt to shapeshift into a chosen

---

[59] Dover Publications, 1992.
[60] For more information about the Elves, see The Pathwalker's Guide article "Dancing Light and Singing Dark": http://www.northernshamanism.org/the-alfar-dancing-light-and-singing-dark.html
For more information about Ljossalfheim, see The Pathwalker's Guide article: http://www.northernshamanism.org/ljossalfheim.html.

animal/other form beginning with your *Hamr*, then move that shape to your Fylgja, as you journey to Alfheim and possibly meet your Elven healer guide. For the entire journey, you will attempt to keep this animal/other form in your Fylgja, and to see, hear, smell, and move with your *Hamr* covering your Fylgja as your chosen animal/other would, as well as move about in the shape of your chosen ally.

It is best to pick an animal/ally you are very familiar and close to, as this helps with your understanding of how and what the creature will look and act like. Be sure it is a real living creature from nature, not a mythical being. You will need a Blót bowl, mead, ale or some other offering, a diabetic lancet to draw blood from your finger, a bundle of herbs of your choosing for hallowing, and a candle.

Practice: Alfarblót Ritual

You will be singing a joik as part of this ritual; a joik that tells the tale below. Remember, joiking has no sentences and very few words. With your intuitive song, you are giving life to the narrative below. Read through it a few times and then work on the joik, which will be an offering to the Alfar. Do this well before you decide to do the rite.

"Many, many years ago, in the homeland, a group of Völvas gathered to celebrate the Alfarblót rite. After studious preparation, the Spá sisters gathered to hear of what was to come. They were led by a Seer on a short walk through the countryside, where they came upon a great Ash tree, standing atop a burial mound. Sensing this wonderful opportunity, the seiðkona's linked hands and minds, becoming one with the tree, one with nature, and one with the Nine Worlds. They sang the way open.

They then saw an opening in the great tree and entered within. As the mist formed, they heard a large black bird circling the Great Tree, screeching out in human speech the words to the sacred song of the Völva. Then a great horn was blown and one of their number rose to recite the opening Galdr, as was done in the days of our ancestors. They then claimed the land on which they were about to work, offering a gift in exchange for the silence of those who would aid them. An Elf rose to tell the folk the stories of Creation, of the Well of Hvergelmir, Muspellheim and of Yggdrasil. The folk set their minds upon welcoming their guests to share this power. In response, the ancestors of land, of blood, and of path gathered near. After the Elf had givin them the healing blessing requested, the seiðkona boarded a ship and set sail to Alfheim."

When the time comes to do the rite: Prepare the space, and yourself, for Utiseta as you usually do. Hallow your space, and call to the four directions: Austri, Sudri, Vestri, Nordri. Place a loose incense blend on your brazier (or, if you don't use a brazier for incense, use a charcoal disc in a bowl or plate) and light it. As the smoke begins to rise, envision your words wafting away with the smoke. Then say the following, or some version thereof:

I call upon you, Alfar, in a time of in-between!

I ask your assistance and blessing, for one who is seeking kinship!

I, [Name], seek to be a co-walker of your healing might!

I ask you to guide my hands, and give me strength,

To keep all creatures great and small from illness,

And protect all in body and soul.

I ask you, great Alfar; to accept me as a worthy Völva/Vitki,

And to send one of your kind as my guide and ally

In the work of healing in Midgard,

And, if needed, the other worlds.

(If divination has indicated that the Alfar are willing to make a relationship of kinship with you, add the following words:)

Carry my Oath out to the four winds, never to be forgotten.

To the north, take this Oath of kinship and infuse it with health.

To the east, take this Oath of kinship, and infuse it with strength.

To the south, take this Oath of kinship, and infuse it with vitality.

To the west, take this Oath of kinship, and infuse it with life.

(Light the candle.)

Hail to you, powerful Alfar, I pay you tribute.

I honor you and ask this one small gift, as a gift I give.

May your power, strength and kenning wash over me [name],

So I might find you supporting me in time of need.

Take a few moments to meditate on what you really wish for your relationship with the Elven race before you sit down to fare forth. Then state the oath you have created in your own words. After saying your words, prick your finger with the lancet and give a few drops of your blood mixed with ale or mead and offer it up to the Elves. Take three deep breaths and begin to Galdr Dagaz, the Futhark rune for change, and Wunjo, the Futhark rune of the Light-Elves, while moving about your space with your drum. Then use the Joiking you created to soul-sing your Ally to you. Focus on feeling your Hamr change and morph; allow your body to move and act as your chosen shape. Don't censor or critique your experience; just let it unfold naturally. See, hear, smell and move like your chosen subject would. Once you have finished and feel able to wear your totem's skin in your Hamr, sit down on your Seidrstallr and prepare to journey to Alfheim.

Now, call your intention. Galdr the Futhark runes Wunjo, Laguz, Raido, Ehwaz, Kenaz, and Algiz. Begin to sing a Vardlokkur which says: "In the name of Saga, let the story unfold! In the name of my Ancestors, let the story be bold! In the names of Freyr and Freya let me arrive upon the shores of Alfheim where my oaths may be told!" Let the melody come naturally; don't worry about it being fine music or poetry.

Thump your Stav nine times and then begin to joik the offering story. After you feel you have given life to your intention with your joik, place your offering in your Blót bowl and say:

This place I name, this land I do claim,
While me and my own are upon it.
Freyr and Freya, You who choose to assist me in my stated purpose,
Whose voice will harmonize with the tune I sing this day,
Your function I honor, your purpose I respect.
For you are Two among the Many, Twin faces of the great mystery!
As a gift calls for a gift, I offer and pray, asking only this:
Till the Stav is pound and the rite is ground,
Let there be frith between us!

(Pour the offering of wine, mead, or milk. Then being a steady Stav beat. Say as you begin your trance state:)

I ask Frey to lend me his magical ship Skidbladnir,
Which can sail on sea or sky,
And be folded like cloth into one's pocket.
I call Inguz to be the ship on which I sail to Alfheim.

Begin to Galdr the Futhark rune Inguz, and see the mist form. Feel your Hamr take on the shape of the animal ally you have chosen while climbing into the boat. Watch the riverbanks for changing terrain, being sure to note where you are in case you want to revisit these places at another time. Once the boat reaches the shore of Alfheim, get out and begin using your animal senses to find the Hall of the Elves.

Upon finding your destination, change back into your common form and wait. The Elven Folk know you are here, and will appear when they are ready. When one shows up, be sure to introduce yourself and be sure make devotional offerings to the Elven being who appears to you before you ask any questions or favors. Accept whatever it is that is told to you, and when the visit is over, again thank your host. Change your Hamr once again into your ally form, and return to the boat. When reaching the shore back to Midgard, leave offerings to Freyr for the use of the boat.[61]

Begin traveling back to the Tree, once again allowing your normal form to return as the veil mist forms around you. Once back in your body, thump your Stav three times to signal that the journey is complete.

Reflect upon what it is you received from the Land of Elves, and what blessings their powers of healing can offer you that is of value to you. Fill the horn with mead and raise it, calling into it the blessings that our allies offer us. Say:

> By land, sea and sky,
> By the bonds above and below,
> As we have given you praise
> Let us receive the flowing blaze
> Of your blessing
> To share by drinking.

Hold up the horn, making a toast to honor all the beings who took part in this journey. Feel free to brag of some accomplishment, boast of some future deed, and of course offer a blessing and then drink a sip, hailing each entity that you worked with during this Utiseta. After your "hail" and your sip, pour out an offering on the ground to our allies to show we are not greedy, nor ungrateful.

---

[61] For offering ideas, and general information about Freyr, see His online shrine on the northernpaganism.org site.

You will be thanking in turn your Alfheim hosts, Freyr, Freya, your Disir, the Ancestors, your animal ally and the landvættir. Say:

My saga was made, the story is told,

May there always be kenning, may I always be bold!

Thump your Stav nine times, and allow the candle to burn out on its own if possible.

Lesson 8/7: Nidavellir and the DuergarBlót.

Svartalfheim is a world divided into two parts: above and below. Above, the Dokkalfar roam singing through dark evergreen forests and mountains. Below, the Duergar, often known as "dwarves" or "dwarrows", have their deep caves and forges. (Yes, you can think "Tolkien dwarves"; he did, after all, steal their descriptions and even their names out of Norse mythology.) The Duergar are master craftsmen; their caves are far from dank, dark places. Instead, they are filled with fiery forges, comfortable dwellings, high halls, and endless amounts of beautiful objects that they have created. If your creativity is blocked or stunted, or if you want to learn greater skill in your crafting, the Duergar are masters of those gifts.

However, their prices are not cheap. They know the value of what they make (and teach), and they will not undersell themselves. They are also not interested in wasting their time on humans who claim to want something but aren't interested in working for it. The Duergar practically invented the term "work ethic"; they have been known to slave for months or years on a creative project, and being in the throes of creative obsession to the point where nothing else matters, and one must have friends and family keep making sure that one is eating, washing, and sleeping, is considered a holy state among them. They have been known to insist that a bargaining human swear to do only their absolute best work on creative projects—no skimping on time or materials or cutting corners—for the rest of their lives, and humans have been known to default on such deals, at which point the Duergar feel that they have the lawful right to lay a curse on the lazy and unfortunate mortal. So be careful what you ask for![62]

Like the AlfarBlót in the last section, we will be opening our Utiseta for a journey to Nidavellir with a DuergarBlót. This ritual has been given to us by Susannah Ravenswing, a sacred smith who works closely with the Duergar.

> Of all of the races of the Nine Worlds, the Duergar are most secretive, and with ample reason, given that they are the makers of the most notable magical objects described in the lore. As a result, they are extremely reclusive and selective about whom they will engage with and even more selective as to whom they admit to their cities beneath the rugged surface of Svartalfheim. Anyone who would seek to visit should know that the Duergar value Substance more than anything. This means that a thing must be as it seems, and a being must be free of glamour or artifice. They have bluntly told me that those bearing Alfar blood are unwelcome in their holdings. The Duergar are acutely aware of the value of their skills as artisans and enchanters and are unwilling to waste time or knowledge on casual encounters. While the Duergar are best known as craftsmen and Master Makers, they are also stalwart warriors and quite prepared to defend their realms with steel. (Unlike the Alfar, the Duergar have always been at home with iron and its working.)
>
> Always begin with divination to determine whether such a journey is to be undertaken. Should the runes YR, LAGUZ, RAIDO, or CHALC appear reversed (or "mirkstave"[63]), do not persist. If the signs are positive, gather the following, the specifics of which are very important:
> - ❖ Fire-making kit OR, if necessary, lighter or matches.
> - ❖ A slab of stone OR wood, covered with hand-woven cloth as harrow or altar.
> - ❖ A recaning stick of mugwort.

---

[62] For another view of the home of the Duergar, read the second half of the Svartalfheim article from *The Pathwalker's Guide* website: http://www.northernshamanism.org/svartalfheim_nidavellir.html.

[63] Not everyone uses reversed runes, referred to as "mirkstave". Whether one chooses to read runes as single meaning or otherwise is up to them.

The Deeper Arts of the Volva

- Deep red OR gold pillar candle.
- Fine Scotch OR Whisky.
- A plate of roast boar OR pork.
- A cluster of quartz OR amethyst crystals.
- A drinking horn.
- An silver OR iron token made by a sacred smith.[64]
- A hand-carved wooden Blót bowl.

Begin the rite by recaning yourself and the space where you are; outdoors is preferable.[65] Place the cloth over wood or stone and arrange the other items on the harrow. Light the candle; holding it in both hands, hail the Duergar of the Four Directions:

(Face North) Hail Norðri!

(Face East) Hail Austri!

(Face South) Hail Suðri!

(Face West) Hail Vestri!

Hail unto You, who faithfully hold high the arching vault of the heavens.

Replace the candle on the harrow. Place the crystal cluster in the center of the Blót bowl and arrange choice bits of the meat around it. Pour a generous portion of the Scotch or Whisky into the horn. Raise the horn and say:

Hail to the Makers,
The Workers of Wonder.
Hail to the Diggers
Who delve far below.
Hail the Gold-Gatherers,
Down in the darkness
Whose songs call the gems

---

[64] Sacred smiths are beginning to relearn their own mysteries, often with the help of the Duergar.

[65] "Recels" is the old Anglo-Saxon word for what modern Americans would generally refer to as "smudge"—a bundle of dried plant material for burning as incense; the verb form is "recaning", pronounced "reek-en-ing", and yes, it is related to the modern English word "to reek". Mugwort was the most common sacred recaning herb, and a mugwort stick for recaning can be handmade or bought.

> That in caverns do grow.
> Hail to the master smiths,
> Lit by the forge-light,
> Billet to blade by their skill
> Is made strong.
> Hail the embroiderers'
> Shining threads gleaming
> Finest of stitches
> Enchanted by song.
> Hail to the Makers,
> The Workers of Wonder.
> Hail to the Duergar,
> The Masters of Art.
> Hail to the Old Ones
> That honor traditions
> So that beauty is born
> Both by hand and by heart.
>
> *Take a sip from the horn and pour the remainder over the contents of the Blót bowl. Say:*
>
> I offer you fair gifts: fine meat and drink,
> The glittering bounty of the deep earth,
> And humbly ask for safe passage,
> Claiming guest rights and knowing
> That I may look but not touch.
>
> *Place the iron or silver token in your left palm and lay your right over it. Galdr the Futhorc rune YR. Henceforth, carry the token in your pouch or pocket when you seek to visit Niflheim.*
>
> *Extinguish the candle. Place the Blót bowl at the base of a very large tree which has agreed to accept the offering or in a small opening beneath rocks.*
>
> *Be advised that this rite will not guarantee you admittance.*

Indeed, after the rite you should draw runes to see if your gifts were accepted. If the omens look positive, prepare for the journey. First, create a song or invocation for the Duergar that is polished and well made. It is all right to get help with this; they appreciate original craftsmanship regardless of whether it is yours or not. If you are stuck for a theme, try composing something for the Four Dwarves of the Directions, who also correspond to the seasons. Remember that while these beings may be a mythological footnote to most humans, they are the Sacred Gods of the Duergar and are much revered.

Prepare the space, and yourself, for Utiseta as you usually do. Sing your usual vardlokkur and mentally orient yourself on the Tree. Point yourself toward Svartalfheim and visualize a glade at the foot of a mountain, surrounded by evergreen trees so tall that they almost Blót out the sky. A small ring of stars can be seen above the clearing, in the center of which stands a empty well with offerings set about it. In front of you is a stone door, carved into the side of the mountain, with no visible means of opening. Call out:

I have made offering, and received reply! Open to me, and I swear I will be a fair guest, and accept what is given to me.

Assuming that the door opens (if it does not, turn back and try again another time), you will be invited into the glowing passageways of Nidavellir by a Duerg guide. Follow the guide, looking around as you go. What do you see, hear, or feel? What sort of place do you go?

Eventually you will be brought through the labyrinthine passages and great halls until you come before a Duergar Lord (or Lady, although they are very rare) who wishes to speak to you. Listen to their words, and if you must ask questions, make them respectful. Offer to sing your song for them, and if they accept, give the best performance you can. Thank them for their wisdom, and allow yourself to be guided out to the doorway and the nighttime glade. Then orient yourself on the Tree and find your way back to your body.

Reflect upon what it is you received from the Duergar, and what blessings they have been generous enough to give you. Fill the horn with mead and raise it, calling into it the blessings that our allies offer us. Say:

By land, sea and sky,
By the bonds above and below,
As we have given you praise
Let us receive the flowing blaze
Of your blessing we share by drinking.

Hold up the horn, making a toast to honor all the beings who took part in this journey. Feel free to brag of some accomplishment, boast of some future deed, and of course offer a blessing and then drink a sip, hailing each entity that you worked with during this Utiseta. After your "hail" and your sip, pour out an offering on the ground to our allies to show we are not greedy, nor ungrateful. You will be thanking in turn your Nidavellir hosts, the Four Duergar Gods, your Disir, the Ancestors, and the landvættir. Say:

My saga was made, the story is told,
May there always be kenning, may I always be bold!
Thump your Stav nine times to end the rite.

Lesson 8/8: The Iron Wood and the JotunBlót.

In Norse mythology, Járnviðr (Old Norse "Iron-wood") is a forest located in Jotunheim, inhabited by trolls, giants, shapeshifters, and giant wolves. The Iron Wood is found in the *Völuspá*, verse 40.[66] Snorri Sturluson quotes this stanza and expands it in his Gylfaginning:

> A witch dwells to the east of Midgard, in the forest called Iron Wood: in that wood dwell the troll-women, who are known as Iron Wood-Women (*járnviðjur*). The old witch (who, by the way is Angrboda, the Hag of the Iron Wood and Loki's first wife) bears many giants for sons, and all in the shape of wolves; and from this source are these wolves sprung. The saying runs thus: from this race shall come one that shall be mightiest of all, he that is named Moon-Hound (Mánagarmr); he shall be filled with the flesh of all those men that die, and he shall swallow the moon.

The form *Járnviðjur* ("Iron Wood-dweller") is nowhere else to be found, but in singular, *Járnviðja* is listed in the *þulur* as a "troll-wife", in 10th century skald Eyvindr Skáldaspillir's *Háleygjatal*, which is referring to the goddess Angrboda.

As we study the Iron Wood, we must remember always that Snorri Sturluson was a devout medieval Christian, so any story he recants is going to have the slant that a true "wild-woman" is inherently unpredictable, dangerous, and to be feared. That also goes for the "uncivilized" places she tended to call home, and for me, that is the wild, untamed Iron Wood.

---

[66] For another view of the Iron Wood, see *The Pathwalker's Guide* website, in the last half of this article: http://www.northernshamanism.org/jotunheim.html.

From Indo-European history and archeology, we can find instances of healers and indigenous shamans who chose to live in the forests on the fringes of "civilization" for the benefits of being one with the wilderness, and in doing so learned the secrets of life and death via the natural world around them. We also find magics deeply being inseparable from the location of forests via the original term for "troll" in Scandinavia. A "troll" was a creature that lives in the forest and is seen as a primal homomorphic being (perhaps equated to our Neanderthal predecessors) by some. Even though a troll is a mythical creature best known in lore with negative connotations, trolls have always been depicted with the name having the original meaning of "supernatural" or "magical" with an overlay of "malignant" and "perilous."

In old Swedish law, *trolleri* (a type of magic wielded by Trolls) was defined as magic intended to do harm, but it should be noted that modern Scandinavian terms such as *trolldom* ("witchcraft")[67] and *trolla/trylle* ("perform magic tricks") do not imply any connection with the mythical beings. Moreover, in the sources for Norse mythology, "troll" can signify any uncanny being, including but not restricted to the Norse giants (Jötnar)[68]. And what gives these trolls, malevolent or not, their power? The wild places in nature where humans seldom have the balls to go!

In Old European folklore, "witch" (and I am talking about before the Medieval diabolic meaning of the term) was a title given to the solitary wisewoman who lived on the fringes of civilization. The term "witch" was originally associated with the spirits of nature, a human conduit who had the wisdom to channel elemental natural forces while possessing unexpected powers constituted a threat to the prevailing order. The simple fact that a witch lived deep within the forest and knew how to live feral

---

[67] For more information on trolldom, see this article by Johannes Bjorn Gardback: http://www.luckymojo.com/trolldom.html. For more on medieval women as healers, see: https://www.huffingtonpost.com/gerit-quealy/forgotten-women-witches-h_b_859230.html.

[68] For more information on the Jotnar, see *The Pathwalker's Guide* website here: http://www.northernshamanism.org/jotnar.html.

meant that she was feared by town dwellers even as they sought out her knowledge of healing.

Prior to the 13th or 14th century (Snorri Sturluson's time), witchcraft had come to mean a collection of beliefs and practices including healing through spells, ointments and concoctions, dabbling in the supernatural, and forecasting the future through divining and clairvoyance, all while staying to the wild fringes of nature and humanity. In England, the provision of curative magic was the job of a "witch doctor" (a term used in England long before it came to be associated with Africa), also known as a "cunning man", "white witch" or "wiseman". Although they did not refer to themselves as witches, these cunning-folk were generally considered valuable members of the community, and generally always found in the wild places. So in the study of European folklore, we find that wilderness locations such as Angrboda's Iron Wood is a place full of power, magic and primal wisdom.

For this third alternate Utiseta, we will attempt to travel to the Iron Wood to meet the cunning Iron Wood Women (járnviðjur) and perhaps get a glimpse of the power of one of my patron goddesses, Angrboda, as well as the wolves who run free there.[69] We will begin with a Blót to Angrboda and the people of the Iron Wood, contributed by Raven Kaldera.

> The beings of the Iron Wood are of that spirit-race that humans call Giants or Trolls (or Jotnar, Etins, Thurses, etc), but that doesn't mean either that they are very large or that they are all slavering, ugly, brutish creatures. They are members of a spirit-race that is very close to Nature and can change their shapes at will, and often take the form of (and even meld with) natural energies such as fire, water, wind, or earth. that why there are fire-etins in Muspellheim, frost-thurses in Niflheim, and sea-etins in the oceans between the worlds. Jotunheim, or "Giant-Home", is populated by mountain-giants, tree-etins, and Jotnar who take on animal shapes. The Iron Wood is inhabited especially by these latter two, and they divine themselves into nine Tribes. As shapeshifters who often go in

---

[69] For information on Angrboda, see Her online shrine at http://www.northernpaganism.org/shrines/angrboda/welcome.html.

strange or patchwork forms, they have different standards for beauty than most modern humans, and we must keep this in mind when journeying there.

Angrboda is the Wolf-Mother, chief of the Wolf Tribe and chief of chiefs of all nine tribes. She is warrior, priestess, sorceress, shapeshifter, the senior wife of Loki and the mother of Hela, Fenrir, and the World Serpent. She is compassionate to the strong who try hard but break, but has little patience for the weak of will. Her wisdom is ancient and bloody, and may be difficult to bear.

For this Blót you will need:

- A liter of whisky (Jack Daniels works well for anything in Jotunheim).
- Chunks of meat, ideally raw.
- A campfire, or at least a candle.
- Crumbled dried Agrimony herb, Angrboda's plant.
- A stick of mugwort, and your drum and stav, if you intend to do the journey there as well.

Ideally, this rite should be done outdoors in the wilderness, far from any tame parks where domestic animals could eat the raw meat and get sick. If you can't make a campfire, light a small candle in a fireproof vessel and be very careful not to knock it over or otherwise be stupid with the flame. When the flame is going, drop a bit of the Agrimony on the flame and burn it as incense. Then lay out the meat and call out:

By the Wolves of the Forest,
By the Serpent of the Ocean,
By the Hound-Beetles that bury the corpse,
By the Tree struck by Lightning,
By the River of Stone Knives,
By the Hyenas that clean up the mess,
By the Alder-Tree that drips with blood,
By the Bear that drowses in the Cave,
By the Ghost of the Great Stag,
I bring you offering and ask for your favor!
Then pour the whisky out onto the earth, saying:
Lady of the Iron Wood,
Bride of Flame, Chieftess of Power,
Mother of Death, Mother of Destruction,
Mother of Liminality, Mother of Wolves,

> Mother of Monsters who cares for the ones
> Deemed too ugly for the weak of heart,
> I ask for your permission to enter your sacred Wood
> And learn the wisdom held therein
> As safely as I may!

Do your divination, see if the runes are positive, and if they are, you may begin the journey to the Iron Wood. You can do the journey in the wilderness area, or go home and do it in your Seiðrstallr. The Iron Wood folk will give you points for doing it in the wilderness, however.

1) If you are home, hallow your Seiðrstallr as you normally would. If you are in the wilderness, light the mugwort stick with the candle, smoke the area, and then carefully put out both the candle and the stick. Perform the Pose of Receiving to begin your journey.

2) Using whatever method you like best (Drumming or Staving) to pick a way of singing your intention to be allowed access to the Iron Wood via Yggdrasil. Be sure your Ek is in check, and that you are entering this ancient sacred woodland for the purpose of gaining wisdom of the powerful cunning women. No big human egos here!

3) See the mist of the portal form before you, and as it fades be aware of the deep, dark vastness of this ancient and primordial forest.

4) Check to see if your Disir is with you. Ask her to take the shape of a wolf, and send her ahead of you to gain permission from the ancient wolves who live here. (For this trip you will keep your Fylgja as the image of your current human form; no shapeshifting for you at this time in the Iron Wood. Only those with Iron Wood bloodlines or special prior permission may shapeshift here.)

5) Begin your journey. As you travel, you may wish to change your Fylgja with your *Hamr* into the shape of a wolf as well, but don't! This Goddess whom you seek will want to see you as you are in the everyday everywhere. Take note of the sights, smells and sounds.

6) When (and if) you come to the Dwelling of the Járnviðjur, change back into your human self, and ask for permission to approach, holding an offering of something that is of great importance to you.

7) If Angrboda does show up to greet you, for the rest of the journey you are not to speak. Just listen and be very quiet, in tune to Her every

move. If Angrboda is welcoming, and appears receptive to your visit, She will take your gift. She might show you some disfigured or strangely "put together" inhabitant of the Iron Wood. *Do not* flinch, or even hesitate in smiling and giving them Welcome. (If you don't know what to say, you can soundlessly bow in honor of its presence.) Angrboda sees the usefulness and beauty in the odd, the different and the malformed. Her daughter is Hela, and Hela's brother is none other than Fenrir, so do not for an instant allow yourself to be repulsed or afraid of what friend she presents to you.

8) Using the skill of empathy, understand her teachings and be keenly aware of when she is finished entertaining your presence.
9) When it is time to depart, simply bow, and whistle for the portal of the mist to form for your return home.
10) Return back to the Tree the way you came.
11) Come back to your body and thump your Stav nine times to signal you are fully back in Midgard.
12) Record your findings in your journal.

Lesson 8/7: More Mind Training.

To better improve our memory and mind when journeying, we are going to attempt to take three items and visualize as clearly as possible their appearance, texture, taste and smell. Don't move on to the following object until you feel you can make each thing as real in your mind as it is in front of you.

An Orange. Take a real orange and peel it slowly. Note everything about this process, from the juice squirting on your hands, to the texture of the peel. Note the smell of the fruit, and how each segment of the orange looks. Finally, take and eat a piece of it, noting the flavor. Then put the orange down and close your eyes. Conjure up an orange in your mind, and repeat the entire process. If you lose concentration, open your eyes, hold the real orange, then close your eyes and begin again until you can relive the entire process in your mind's eye.

Flame. Now take a plain white candle, and place it in a holder. Note its size, what it feels like in your hand, and how it looks to you, including the holder. Take a match or lighter and lite the wick. Notice how the flame takes life, and how that looks and smells. Watch it burn for a minute or so, noting the flame and if its shape changes size and intensity, then blow out the candle. Close your eyes and repeat the entire process in your mind. Again, if you can't clearly picture the candle-lighting process, open your eyes and retrace your steps.

Reflection. Finally, go to a mirror. Stare at your own face, noting every detail of your features. Feel your face with your hands and note what that feels like to your hand receptors as well as to your facial nerve endings. When you feel ready, close your eyes and repeat the entire process, never actually touching your own face. Again, if you lose concentration, open your eyes and go through looking and touching your face in the mirror.

Lesson 8/8: Reading Material.

1) Read and work on the last two chapters of *Neolithic Shamanism*—"The Black World" and "Broken Promises".

2) Read at least five more of the online God-shrines, and ask via Futhark/Futhorc or your own personal runes whether any of them would be interested in teaching or aiding you.

3) Read more of the other books on the Required Reading list.

4) Make sure that you are doing some kind of physical practice that combines moving the body with moving the body's energies.

5) Do a daily rune draw. If you do any other divination, practice your divination protocol.

Lesson 8/10: Immersion into the Völuspá, Verses 50–55.

50. How is it with the Æsir? How with the Alfar?
All Jötunheim roars; the Æsir are in council.
The dwarfs groan before stone doors,
the wise ones of the rock-wall.
Know ye yet, or what?

51. Surt fares from the south with the bane of branches;
shines from the sword the Val-gods sun.

The stony hills gnash, gifur totter;
men tread the Hel-way, and heaven is cloven.

52. Then comes Hlin's second grief,
when Odin goes to fight with the wolf,
and the bright slayer of Beli with Surt.
Then will Frigg's sweet-scent god fall.

53. Then comes the great Victory-father's son,
Vidar, to fight with the deadly beast.
In the mouth of Hvethrung's [Loki's] son, he made stand
a sword in the heart; Then he avenges his father.

54. Then comes the mighty son of Hlódyn:
Odin's son goes to fight with the wolf;
in his rage will slay the worm, Midgárd's Veor.
All men will abandon their homes.
Nine feet will go Fiörgyn's son,
bowed by the serpent, who feared no foe.

55. Sun turns dark, earth sinks in sea,
hurl from heaven the bright stars,
fire's breath assails the all-nourishing tree,
high flames play against heaven itself.

Month 9: Time and Seasons.

For this last chapter I am going to share the year-long trip around the sun. By now hopefully you have a good moon practice going with your monthly Utiseta; however, now it is important to further your practice by participating in the seasonal dance of Jord and Sol, the two goddesses who orchestrate the song to the wondrous turning of life.

I feel that by immersing oneself into the flow of Jord's changing faces, along with the fluctuating presence of Sol, we then can truly connect to the life forces going on all around us every day. By implementing sacred ceremony we actually interact with these forces as we step into our power fully and joyously as Völvas or Vitkis though experiencing the flow and current of life and Wyrd.

This month and our last chapter will bring together all the other work we have done into balance and application by uniting above with below—the microcosm with the macrocosm, thereby completing our training. By taking our spiritual work into the real world, we bring our practice to life.

This book can only be made a complete "course" when we learn the language of ritual and sacred pantomime. And as I learned in French class, a language can only be truly understood when its spoken often and within all venues of your daily life.

Lesson 9/1: Moving with the Seasons.

Your first lesson this month is very simple. Where are you in the year? Read through the next section of the book, Sacred Ceremony, and find out what holy day is coming up. Find a way to celebrate it by adopting the ritual for yourself as a solitary rite, or gather some of your friends to help celebrate it.

It's important to remember that this spiritual practice does not exist in a vacuum. It is part of a religious context, and celebrating the holidays reminds us that this. For the next year, you will slowly build the Norse/Germanic holidays into your life. If you can't do them all, at least do something for the main holy days such as Ostara or Freyfaxi or Yule. Cook something special, light a candle and read out a prayer or invocation, put up some house decor, invite friends over for a small celebration, anything that reminds you to take a breath and be grateful for each season, and thus each new year you are alive.

Lesson 9/2: Making a Sigil.

The term sigil derives from the Latin *sigillum*, meaning "seal", though it may also be related to the Hebrew *segula*, meaning word, action, or item of spiritual effect, or talisman. The current use of the term is derived from Renaissance magic, which was in turn inspired by the magical traditions of antiquity.

In medieval ceremonial magic, the term sigil was commonly used to refer to occult signs which represented various spirits which the magician might summon. The grimoires (magical training books) often listed pages of such sigils. A particularly well-known list is in *The Lesser Key of Solomon*, in which the sigils of the seventy-two princes of the hierarchy of the Christian Hell are given for the magician's use. Such sigils were considered to be the equivalent of the true name of the spirit and thus granted the magician a measure of control over the beings

There are infinite ways to make and use sigils, but the best-known way in Heathenry is to make them with Norse Futhark runes. Below I will show how to do it with our own alphabet to demonstrate in simplicity, but to match a spell done in Seiðr; simply replace Norse Futhark runes for our modern Roman letters, being sure they are spelling out correctly your magical incantation. (If you work with the Anglo-Saxon Futhorc runes, they work even better for use with the modern English alphabet, as English is descended from Anglo-Saxon.[70]) On the other hand, you can also use your own personal runes, if they have letter value.

Write out a Sentence such as, "I will be Queen of the Mongrels".

Remove all the vowels from the sentence, and rewrite all the remaining Letters, "wllbqnfthmngrls."

---

[70] For information on writing modern English with the Futhorc symbols, see this online article: http://www.northernshamanism.org/writing-english-in-runes-for-magical-purposes.html

Next, remove all the repeating Letters. So it's now just a string of non-repeating consonants, "WLBQNFTHMGRS".

Take what letters are left and translate them with the corresponding Futhark rune (or Futhorc rune) letter value.

Make a symbol by combining the form of the remaining letters. You can combine the letters into a geometric shape; then morph the geometric shape of the combined letters till it looks aesthetically pleasing to you, and the combination of the letters are hidden.

Charge the Sigil, holding it in your mind during an altered state of consciousness. You can use any means to achieve this altered state, such as Galdr, meditation, dancing, sexual release, chanting, yoga, ritual, etc.

After charging your Sigil, destroy all the things you've written to make the Sigil. Let nothing be a reminder of its meaning.

Carry the Sigil on your person, or keep it within your environment, until you feel the intent for the Sigil is manifesting.

While using your Sigil, forget the Symbol's meaning, and forget the desire behind the original sentence completely. Remembering the desire ruins the ultimate effect.

Once your Sigil has done its work, destroy the Sigil itself entirely.

Lesson 9/3: A Ritual of Runes, Futhark and Otherwise.

This ritual is for those of us who need a little boost of self-empowerment. I have had moments in my life where I doubt my own destiny, my worth to my Gods and my community, or even my skills as Volva, due to issues of Orlog, or the life-tempering of Wyrd that I haven't worked through yet. Don't let the simplicity of this ritual fool you; it is very effective in initiating powerful changes through the use of Futhark runes, and by learning the art of creating personal runes infused into your multilevel intricate being.

Materials:
- ❖ A set of colored markers, paints, or pencils including red, orange, yellow, green, light or sky blue, dark blue, violet or purple, black, grey, white, silver, and gold. (I have used paints or fabric paints for the last three, sometimes for all of them.)

- ❖ Cloth or paper on which all the colors will show up (beige or brown for example).
- ❖ A list of the personal runes you associate with yourself at this time that give you power and strength.
- ❖ A red candle.
- ❖ Fiery incense, such as sage or cedar.
- ❖ A bowl of fresh dirt.
- ❖ Mead for offering.
- ❖ Your blót bowl.

The purpose of this ritual is to tap into your own personal life-force and amplify it into a personal statement of self-confidence and strength; then via chanting your own runes and drawing a physical mandala of manifestation you send this energy of change into the multiverse. Afterwards, when you feel yourself dragging in one area or another, concentrate on the mandala by locating the appropriate Futhark rune in the appropriate color for a bit, and you will find yourself tapping back into the energies you established in the ritual when you sang out your personal runes. (I hung the finished sigil on my wall where I could see it every day to reinforce its lessons, as well.)

Ritual:

First, establish your working space, after you've gathered all your materials together. Make sure you have a comfortable place to sit and draw or paint; you'll be here a while. (When I'm doing a spell-working such as this in my temple space, I do not generally go through an elaborate space-cleansing and space-casting ritual—unless the temple feels that it needs it! I start by calling in the directions and visualize them forming a sphere of power centered around the altar.)

Face the east and say:
Austri, Spirits of the East, powers of Air,
I ask that you be present at this spell-working.
Help me find inspiration and visualize the runes clearly
That I may partake of their essence.

Face the south and say:
Suðri, Spirits of the South, powers of Fire,
I ask that you be present at this spell-working.
Help me find the spirit within
To empower the runes and tune into their energy.

Face the west and say:
Vestri, Spirits of the West, powers of Water,
I ask that you be present at this spell-working.
Help me to seek the mystery within,
That the runes I draw here
May work upon my emotions for my Highest Good.

Face the north and say:
Norðri, Spirits of the North, powers of Earth,
I ask that you be present at this spell-working.
Help me to manifest the runes in the third-dimensional world
So that their energies may become a part of my physical existence.

Face the sky and say:
Freya, you who gift us with Seiðr:
I ask that you watch over me in this spell-working.
Lend me your wisdom so that I may safely link my inner vision with the outer Self.

Place your hands on the bowl of earth and say:
Skadi, I ask that you watch over me in this spell-working.
Let me ground myself deeply in you
And draw on your strength and energy to sustain me in my work.

Face your altar in the center of the circle and say:
Sacred Disir, Spirit that guides me,
Ancestors, of whom we are all descended aspects,
Unite this sphere into a protected space

For the wyrd-working I plan to do here.

Once you feel centered. pour some mead in your blót bowl and say:
Norns who gave us Wyrd,
Accept this gift for a gift!
Grant me kenning in my galdr of summoning my own runes this day,
From the well of Urd,
That I might know true empowerment!

Place the bowl of mead back on your altar. Begin to raise energy by chanting your personal runes (hidden occult kennings) in a rhyming fashion; chanting with strength, building in speed, volume and intensity each round of your personally created Galdr. Raise energy through chanting, drumming, shaking or dancing (or whatever other method you use for magickal work). The energy for this spell will be drawn primarily out of yourself, because you are attempting to change your own internal energy states.

- ❖ Now to the work. Meditate on the Futhark rune Sowelu in red. Speak its name. Red symbolizes the lifeforce, and Sowelu as a sigil brings to the lifeforce the energy of essential power. This Futhark rune will link and empower all the other Norse letters.
- ❖ Once you have visualized this Futhark rune and felt its energy, draw it in red in the center of your sheet of paper or cloth. We are going to encircle Sowelu with seven more Norse letters in rainbow colors, corresponding to the Norse Hvel (akin to the concept of chakras) plus one in white to unite them with the source, then we will bind the energy with four Futhark runes at the cardinal points.
- ❖ Next, meditate on the Futhark rune Teiwaz in red. Speak its name. Here, red represents strength and protection—the essential warrior within. Once you have visualized it and felt its energy, draw it in red below Sowelu. (This corresponds to the root Hvel at the base of the spine.)
- ❖ Next, meditate on the Futhark rune Uruz in orange. Speak its name. Here, orange represents vitality, and the rune brings in the essence of potency, courage, and strength. Once you have

visualized it and felt its energy, draw it in orange above and to the left of Teiwaz, below and left of Sowelu. (This corresponds to the sacral or sexual Hvel below the navel.)

- ❖ Next, meditate on the Futhark rune Mannaz in yellow. Speak its name. Here, yellow represents the intellect, and Mannaz is a request for self-knowledge. When you have visualized it and felt its energy, draw it in yellow above and to the left of Uruz, directly left of Sowelu. (This corresponds to the power or ego Hvel at the solar plexus.)
- ❖ Next, meditate on the Futhark rune Fehu in green. Speak its name. Here, green represents expansion, and Fehu abundance, prosperity, growth, and universal love. When you have visualized it and felt its energy, draw it in green above and to the right of Mannaz, above and left of Sowelu, lined up with Uruz. (This corresponds to the heart Hvel in the center of the chest.)
- ❖ Next, meditate on the Futhark rune Wunjo in sky blue. Speak its name. Here, the light blue represents expression and communication, and Wunjo spiritual gain, joy, and self-achievement. When you have visualized it and felt its energy, draw it in light blue above Sowelu, lined up with Teiwaz. (This corresponds to the throat Hvel.)
- ❖ Next, meditate on the Futhark rune Laguz in dark blue or indigo. Speak its name. Here, the indigo represents synthesis, and Laguz inner wisdom. When you have visualized it and felt its energy, draw it in dark blue below and to the right of Wunjo, above and to the right of Sowelu, aligned with Fehu. (This corresponds to the third eye Hvel in the center of the forehead between the eyes.)
- ❖ Next, meditate on the Futhark rune Kenaz in violet or purple. Speak its name. Here, the purple represents spirituality, and Kenaz spiritual guidance. When you have visualized it and felt its energy, draw it in violet to the below and to the right of Laguz, to the right of Sowelu and even with Mannaz. (This corresponds to the crown Hvel at the top of the head.)
- ❖ Next, meditate on the Futhark rune Algiz in white. Say the letter. Here, the white represents healing and integration, and Algiz

spiritual assistance, shielding, and protection. When you have visualized it and felt its energy, draw it in white below and to the left of Kenaz, below and to the right of Sowelu, even with Uruz. (This represents the body's connection to the Higher Self and Spirit—the universal Mind of the Universe, if you will.)

- ❖ Now that the central pattern is complete, and we've linked your life-force into the Higher Self, we'll surround the pattern with your own runes (your own wordings of hidden occult secrets spoken in rhyme) to bind and activate the desired qualities. First, before saying your rune, draw on the Futhark letter Isa in silver. Chant your own rune of change. Here, the color silver represents receptivity to the changes you wish to make in your ego self, and the Futhark rune Isa is the inner journey of static freeze you have embarked upon. When you have visualized it and felt its energy, draw in silver the letter Isa to the left of Mannaz and Sowelu.

- ❖ Next, meditate on your own rune of your needs. Begin the chant your own personal rune of need. Here, meditate on the color grey, which represents flexibility, and then draw the Futhark rune Nauthiz to signify the endurance, persistence and resolve that you will need to accomplish the changes you desire. When you have visualized it and felt your own runes' energy of need, draw the Futhark rune Nauthiz in grey above Wunjo and Sowelu.

- ❖ Next, meditate on Mannaz again, this time seeing a gold light, and begin to chant your own personal rune of connection. Here, the gold represents activity, and the Futhark rune Mannaz represents self-activation. The rune of your own creation activates the energies of the others you've linked with to accomplish the changes you desire. When you have visualized it and felt its energy, draw another Mannaz Futhark rune in gold to the right of Kenaz and Sowelu. (You should have a horizontal line formed through the center with the letters Isa, Mannaz, Sowelu, Kenaz, and Mannaz again.)

- ❖ Finally, meditate on the power of disruption and thorough changes. See the color black as you chant your own personal rune that symbolizes the upheaval that lasting changes may bring. Here, the black represents release, so draw the Futhark rune Hagalaz, as it represents the energy of change and transformation. You are releasing the energy of your spell onto the Inner planes to do its transformative work. When you have visualized it and felt its energy, draw Hagalaz in black below Teiwaz and Sowelu, saying Hagalaz's name out loud. (You should now have a vertical line of letters through the center with Nauthiz, Wunjo, Sowelu, Teiwaz, and Hagalaz.) Visualize the energy of the circle made by your creation of your own runes and the Futhark runes, all used as sigils being bound into your work.

- When you feel your ritual is done, thank Skadi (as the personified power of the wilderness inside you), and the Nornir, your Disir, and Ancestors, by offering up the mead and honoring and thanking each in turn. Thank the spirits you invoked in all seven directions for their presence and help by offering up some mead in turn. Be sure to give thanks for their presence and aid in this work.
- Open the Space, and say: *To all spirits visible and invisible that have been present in this ritual, depart in peace, my thanks and blessings.* Pour the rest of the mead on the ground
- Put your runic mandala up somewhere so that you can see it and meditate on it daily to achieve its affects in your life.

Note: This ritual makes the rune energies that were part of you part of the Nine Worlds, and attunes your spirit-self to them so that they will be available to you at need. The written Futhark runes on your mandala work as sigils to continue the spoken rune portion of this work. When you find the work has manifested sufficiently, be sure to destroy the mandala.

Lesson 9/4: Integrating It All.

As you go through the next year, working the celebrations into your life, remember to also work this belief system into your every day as well. This is not just something to practice on holy days and when you are called to do work for someone. Find small ways to work in your own spiritual customs from this cosmology. Let it become your own. When you eat, bless your food. When you see the Sun and Moon, acknowledge them. When you lie down to sleep, bless the forces that have brought you through this day. This is more than just religious worship; it is maintaining relationships with the spirits that you will be working with for a long time.

As a poetic example of how to do this, we have obtained permission from Seawalker to use his poem "Epilogue" in this book.[71]

> I rise, and the sun breaks golden
> Over the horizon. Hail Sunna, it is already
> Seven-thirty. I bow to Her and stretch, salute
> Her glory with my hamstrings. A little pain,
> A little pressure, and my sacrifice to the Morning.
> I sit bleary in the bathroom. My waste goes down
> The hole, and I thank the Dragon, thank all Life
> That there is a hole, a down, a place for waste
> Where it can become renewed. Fifteen minutes
> Of enforced idleness each morning. I will not
> Be idle, I will weave mindfulness into even
> This ambivalent moment. Hail to the Gods of
> Life and Death, may they sustain me.
>
> And all that I do is an act of worship,
> So long as it is done with knowledge of
> The Gods standing behind my shoulder.
> My hof my hearth, my horn my hands,
> There is nothing in my life that is not sacred,
> Because I have made it so.
>
> Newspaper opens, classifieds are scanned
> With a glance. Today, nothing. Ullr, send me game,
> Make my sight keen, let my eyes miss nothing.

---

[71] From *Northern Tradition for the Solitary Practitioner*, Krasskova and Kaldera, New Page Press 2011.

Give me the chance to find that right livelihood,
That I might turn from hunter to trapper in the office.
Odin, may my tongue woo them, may my deeds
Cause admiration. Frey, give me patience to do the
Honorable work, even when I am tired, for the mouths
Of those I love must be fed. I will make a garden
Out of whatever wilderness I am given to tame.

And all that I do is an act of worship,
So long as it is done with knowledge of
The Gods standing behind my shoulder.
My hof my hearth, my horn my hands,
There is nothing in my life that is not sacred,
Because I have made it so.

Apples red-cheeked at the market, I buy
Six for me, the seventh for Iduna, to give
To a friend who reminds me of Apple-Woman
But who is poor, scrambling for food,
And she should have it. I wish prosperity
Into the ruddy flesh. On the way home
I stoop, I stack three stones in a pile
Because Someone would be pleased by it.
I move on, never knowing who would see
My tiny cairn and stop in their tracks,
Heart pounding, a message written only
For them, that no one else could read. I am
The pen only, and happy to be a tool
In the hand of greater Things. Bent over,
I see litter within my reach and pick it up,
Because to pass it would sink me neck-deep
In pious hypocrisy. O Gods, let me help
Where I can, let my tracks through this my Midgard
Leave a trail clearer and brighter than the
Mourning earth I reverently approached.

And all that I do is an act of worship,
So long as it is done with knowledge of
The Gods standing behind my shoulder.
My hof my hearth, my horn my hands,
There is nothing in my life that is not sacred,
Because I have made it so.

The moon rises in the window, nearly full,
A reminder of time passing. Hail Mani. I catch
The pale flash of reflection in my cup of tea.
Dinner eaten at night, and a small portion
Of food set aside, a small plate of sharing,
Perhaps a cup of drink. I can afford it, my larder
Is not so small that I cannot share with an honored
Guest. Perhaps it goes to feed my ancestors,
On the harrow set with photographs, bones, stones, folded
Paper cranes. Perhaps it goes to a God-altar, whoever
I have invited to dine that day. Afterwards, when They
Are done, out to the fields go the scraps for the woodland
Creatures, mouths of the landvaettir. Drink is poured
Into the thirsty garden. Milk, wine, water. There will be
No waste, I tell the Dragon, walking the line
Between loving Them and caring for Their creations.

And all that I do is an act of worship,
So long as it is done with knowledge of
The Gods standing behind my shoulder.
My hof my hearth, my horn my hands,
There is nothing in my life that is not sacred,
Because I have made it so.

Lesson 9/4: Body, Mind, and Soul.

As these lessons draw to a close, our last lesson will simply be a reminder about the importance of combining the Body (*lyke*) and the mind (*hugr*) as well as all the soul-parts we have come to know. In a Tradition such as the Arts of the Völva, through our work with all our parts of the soul; we come to see we can change, grow, strengthen, and come into alignment with our Souls work and our skillsets of Song, Staff and Runes.

You will continue this work long after this book is done by observing yourself (in regular ritual as well as in the mundane world) and noting which parts are most developed, and which still need work. You might be out of balance in one way or another, as each new day brings new challenges from the outside world. For example, while it is unwise to be wholly controlled by our animal nature, the *lyke*, it is equally unhealthy to ignore its instinctive wisdom and exist solely on an intellectual plane via the *Hugr*.

We also want to have ease of access into the spiritual realm, and this can only be accomplished when we truly know and recognize our *Hamr*, our *Fylgja* and our *Hamingja*, but the Völva's way is not to leave her body behind and strive for a purely spiritual existence. It is crucial when doing this lifelong work that our own God Soul, our *Disir*, is embodied. Our entire spirituality must be embodied. All souls are one, through all of time, rooted in our body in this lifetime. When we are unaware or ignorant of our entire potential as both organic and spiritual entities—or when we are out of touch with the various parts of ourselves—we are more easily prone to being controlled by random events, emotions, or stray thoughts.

Reconnection with our ancient selves, particularly with the help of our Landvættir and our Ancestors who walked this earth so many thousand eons ago, can lead us from the disconnection that our society have created towards Jord. Living with all of our parts disconnected with the Natural Order can simply make our lives much more difficult and painful than they need to be, keeping us stuck in old patterns and unhealthy family, work, or spiritual situations.

Lack of "knowing thyself" is a splintering of pieces of ourselves from each other. Soul alignment is a central spiritual practice, in that it re-knits our spirits and can, in the long term, help us to refashion the ways in which we live with one another. The tools in this book began this process by hopefully introducing you to connection between the psychic and the physical. My hopes is that you, in a few months' time, have been given sufficient resources to be a proficient Völva/Vitki, and the possibility of you becoming whole, balanced, strong, happy and open to the abundance of All the Nine Worlds.

You've only just scratched the surface, but my hopes is you continue this journey and flourish in your self-discoveries, and then share with others what *you* have seen in the well of Urd.

Lesson 9/5: Final Immersion Into the Völuspá: Verses 57–63

57. She sees arise, a second time,
earth from ocean, beauteously green,
waterfalls descending; the eagle flying over,
which in the fell captures fish.

58. The Æsir are found on Ida's plain,
and of the mighty earth-encircler speak,
and of the great-god's ancient runes.

59. Then again shall the wondrous
golden tables be found in the grass;
those they had owned in early days.

60. Unsown shall fields produce,
bale may all be better; Baldr shall come;
They inhabit, Hödr and Baldr,
Hropt's victory-walls
the sanctuaries of the gods of the slain
Know ye yet, or what?

61. Then can Hoenir choose by lot,
and the sons of two brother's inhabit
wide Windheim.
Know ye yet, or what?

62. She a hall sees standing brighter than the sun,
bedecked with gold, on Gimle:
there shall the righteous people dwell,
and forever more enjoy happiness.

63. There comes the dark dragon flying
the snake from below, from Nida-fells.
Bearing on his wings flying over the plain,
Nidhögg, a corpse. Now she will sink.

    May the Gods bless your journeys, and may the Norns weave you a beautiful tapestry of Wyrd. Be true to yourself, be true to the Ancestors, and be true to those you call Kith and Kin.
    Hailsa!

Ivy C. Mulligan
Summer solstice, 2018

Sacred Ceremony

Sacred Calendars

I was the Director of Religious Affairs for The Asatru Community, Inc., and the Blóts and seasonal ceremonies in the next section of the book come from the collective practices of that community.

The Asatru Community (TAC) is an all-inclusive Heathen teaching organization started by a very progressive young man name Seth Chagi. The vision was to create a modern-day Asatru community where today's Heathens could find guideposts to navigate the reclaiming process of ancient Heathenry in the 21st Century. I feel TAC has met that vision and is moving beyond its tentative beginnings, helping us all create a viable new Tradition to bring into the future, keeping our ancestors' love and veneration of the Old Ways very much alive and well.

The seasonal celebrations I will share here are a modern compilation of many Northern European seasonal rites. There is much debate upon what are truly authentic "Heathen" celebrations and what is modern-day "Wiccatru". I have found that the Norse/Germanic peoples did what celebrations they were prompted to by the seasons, and more importantly, they chose times to gather that were convenient to pause in their survival labor for a short time.

I will include the calendar from The Asatru Community as I am the DORA and a Gythia for them; I feel TAC's resources are invaluable today for any Völva or Vitki in their reclaiming work, as we are Heathens after all! I will also include the Anglo Saxon and Icelandic calendars, as well as the "Neo-Pagan" wheel of the year, thereby hopefully giving you the reader choices on when or how you celebrate the seasonal changes of Jord and Sol. The biggest point is to actually do the rituals. Do not get paralyzed by any fears that the ceremony, Blót, time of year, or name is "right" or "wrong". Hearken to your own inner kennings—your soul and heart are more in tune with the World than you know. [72]

---

[72] For an alternate book of seasonal and specific rituals to inspire you, see *Horn and Banner: Rituals for the Northern Tradition.* (Asphodel Press, 2012.)

The Old Anglo–Saxon Calendar:

This is a Germanic calendar that had been brought to England from mainland Europe by Anglo-Saxon settlers, and was used to divide the year into twelve (or sometimes thirteen) lunar months.[73] The earliest and most detailed account we have of this pre-Christian calendar comes from St. Bede, an 8th-century monk and scholar based in Jarrow in northeast England, who outlined the old Anglo-Saxon months of the year in his work "De Temporum Ratione."

The first month, January, Bede explained, corresponds to an Anglo-Saxon month known as Æftera Geola, or "After Yule"—the month after Christmas.

February was Sōlmōnath, a name that apparently derived from an Old English word for wet sand or mud, and according to Bede, it meant "the month of cakes," when ritual offerings of savory cakes and loaves of bread would be made to ensure a good year's harvest. It's plausible that the name Sōlmōnath might have referred to the cakes' sandy, gritty texture.

March was Hrēðmonath to the ancient Anglo-Saxons, and was named in honor of a little-known pagan fertility goddess named Hreða, or Rheda. Her name eventually became Lide in some southern dialects of English, and the name Lide or Lide-month was still being used locally in parts of southwest England until as recently as the 19th century.

April corresponds to the Anglo-Saxon Eostremonath, which took its name from another mysterious pagan deity named Eostre. She is thought to have been a goddess of the dawn who was honored with a festival around the time of the spring equinox, which, according to some accounts, eventually morphed into our festival of Easter. Because no account of Eostre is recorded anywhere else outside of Bede's writings, this seasonal festival is still hotly debated in the heathen community, however, the

---

[73] For a more detailed desscription of the Anglo-Saxon calendar, I refer to you the website of A.H. Gray, an Australian author/historian/archaeologist. Her website can be found at: https://ahgray.wordpress.com/2014/02/16/seasons-and-festivals-time-in-anglo-saxon-and-viking-england/

Oxford English Dictionary states: "it seems unlikely that Bede would have invented a fictitious pagan festival in order to account for a Christian one."

May was Thrimilchimonath, or "the month of three milkings," when livestock were milked often due to bountiful grass feed and the newborn offspring stimulating their milk.

June and July were two months lumped together, called as Liða. Liða is an Old English word meaning "mild" or "gentle," which described the period of warm, seasonable weather either side of the summer soltice we call midsummer. Each month had its own name; June was sometimes known as Ærraliða, or "before-mild," and July was Æfteraliða, or "after-mild." In what we know now as "leap years", a "leap month" was added to the calendar at the height of the summer, which was Thriliða, or the "third-mild".

August was Weodmonath; the "plant month" due to the growing season.

September, or Hāligmonath, meant "holy month," when celebrations and religious festivals would be held to celebrate a successful summer's crop.

October was Winterfylleth, or the "month of the winter full moon," because winter was said to begin on the first full moon in October.

November was Blōtmonath, or "the month of blood sacrifices." This month's late autumnal sacrifice would have been because any older or weak livestock that seemed unlikely to survive the bad weather ahead would be killed both as a stockpile of food, and as an offering for a safe and mild winter.

Use of the Germanic calendar dwindled as Christianity—which brought with it the Roman Julian Calendar—was introduced more widely across England in the Early Middle Ages. It quickly became the standard, so that by the time that Bede was writing he could dismiss the "heathen" Germanic calendar as the product of an "olden time."

The Old Icelandic Calendar:

The Old Icelandic/Norse calendar was based around the solstices and equinoxes as these were, and are, very important in these northern regions of the world.[74] Iceland has very short days in the winter and the coming of the Winter Solstice marks the rebirth of the year and the promise of the long days and light nights of the summer. Because of this, the year begins around the Winter Solstice.

The year consists of twelve months of thirty days, with an extra four days in the middle of summer called *Sumarauki*. This produces a year of 364 days, i.e. exactly 52 weeks. To account for leap years, an extra seven days are added to Sumarauki after five or six Gregorian years. This ensures that each date in the calendar falls on the same day of the week each year. For example, leap years in the first two decades of the 21st century occur in 2001, 2007, 2012 and 2017. In some places, the months were just "summer" and "winter", divided into six parts—"the sixth summer", etc. In other places and times, they had actual names.

Sumar 1: April–May. Also known as *I fyrsti manoðr* (the first month), *gaukmánuðr/gaukmámaðr* (cuckoo month), or *sáðtíð* (seed time).

2. Sumar 2: May–June. Also known as *annar manoðr* (second month), *eggtíð* (egg time), and *stekktíð* (lamb-fold time).

3. Sumar 3: June–July. Also known as *þriþi manoðr* (third month), *sólmánuðr/sólmánaðr* (sun month), and *selmánuðr/selmánaðr* (*shieling* month; *shieling* is the yearly move to the fields to be with the herds).

4. Sumar 4: July–August. Also known as *fiorþi manoðr* (fourth month), *miðsumar* (midsummer), and *heyannir* (hay time).

5. Sumar 5: August–September. Also known as *tvimanoðr/tvimánaðr* (double month), and *kornskurðarmánuðr/ kornshurðarmánaðr* (corn cutting month).

---

[74] For a more detailed description of the holidays of the Icelandic Calendar, I refer you to the website of Haus Rheinwood: http://rheinwood.weebly.com/seasonal-celebrations.html

6. Sumar 6: September–October. Also known as *setti manoðr* (sixth month) and *haustmánuðr/haustmánaðr* (harvest month).

7. Vetr 1: October–November. Also known as *vetr* (winter), or *gormanoðr/gormánuðr/gormánaðr* (slaughtering month).

8. Vetr 2: November–December. Also known as *ylir* (yule), or *frermánuðr/frermánaðr* (frost month).

9. Vetr 3: December–January. Also known as *mörsugr* (fat sucker), *jólmanoðr* (yule month), or *hrutmánuðr/hrutmánaðr* (ram month).

10. Vetr 4: January–February. Also known as *þorri* (Þórr's month), or *miðvetr* (midwinter).

11. Vetr 5: February–March. Also known as *gói* (meaning unknown).

12. Vetr 6: March–April. Also known as *einmanoðr/einmánuðr/einmánaðr* (one month, meaning the last month).

The Asatru Community Inc. Calendar:

January/Snow Moon

January 9: Remembrance for Raud the Strong (a Norwegian chieftain whom Olaf Tryggvason killed for refusing to convert. The end of a metal horn was put down Raud's throat; a poisonous snake was then put into the horn and the other end heated to drive it along).

January 14: ThorraBlót: This holiday began the Old Norse month of Snorri. It is still observed in Iceland with parties and a mid-winter feast. It is of course sacred to Thor and the ancient Icelandic Winter Spirit of Thorri. On this day, we should perform Blót to Thor and invite the mighty Asaman to the feast.

January 31: Disting/DisaBlót. Also called "Charming of the Plough" after the Anglo-Saxon spell and ceremony. Recorded as a regular feast only in Sweden, this blessing takes place January 31st. The name means "Thing (assembly) of the Goddesses". In Sweden, it was the first public moot/fair and market of the year; in Denmark, this is the time when the first furrows were ploughed in the field. This is a feast of new beginnings, at which the work in the fields for the growing season to come is blessed. For "Charming of the Plough" the equipment would be "charmed" as well as the field and seed so that the crops would be in abundance. The Landvættir/land wights would be honored and thanked for their help in the planting, growing and eventual harvest.

February/Horning

February 2: Barri: This is the day we celebrate the wooing by Ingvi Freyr of the maiden Gerd, a symbolic marriage of the Vanir God of Fertility with the Mother Earth. It is a festival of fertility, the planted seed and the plowed furrow. For those of you who garden, this is the time to plant seeds indoors, to later be transplanted in the summer garden.

February 9: Remembrance for Eyvind Kinnrifi (whom Olaf Tryggvason tortured to death when he refused to convert, by putting a metal brazier filled with burning coals on his belly).

February 14: Folk etymology has led to this day being called "Feast of Vali" in modern Asatru. Saint Valentine has no associations with Vali, nor to the thinly disguised Roman Lupercalia rites which take place on this day. However, many Heathens still honor this God on February 14th.

March/Lenting

March 9: Day of Remembrance for Oliver the Martyr, who persisted in organizing underground sacrifices to the Gods and Goddesses despite decrees by St Olaf the Lawbreaker forbidding such activities. Betrayed by an informer, he was killed by Olaf's men while preparing for the Spring sacrifice in the village of Maerin, Norway. Many other men whose names are lost to us were also killed, mutilated, or exiled for taking part in such sacrifices.

Ostara/Summer Finding: Spring Equinox near March 21st

Ostara is celebrated on the spring equinox around March 21. This feast marks the beginning of the summer half of the year. It is a celebration of fertility and a fire festival (fire used to represent the sun). It is named after the goddess Ostara (Anglo-Saxon Eostre), who was such an integral part of heathen Germanic culture that the Christians stole and absorbed it as their own spring feast of the Paschal holiday, and it was converted to the Christian Easter. This was all done to get more heathens to convert to their Christian beliefs. Her name is related to the Germanic words for "east" and "glory"; she was the embodiment of the springtime and the renewal of life.

At the equinox, the sun rises directly in the east and sets directly in the west. In the northern hemisphere, before Ostara, the sun rises and sets more and more to the south, and afterwards, it rises and sets more and more to the north. Spring equinox is the beginning of spring in the northern hemisphere. The holiday is a celebration the rejuvenation of the Earth, fertility and growth; traditional decorations include budding boughs, flowers, decorated eggs and the rabbit motif. Mating season starts early in the spring especially for rabbits and birds. Male hares could be seen jumping around wildly and acting crazy. This is where the phrase "Crazy as a March hare" comes from.

Heathen folk customs associated especially with Ostara's feast include the painting and hunting of Easter eggs, which, according to German tradition, were brought or laid by the "Easter Hare". The Hare was the holy beast of Ostara, slain and eaten only at her blessing. In Germany, bakeries sell hare-shaped cakes at this time of year. Fires were also kindled on the hilltops at dawn, especially in Germany. Another common folk-custom which still survives in rural areas is the performance of plays at which Summer battles with Winter and drives him out, or at which an effigy embodying Winter is beaten, burned, or drowned.

Today, Ostara is seen as the feast to awakening the Earth, the gods and goddesses, and the human soul. Life becomes brighter and more joyful after the Ostara feast has been rightly held.

March 28: Ragnar Lodbrok Day: Ragnar was one of legend's most famous Vikings. On this day in Runic Year 1145 he raided Paris. It just happened to be Easter Sunday. Today, toast Ragnar and read from his Saga.

April/Ostara

April 9: Remembrance for Haakon Sigurdsson (Haakon the Great), one of the Jarls of Hladhir, a great defender of Heathenism in Norway during the brutal period of forced conversion to Christianity.

April 15: SigrBlót/Sumarsdag: Today we celebrate the first day of Summer in the Old Icelandic calendar. In Iceland, it had strong agricultural overtones, but elsewhere in the Nordic world, it was a time to sacrifice to Odin for victory in the summer voyages and battles.

April 22: Yggdrasil Day: On this day, we realize the great significance that the World Tree plays in our culture, heritage, and spirituality. It is from the World Tree that we came, and it shelters and nurtures the Asatru today, and will offer refuge come Ragnarok. Trees are the lungs as well as the soul of Midgard.

May Eve/Walpurgis Night: April 31st - May 1st

Waluburgis Night (Valborgsmassoafton in Swedish, Vappu in Finnish, Walpurgisnacht in German) is a holiday celebrated on April 30, in Finland, Sweden and Germany. It is named after a woman called "Valborg" (alternative spellings are "Walpurgis", "Wealdburg", or "Valderburger") born in 710 somewhere in Dorset/Wessex as a niece of Saint Boniface. Together with her brothers she later travelled to Württemberg, Germany where she became a nun and lived in the convent of Heidenheim, which was founded by her brother Wunibald. Valborg died on February 25, 779 and that day still carries her name in the Catholic calendar. However, she wasn't made a saint until May 1 in the same year, and that day carries her name in the Swedish calendar.

Viking fertility celebrations took place around April 30 and due to Valborg being declared a saint at that time of year, her name became associated with the celebrations. Valborg was worshipped in the same way that Vikings had celebrated spring and as they spread throughout Europe the two dates became mixed together and created the Valborg celebration.

Waluburgis is one of the main holidays during the year in both Sweden and Finland, alongside of Yule and Midsummer. One of the main traditions is to light large bonfires, and for the younger people to collect greens and branches from the woods at twilight, which were used to adorn the houses of the village. The expected reward for this task to be paid in eggs. The tradition which is most spread throughout the country is probably singing songs of spring. The strongest and most traditional spring festivities take up most of the day from early morning to late night on April 30.

Historically Walpurgisnacht is derived from heathen spring customs, where the arrival of spring was celebrated with bonfires at night. With the

Christianization of Germany these old customs were condemned as heathen.

No true Germanic Heathen name survives for May Eve; the German Walpurgisnacht is derived from the well-documented Christian St. Walpurga. To avoid confusion, and because no better name survives, many Germanic heathens have replaced "Walpurga" with the name of the second-century Germanic seeress "Waluburg". This festival marks the beginning of summer in Scandinavia. In all the Germanic countries, it is a time when witches are particularly active, a belief memorialized in Goethe's description of the witch-moot on the Brocken (Faust, Act I) and Mussorgsky's "Night on Bald Mountain". It is also the Germanic equivalent of Valentine's Day and a night of love: young men are expected to go out into the woods to gather green branches and wildflowers with which they decorate the windows of their beloveds. For both these reasons, Heathens consider Freya to be the ruler of this festival, as she is mistress of both witchcraft and love. The traditional "Maypole" or "May Tree" is also a part of the celebration of this feast; in Scandinavia, the "May Tree" is carried about in processions, a practice which probably goes back to the Vanic fruitfulness-procession of earliest Heathen times. Fires were kindled on grave mounds or other high places on this night; it is traditional for folk to leap through the flames for luck. A fire kindled by friction (the "need-fire") might also be used to protect cattle against illness or cure them.

May/Merrymoon

May 1: May Day: The first of May is a time of great celebration across Europe, as the fields get greener and the flowers decorate the landscape with colorful confusion. Freya turns her kindly face to us after the night of Walburg. Celebrate the birth of Spring and the gifts of Freya on this day.

May 9: Remembrance for Gudrod of Gudbrandsdal, whose tongue was cut out by the Norwegian king St. Olaf (not to be confused with Olaf Tryggvason despite the similarity of names and methods. St. Olaf, otherwise known as "Olaf the Fat" or "Olaf the Big-Mouthed", was canonized for his efforts to convert Norway by fear, murder and torture). This Norwegian martyr spoke out against the tyranny of the Christian fanatic Tryggvason, and urged others to resist him. For this, the king had his tongue cut out.

May 20: Frigga Blót: Today we rejoice in the warmth and splendor of Spring. A traditional time for a Kindred campout, perform Blót to honor the All-Mother and thank her for the health and vitality of the Family, Kindred and Tribe.

June/Midyear

June 8: Lindisfarne Day: On this day in the year 1043 Runic Era (793 CE) three Viking ships raided the Isle of Lindisfarne, officially opening what is the Viking Age.

June 9: Remembrance for Sigurd the Dragon slayer (known in German versions of the story as Siegfried). Sigurd the Volsung is the model hero. His wooing of the Valkyrie Brynhild, the winning of the treasure of the Nibelungs, and slaying the dragon Fafnir, are priceless parts of our Asatru heritage.

Midsummer: Summer Solstice near June 21st

Midsummer is the religious celebration held at the summer solstice. This feast usually falls around June 20-21. Midsummer-related holidays, traditions and celebrations are found in all the Germanic countries of Northern Europe. Midsummer's eve is considered the second greatest festival of the Germanic holy year, comparable only to the twelve days of Yule. The Summer Solstice is the date with the longest day and hence with the shortest night.

Certain celebrations take place on the evening of the summer solstice. Great roaring Bonfires, speeches, songs and dancing are most traditional. Folk traditions include the making of wreaths, the kindling of fires, the burning of corn dollies (human figure made of straw), and the adornment of fields, barns, and houses with greenery.

Midsummer is particularly a time to make blessings to Baldur. Model Viking ships are also sometimes made from thin wood, filled with small flammable offerings, and burned. Midsummer is the high point of the year, the time when deeds are brightest and the heart is most daring. This is the time when our Viking forebears, having their crops safely planted, sailed off to do battle in other lands. It is a time for action and risk, for reaching fearlessly outward. Other traditional events include raising and dancing around a huge maypole. Before the maypole is raised, greens and flowers are collected and used to "may", the entire pole. Raising and dancing around a maypole to traditional music is primarily a fertility ritual.

The holiday is considered the time of the death of the Fair God of sunshine, Baldur and thus the turning point at which summer reaches its height and the Sun shines longest, but at the same time it is when the days will soon begin to shorten and the Earth is beginning its slow descent into winter again. For that reason, some groups prefer to honor the Goddess Sunna for she is the Sun that shines on crops during the summer months. It is important to note that midsummer is actually the first day of summer and not the middle.

One idea for midsummer is to remain awake all night and mark the shortest night of the year, then rise at sunrise to perform a "Greeting of Sunna" Blót to her. Another midsummer custom is the rolling of a flaming wagon wheel down a hill to mark the turning of the wheel of the year. If fire would otherwise be a hazard, one could parade a wheel covered with candles for similar effect.

July/Haymoon

July 9: Day of Remembrance for Unn the Deep Minded: Unn was a powerful figure from the Laxdaela Saga who emigrated to Scotland to avoid the hostility of King Harald Fairhair. She established dynasties in the Orkney and Faroe Islands by carefully marrying off her granddaughters. As a settler in Iceland she was considered one of the great chieftains as she continued to exhibit all those traits which were her hallmark—strong will, a determination to control, dignity, and a noble character. In the last days of her life, she established a mighty line choosing one of her grandsons as her heir. She died during his wedding celebration, presumably accomplishing her goals and having worked out her *orlog* here in Midgard. She received a typical Nordic ship burial, surrounded by her treasure and her reputation for great deeds.

July 29: Stikklestad Day: Olaf the Lawbreaker ("St. Olaf") was killed at the battle of Stikklestad on this date in the year 1280 R.E. "Olaf the Fat" acquired a reputation for killing, maiming, and exiling his fellow

Norwegians who would not convert to Christianity, and for carrying an army with him in violation of the law to help him accomplish his oppression. Today, honor the warriors who brought justice to the Lawbreaker.

August/ Harvest

Freyfest/Freyfaxi/Lammas: August 1st

The name Lammas is taken from an Anglo-Saxon heathen festival which was forcibly Christianized. The name (from *hlaf-mas*, "loaf festival") implies that it is a feast of thanksgiving for bread, symbolizing the first fruits of the harvest. Heathens mark the holiday by baking a figure of the God Freyr in bread, and then symbolically sacrificing and eating it.

Again, no purely Heathen name has survived for this festival, which takes place at the beginning of August. This was the time when the first fruits of harvest were brought to the church as gifts, taken over from Heathen custom. In English and German tradition, the First Sheaf was often bound and blessed as an offering to Heathen deities or the spirits of the field at the beginning of harvest, just as the Last Sheaf was at its end. English folk custom also includes the decoration of wells and springs.

In Heathenry today, the feast is especially thought of as holy to Freyr as a fertility God, Thor as a harvest God and his wife Sif, whose long golden hair can be seen in fields of ripe grain. The warriors who had gone off to fight at the end of planting season came back, loaded with a summer's worth of plunder and ready to reap the crops that had ripened while they were gone. Loaf-Feast is the end of the summer's vacation, the beginning of a time of hard work which lasts through the next two or three months, while we ready ourselves for the winter.

Freyfaxi marked the time of the harvest in ancient Iceland. Today the Asatru observe this date as a celebration of their harvest with Blót to Freyr and a grand Feast from the gardens and the fields. Any grains harvested are made into breads and other seasonal fruits and vegetables are included in the feast. Preserving foods from the harvest is also done this time of year. Some groups gather to help each other preserve food for the winter.

August 9: Day of Remembrance for Radbod. On this date, we honor Radbod, a king of Frisia who was an early target of Christian missionaries.

Just before his baptism ceremony, he asked the clergy what fate had befallen his ancestors who died loyal to Asatru. The missionaries replied that Radbod's Heathen ancestors were burning in Hell, to which the king replied: "Then I will rather live there with my ancestors than go to heaven with a parcel of beggars." The baptism was cancelled, the aliens expelled, and Frisia remained free.

September/Shedding

September 9: Day of Remembrance for Herman of the Cherusci. Few mortals have been privileged to serve our Folk as did Herman, a leader of the tribe called the Cherusci. He defeated Varus's three Roman Legions in 9 C.E. Herman was very aware of his duties not only as a member of his tribe but also as an Asaman—indeed, the two were probably inseparable with him. Shedding is the ideal time to give him praise, because the crucial battle for which he is remembered was fought during this month.

Fall Feast/HausBlót: Autumn Equinox near September 21st.

Fall-feast is another joyous festival in the Asatru holy calendar. It falls on the Autumn Equinox, and is the beginning of autumn in the northern hemisphere. Also called Winter Finding, Fall Fest represents the second harvest of the season.

Bonfires, feasting, and dancing played a large part in the festivities. Even into Christian times, villagers cast the bones of the slaughtered cattle upon the flames, cattle having a prominent place in the pre-Christian Germanic world. (Folk etymology derives the English word "bonfire" from these "bone fires".) With the bonfire ablaze, the villagers extinguished all other fires. Each family then lit their hearth from the common flame, bonding the families of the village together.

Practically speaking it marked the beginning of the gathering of food for the long winter months ahead, bringing people and their livestock in to their winter quarters. To be alone and missing at this dangerous time was to expose yourself and your spirit to the perils of imminent winter. In present times, the importance of this part of the festival has diminished for most people. From the point of view of an agricultural people, for whom a bad season meant facing a long winter of famine when many would not survive until spring, it was paramount.

At the equinox, the sun rises directly in the east and sets directly in the west. In the northern hemisphere, before the autumnal equinox, the sun rises and sets more and more to the north, and afterwards, it rises and sets more and more to the south.

In ancient times, our European ancestors celebrated their Harvest Feast, and found many reasons to be thankful and to celebrate. Our people have done this for as long as we can trace our history. Although what our people have felt thankful for has certainly changed over the many years. Remember that as you sit down this year with your family, you're participating in an ancient tradition. It's a great time to figure out what you're thankful for, or for your kindred to hold a Blót of thanks.

October/Hunting

October 8: Day of Remembrance for Erik the Red. Remember the founder of Greenland, (exiled for murder he sailed west to Greenland) and father of Leif Erikson, the founder of Vinland. Erik remained loyal to Thor even when his wife left the Gods and refused to sleep with her Heathen husband.

October 9: Day of Remembrance for Leif Erikson. This is a day that even the U.S. Government admits should be dedicated to the man who beat Columbus to the shores of Vinland by over 500 years.

October 14: VetraBlót: In the Old Icelandic Calendar, winter begins on the Saturday between the 11th and 17th. VetraBlót celebrates the bounty of the harvest, and honors Freya and the fertility-and-protective-spirits called Disir that She leads. (Often the Disir are seen as our female ancestors). Give glory to Freya and pour a libation of ale, milk, or mead into the soil an offering to the Disir and the Earth itself.

Winter Nights/Vetrnaetr: October 31st.

Winter Nights is held on the 31st of October. Winter nights marked the last of the harvest and the time when the animals that were not expected to make it through the winter were butchered and smoked or made into sausage. The festival is also called "Elf-Blessing", "Dis-Blessing", or "Frey-Blessing", which tells us that it was especially a time of honoring the ancestral spirits, the spirits of the land, the Vanir, and the powers of fruitfulness, wisdom, and death. It marks the turning of the year from summer to winter, the turning of our awareness from outside to inside. Among the Norse, the ritual was often led by the elder woman of a family—the ruler of the house and all within.

One of the most common harvest customs of the Germanic people was the hallowing and leaving of the last sheaf in the field, often for Odin and/or his host of the dead, though the specifics of the custom vary considerably over its wide range. The Wild Hunt begins after Winter Nights, and the roads and fields no longer belong to humans, but to ghosts and trolls.

The Winter Nights feast is also especially seen as a time to celebrate our kinship and friendship with both the living and our earlier forebears. It marks the beginning of the long dark wintertime at which memory becomes more important than foresight, and when old tales are told and great deeds are toasted as we ready ourselves for the spring to come. It is a time to think of accomplishments achieved and those which have yet to be made. Winter Nights also marks the beginning of a time of indoor work, thought and craftsmanship.

This festival and feast celebrated the accessibility, veneration, awe, and respect of the dead. This was also a time for contemplation. To the ancient Germanic people, death was never very far away, and it was viewed as a natural and necessary part of life. To die was not as much of a surprise or tragedy it is in modern times, and death as not viewed as something "scary" or "evil". Of higher importance to the Germanic people was to live and die with honor, and thereby live on in the memory of the tribe to be honored at this great feast.

Starting on this night, the great divisions between the worlds are somewhat diminished, which can allow the forces of chaos to invade the realms of order, the material world conjoining with the world of the dead. This is when the Wild Hunt began, in which the restless spirits of the dead and those yet to be born walked amongst the living. The dead could return to the places where they had lived, and food and entertainment were provided in their honor. In this way, the tribes were at one with their past, present and future.

As another example of the Germanic Heathen calendar changing to convert more pagans to Christianity. Winter nights on October 31 became "All Hallows Eve" and November 1st was declared "All Saint's Day".

November/Fogmoon

November 9: Remembrance for Queen Sigrid of Sweden. Wooed by Olaf Tryggvason, the relationship ended sharply when she told him that she had no intention of leaving the gods of her fathers and he slapped her across the face. She was the chief arranger of the alliance that brought him down.

November 11: Feast of the Einherjar, in which the fallen heroes in Valhalla and in the halls of the other Gods and Goddesses are remembered.

November 27: Feast of Ullr and Skadi, and Wayland the Smith's Day celebrating the greatest of Germanic craftsmen.

December/Yule

December 9: Remembrance for Egill Skallagrimsson. Odin was his God, and the blood of berserkers and shape-shifters ran in his family. His lust for gold and for fame was insatiable, yet the same man was passionately moved by the love of his friends and generously open-handed to those who found his favor. The same brain that seethed with war-fury also composed skaldic poetry capable of calming angry kings. Can it be by accident that Egil worshipped Odin, the great solver of paradoxes and riddles?

Yuletide: Sunset of the Winter Solstice, December 20-21.

Yuletide is the pre-Christian Germanic Midwinter celebration. The name Yule may be derived from the Old Norse *hjol*, meaning "wheel", to identify the moment when the wheel of the year is at its lowest point, ready to rise again. *Hjol* has been inherited by Germanic and Scandinavian languages from a pre-Indo-European language level, and is a direct reference to the return of the Sun represented as a fiery wheel rolling across the heavenly sky. Yule celebrations and traditions at the winter solstice predate Christianity by thousands of years. There are numerous references to Yule in the Icelandic sagas, and in other ancient accounts testifying to how Yule was actually celebrated. It was a time for feasting, giving gifts, drinking and dancing.

The Yule holiday is the most important and most popular of all the native Germanic spiritual celebrations. Yule marks the return of the God Baldur from the realm of Hel and the loosening of winters grip on the frozen Earth. The commencement of the Yuletide celebration has no set date, but is traditionally twelve days long, with the start of the festivities beginning at sunset on the winter solstice. In the northern hemisphere, this date usually falls on or around December 20 or 21. This Germanic Heathen holiday was forcibly stolen by early Christian missionaries and became known as the "twelve days of Christmas".

The first night of Yule is called Mother Night, when Frigga and the Disir (female ancestral spirits) are especially honored. Mother Night is appropriately named, as it represents the rebirth of the world from the darkness of winter. This is the date with the shortest day and the longest night of the year. A traditional vigil from dusk to dawn is held on the Mother Night, to make sure that the sun will rise again and welcome her when it does.

Yule is the season at which the gods and goddesses are closest to Midgard: our deities were called "Yule-Beings" by the Norse, and Odin himself is called *Jólnir*, the "Yule One", and may be partly where the image of Santa Claus is derived from. Yule is also the season during which the dead return to earth and share the feasts of the living. Elves, trolls, and other magical beings roam freely, and must either be warded off or invited to come in friendship and peace. Yule is the time of the year at which the Wild Hunt—Odin's host of the restless dead—rides most fiercely; it is dangerous to meet them, but gifts of food and drink are left out for them, for they can also bring blessings and fruitfulness.

Yule is a time for dancing, feasting and family. Sun wheels are sometimes burned as part of folk festivities. It was the practice in Germanic Heathen times to swear oaths on a hallowed boar. This survived in Swedish folk-custom; a large boar-shaped bread or block of wood covered with pigskin was brought forth at Yule for this purpose through the beginning of this century. Boar-cakes are used for Yule-oaths by most Heathens today. Especially meaningful oaths were also sworn on the horn or cup while drinking at the Yule-feast. The "New Year's Resolution" is a diminished form of the holy Yule Oath. The fir or pine-tree which is carried into the house and decorated is an ancient Germanic custom, brought to America by German immigrants.

The tree on which holy gifts are hung was Heathen in origin representing Yggdrasil. In Germany, those who kept the old custom hid it inside so the church authorities wouldn't notice, but in England and Scandinavia, the trees and various spirits received their gifts outside. In those latter countries, it was a candlelit and ribbon-bedecked wreath, the ring of which may have reflected the oath-ring or the Yule sun-wheel, that was traditionally brought in to decorate the home. The Yule-log is also an old Heathen custom. This log was supposed to burn all night during the longest night of the year to symbolize life lasting even in the time of greatest darkness, its fire rekindling the Sun in the morning. Its ashes or pieces were used as protective amulets during the rest of the year. Those who lack large fireplaces often use 24-hour candles instead.

The twelve days of Yule are largely devoted to baking cakes, cookies, and breads and making the unique decorations which beautify every Heathen home at this holiday season. There are, for example, intricate paper cutouts to make and put on the walls; stars, wooden toys, straw Goats and Wild Boars to hang on the Yule tree. The straw animals, which are still widely found throughout Sweden, are intimately related to ancient Norse Germanic mythology; originating in legends of the sacred animals of the gods; the Goats of Thor (Yule Goat—*Julbock* in Swedish), and the Wild Boar of Freyr (Yule Boar—*Julgris* or *Julegris*—also Swedish).

Most of the symbols associated with the modern holiday of Christmas (such as the Yule log, Santa Claus and his Elves, Christmas trees, the Wreath, the eating of ham, holly, mistletoe, etc.) are derived from traditional northern European Heathen Yule celebrations. When the first Christian missionaries began trying to force the Germanic peoples to Christianity, they found it easier to invent a Christian version for popular feasts such as Yule and allow the celebrations to go on largely unchanged, rather than trying to suppress them. Halloween and Easter have been likewise assimilated from northern European Heathen religious festivals.

December 31: Twelfth Night. This culminates the traditional twelve days of Yule, each day of which represents a month of the preceding year in miniature. Reflect on the past year. Take stock and lay a course for the future. Make New Year's resolutions in the old way by swearing your oath on a sun wheel of evergreen, Yule wreath, or on your Hammer.

The Modern Pagan Calendar

The "Wheel of the Year" is an annual cycle of seasonal festivals, observed by many modern Pagans, whether they identify with the term Witch, Druid, Heathen, or just Pagan. Many Modern practitioners of these traditions of Paganism, if not part of the "reconstructionist" movement of their chosen paths, are also known as Neo-Pagans.

This seasonal calendar consists of either four or eight festivals; either the solstices and equinoxes, known as the "quarter days", or these plus the four midpoints between, known as the "cross quarter days". The contemporary eightfold Wheel of the Year is a modern innovation. Many historical pagan and polytheist traditions did celebrate the equinoxes, solstices, and the days approximately midway between them for their seasonal and agricultural significance. Generally, European cultural communities observed four main celebrations a year, sometimes with smaller, more local festivals as well, but none were known to have held all eight as seen in the modern, culturally syncretic "wheel" that is popular in Modern Paganism.

Since the mid-20th century, British Paganism had a strong influence on early adoption of an eightfold Wheel. By the late 1950s, the Wiccan Bricket Wood coven and the Order of Bards, Ovates and Druids had both adopted eightfold ritual calendars, in order to hold more frequent celebrations. This also had the benefit of more closely aligning celebrations between the two Pagan orders. Due to early Wicca's influence on Modern Paganism and the syncretic adoption of Anglo-Saxon and Celtic motifs, the most commonly used English festival names for the Wheel of the Year tend to be Celtic and Germanic, even when the celebrations were not based on those cultures.

The American Ásatrú movement adopted, over time, a calendar in which the Heathen major holidays figure alongside many Days of Remembrance which celebrate heroes of the Edda and the Sagas, figures of Germanic history, and the Viking Leif Ericson, who explored and settled Vinland (North America). These festivals are not, however, as evenly distributed throughout the year as in Wicca and other Heathen denominations.

The festivals celebrated by differing sects of modern Paganism can vary considerably in name and date. Observing the cycle of the seasons has been important to many people, both ancient and modern, and many contemporary Pagan festivals are based to varying degrees on folk traditions.

The precise dates on which festivals are celebrated are often flexible. Dates may be on the days of the quarter and cross-quarter days proper, the nearest full moon, the nearest new moon, or the nearest weekend for secular convenience. The festivals were originally celebrated by peoples in the middle latitudes of the Northern Hemisphere. Consequently, the traditional times for seasonal celebrations do not agree with the seasons in the Southern Hemisphere or near the equator. Pagans in the Southern Hemisphere often advance these dates by six months to coincide with their own seasons. The holidays are:

Yule, Winter Solstice—December 20–22
Imbolc or Oimelc—February 2
Ostara or Eostre, Vernal Equinox—March 20–22
Beltane, May Day—May 1
Litha, Summer Solstice—June 20–22
Lammas, Loaf Celebration—August 1
Mabon, Autumn Equinox—September 20–22
Samhain, Halloween—October 31

Blóts and Sumbels

Blót is the term for "sacrifice" in Norse paganism. A *Blót* could be dedicated to any of the Norse Gods, the spirits of the land, and/or to ancestors. The sacrifice involved aspects of a sacramental meal or feast. The cognate term *blōt* or *geblōt* in Old English would have referred to comparable traditions in Anglo-Saxon paganism. The verb *Blóta* meant "to worship with sacrifice", or "to strengthen". In ancient times the sacrifice usually consisted of animals or war prisoners, in particular pigs and horses. The meat was boiled in large cooking pits with heated stones, either indoors or outdoors. The blood was considered to contain special powers and it was sprinkled on the statues of the gods, on the walls and on the participants themselves.

Historically a blōt was a sacred moment when the people gathered around together offering hard-earned sacrifice in thanksgiving and communion with the Gods, Ancestors, or the Elves. They would fill a bowl with the blood of the sacrificed animal and upon offering it as a gift the Norse Cosmology, they would then bless each other with the remaining blood before pouring it out to the Landvaettier as a gift of gratitude.

The Sumbel was a round or two of oath-making and boasts given to the gods for the idea the person sumbeling would be noticed and blessed by the Gods who were listening. The Old English noun Sumbel is usually translated as "feast", and forms various compounds such as *symbel-wyn* ("joy at feasting"), *symbel-dæg* ("feast day"), *symbel-niht* ("feast-night"), *symbel-hūs* ("feast-house, guest-room"), *symbel-tīd* ("feast time"), *symbel-werig* ("weary of feasting") etc. There is also a derived verb, *symblian* or *symblan*, meaning "to feast, carouse, enjoy one's self".

Today Heathens perform a Sumbel by filling a Horn with a favorite drink that is passed around and blessed from participant to participant. Each participant then has a chance to make a boast of their talents, or to ask for blessings pertaining to an approaching endeavor, to give thanks to the Gods, or to even offer an oath to the gods or to the community. The drink was usually beer or mead but among the nobility it could be imported wine. The old prayer was *"til árs ok friðar"*, meaning for a good year and frith (peace). They ask for fertility, good health, a good life and peace and harmony between the people and the powers.

Tools of the Trade.

Although tools are not a necessary factor in veneration of the Gods, wights, and ancestors, they do add touchstones that aid in the process of switching gears from stepping out of the mundane world into the arena of the sacred.

Since our early years as a species, humans have stood out from other mammals by using tools to make our tasks at hand more successful, and with our art of worship we are no different. This lesson will get us familiar with the small list of ritual items used by most followers of Asatru. None of these things are mandatory to perform Blóts and Sumbels; however, they set the stage for your spirit by signaling deep within your soul (when touched, viewed or held) that you are leaving the world of Midgard for a time, and standing in a space that is the sacred interface with the Gods and wights of the Nine Worlds, the Ancestors, and the Landvaettir inhabit.

Finally, the tools we use and the reasons we use them are given to us by the ancestral sources. That connection to the way our ancestors practiced rekindles a connection to them and provides the Gods, Alfar, Disir, and Vaettir a familiar symbolic gesture. We let them know we are reclaiming the old ways and respect them.

Though some ways of Asatru practice have been altered to support the 21st century we live in (for example, we no longer practice human sacrifice) we do still use offerings of mead/alcohol and valuable items. Here is a basic list of ritual items:

- *Alu:* Ale (beer brewed without hops or other bitters). *Alu* is a primitive Old Norse word that occurs in magical runic inscriptions. The ancient Norse saw alcoholic beverages as mythical conveyers of inspiration.
- **Bolli** or **Hlautbolli**: Blót bowl for holding consecrated liquid used in sprinkling. Originally, the blood of a sacrificed animal would be caught in the Hlautbolli. It acted as a vessel to carry the energy of the sacrifice to where it was directed.
- Drekk(j)a(r) Horn: Drinking horn, used to hold liquid for consecrating with a God's or Goddess' might and essence during a Blót. Some is poured into the bolli for a libation and for sprinkling. The

rest is drunk by Blót participants. Drinking horns are clean hollow cattle or sheep horns with some sort of lining and stand.
- Gandr/Stav: Magic or ritual staff.
- Recel: Incense. Derived from an Anglo-Saxon word meaning "to smoke." Use with a pot, censer, or incense-burner. Used to clear sacred space. The Gothi or Gythia stops and censes each person, and that person often "bathes" him/herself in the ritually cleansing smoke.
- Hörgr/Stalli: An altar for Heathen worship. A Hörgr is usually made of piled stones, where as a Stalli may have a seated area included. Also called a "harrow".
- Hof: a Heathen temple.
- Moot Horn: a cow's horn made into a blowing horn by carving the pointy end and putting a hole in it. A Moot is a word for a Heathen Gathering. So is an Althing (with more legal overtones), and the horn is blown to call everyone to the moot.
- Oath Ring: An arm ring, silver or bronze, to swear religious oaths on.
- Teinn: Twig or branch used to sprinkle consecrated liquid on altar and Blót participants. Traditionally we put it back under the tree or shrub it came from when we are done, along with a bit of the consecrated liquid as a small gesture to the plant for its sacrifice.
- Hamarr: "Hammer, hallow this sacred space/temple and hinder (the entry of) all evil things." This is the most modern adaptation of Asatru ritual tools, but its use is acquired from the idea that at Norse weddings, Thor's hammer was placed in the bride's lap.

Again, don't feel that you must have all or any of these tools to start your regular practice of meeting with the Gods. For a worst-case scenario, grab a paper cup, fill it with water, and hail all the spirits of our Norse universe that walk along side of us every day! The main point is that we remember to include them in our daily run, to whisper thanks for our experiences, and to give a heartfelt "Hail and well met!" to the forces that shape our spiritual lives. The ritual items are to remind us that we have an incredible experience being humans in Midgard.

Seasonal Rituals

For the next section I am including the actual Blóts of The Asatru Community, Inc. Org.; used with permission, and written by TAC organizers Seth Chagi and the late Sage Nelson. They are usually performed by Godis and Gythias ("Godmen" and "Godwomen") who are the clergy for the modern Heathen community. These are given as examples to get you started if you have never performed a seasonal Blót or formal ceremony. Feel free to change, re-form, and coalesce whatever elements into your personal practice you find relevant and meaningful.

We will begin our seasons of Ritual by honoring She who is "The Lady", thereby implementing a couple of the ritual poses learned these last nine Months. By beginning and ending your year with the Blessings of God-Herself, you will find the richness and depth missing from the practice of so many modern-day Heathens who choose for whatever reason to avoid the deeper Arts of the Völva.

Blót of Freya and Our Disir.

Altar: Upon cloth of grey place the last sheaf of grain harvested for the year, and the last vegetables pulled from the ground. Place there also many tankards of mead.

Offerings: Food to the Ancestors. Also divination.

Daily Meal: Porridge and root vegetables.

The Völva holds the ceremonial horn, and standing in the Posture of Blessing, faces north and opens the circle with the traditional blessing:

Nordri! Hail to the North, hold and hallow this holy stead.

Völva faces East and speaks:

Austri! Hail to the East, hold and hallow this holy stead.

Völva faces South and speaks:

Sudri! Hail to the South, hold and hallow this holy stead.

Völva faces West and speaks:

Sudri! Hail to the West, hold and hallow this holy stead.

Völva return to the North position and speaks:

In the name of Thor we call to the ancient Gods and Goddesses, all. May this Horn, symbol of Mjolnir and symbol of the precious mead of inspiration, reaffirm the abundant kenning and power of our Goddess and of our people. I consecrate this place of community and frith, banishing from it all impure influences. May our minds in this consecrated place likewise be sanctified, as is our will to the just services of the Nornir, ancient goddesses of fate of our people. As Heimdall guards the Bifrost, may this place be warded against all forces unharmonious to our purpose here this day. Wights of the land, wherever we may be, give us your blessing this Rite!

The Völva lights candles representing the need-fire, stands forth and pours out the first tankard of mead as a libation, and speaks:

Hail to the Disir!
Hail to the mothers, the grandmothers,
The great-grandmothers, and their mothers,
The ancestral wombs from whence we all came!
Hail to those wise eyes that watch our families!
The red line of blood extends back into the mists,
Umbilical to umbilical, we all came through
That line of doors, as will those who come
After us into the world.

Völva stands forth and pours out the second tankard of mead, and says:

Hail to Freya the Vanadis!
Lady of the Vanir whose soul
Is bound to the Earth, the seeds that grow
And yet stretches forth into the mists!
In the winter we hail you as Lady of Love,
Warming our cold nights with your smile.
In the spring we hail you as Earth-Awakener,
Breaking open the seed that sprouts.
In the summer we hail you as Gatherer of Warriors,
Taking those to your breast who catch your eye.
In the autumn we now hail you as Lady of Seidh,
Wise sorceress who speaks with spirits.
Open the veil of vision for us, wise Vanadis,

And may our sight penetrate down the line of blood to the future.

Using your Pose of Receiving, open up to your Disir, and then arise and pour out a tankard of mead for your own grandmother. Then divination shall be done, in Freya's name, for any questions that may have arisen during the past weeks. Finally, the Völva proposes a toast:

Nature is symbolized
By the Mother Goddess of Midgard.
Nature contains nature;
Nature rejoices in her own nature;
Nature surmounts Nature;
Nature cannot be amended, but by her own nature.
We raise a horn to the Mother Goddess of the world.
We raise a horn Our Disir, and to Freya, The Lady of all Gods!
Let us now raise a toast
And give praise and blessings
To these Goddesses of our destiny!
To their life and light and to the eternal good.
Hail the Goddess's of Seiðr and of Wyrd!
Hail Freya and the Disir!

Mead horn is filled and Völva consumes some. A small portion of what is left over is poured onto the ground for the Ancestors.

The light grows weaker
The ground is dark beneath out feet
The veil between the worlds is thin
As our ancestors before us
We prepare ourselves
For the harsh seasons which lie ahead.
Great lives are lived from patterns of great convictions.
Our daily conduct is based upon our convictions.
Our inward ethics have their source in our convictions.
Our Gods, time, space and the great laws—
These are what bind our universe together.
We stand before our Gods,
As our ancestors have stood before our Gods,
With boldness of spirit

And unwavering perseverance in all life's challenges.
Our family, hearth and home,
And the unity that binds our people
We covet above all earthly things.
Goddess of our Ancestors:
We give praise and thanks to thee
And perform this festive Blót in your honor.
Hail the Goddess,
Hail the Folk,
And hail to the Disir!

Völva faces altar and thumps Stav three times in five-second intervals, then says:

Spirits of Urd, we thank you for your presence here in this circle. We ask for your blessing and while you depart to your noble realm we bid you hail and farewell. I hereby release any Spirits that may have been imprisoned by this ceremony. Depart now in peace to your abodes and habitations. The Blót is now ended.

Yule Blót

Hallowing: Godi holds the ceremonial hammer and opens the circle with the traditional blessing. In the Elhaz position, standing facing North, the Godi speaks:

Hammer to the North, hold and hallow this holy stead.

Godi faces East and speaks:

Hammer to the East, hold and hallow this holy stead.

Godi faces South and speaks:

Hammer to the South, hold and hallow this holy stead.

Godi faces West and speaks:

Hammer to the West, hold and hallow this holy stead.

Godi return to the North position and speaks:

In the name of Thor we call to the ancient Gods and Goddesses – all. May this Hammer, symbol of Mjolnir and symbol of Thor, reaffirm the abundant strength and power of our Gods and of our people. I consecrate this place of community and frith, banishing from it all impure influences. May our minds in this consecrated place likewise be sanctified, as is our will to the just services of Odin, ancient god of our people. As Heimdall guards the Bifrost, may this place be warded against all forces unharmonious to our purpose here this day. Wights of the land, wherever we may be, give us your blessing this day.

Godi now lights candles, then faces circle, holding a filled ceremonial mead horn high with both hands, and speaks:

Gods of the Aesir and Vanir
You come to us this Winter Solstice
As a longship through the ageless, misty sea –
Reaching its port of call
As helmsmen to our folk
Through aeons you have watched us.
We lift this horn of mead to you,
Lords of the two horizons,
Bequeath to us the token of your guidance.
Now may the days grow ever longer,
May the light shine forth from the sky,
Turning the tide of winter.
Here do we burn the mighty Yule log
And celebrate the cycle of the new year.
To you we now hail the sun's rebirth.
Ring out the old,
Ring in the new,
Ring out the false,
Ring in the true.

Attendant reads:

The origin of the word Yule comes from a Northern European word "jol". The feast known as Jolnir was celebrated as a fire festival of light honoring Odin. In the early Anglo-Saxon language, the word Yule derived from "geola", which means "the yoke" of the year. Yule literally means "wheel", when the sun is at its lowest ebb, but is reborn to regenerate the earth in spring. Yule is the shortest day flanked on each side by the longest nights. It is a time to welcome the sun back from its slumber and exchange tokens of joy with friends and family.

The Yule season runs a magical twelve days, starting on Mother's Night, December 20th to December 31st, and is considered the holiest feast of the festival cycles. The twelve days of Yule represent the twelve months of the year in microcosm.

Mother's Night is so named as it is the day when night gives birth to a new sun. The twelfth night is ended with much oath-making and celebration. Norsemen were known to make their oaths on the backs of a live boar in honor of Freyr and his trademark battle boar, Gullinbursti.

The right eye of Odin represents the sun, as does the solar wheel symbol. Yule is a sun festival held in honor of Odin as well as Thor and Freyr. As Balder is the god of Midsummer's sun, Freyr is the god of the Midwinter sun. To the Romans the Yule tradition was the festival of Sol Invictus, the undefeated sun, which included the celebration of Saturnalia, an intense time of merry-making.

Yule involves both matriarchal and patriarchal symbology. As the Mother Goddess gives birth to the Sun God, she then rests through the cold months which belong to the newborn infant god. In the Norse Yule festivals, the dead were always commemorated and believed to be present in spirit. Yule sacrifices were known to be offered for growth.

It has been an unbroken custom to use the evergreen tree as the foremost symbol of the Yule season, as it remains green the year round. The evergreen tree is a token of that which never dies, "everlasting" life eternal, akin in this respect to the world tree Yggdrasil. The druids are known to have tied gilded apples to the Yule tree as a symbol of fire in honor of the Allfather Odin.

Burning the Yule tree holds its origins in man's effort to return the gift of fire to the gods by burning a tree along with sacrificial gifts. These burnt offerings would also be characterized in the form of bonfires and the Yule log. The Yule log is traditionally oak, ash, or beech and directly associated with fire as the purifying emanations of the Sun God. The log is personally cut and brought into the house with ceremony on the eve of Yule, and ignited with a piece of the previous year's Yule log, if available.

The Yule candle is another symbol of light in the darkness of winter. Customarily, it was a large ornamental candle, usually blue, green, or red in color, which is lit at the beginning of Mother's Night. Often it is displayed in the window of a home to signify good will.

Holly and mistletoe are also a popular standard of the old tradition, and particularly spiritual to the Druids. It was believed that all who passed under the mistletoe were kissed by Freya, our goddess of fertility. Additionally, mistletoe was the fateful poison which brought the demise of the heretofore invincible Balder, the god of the summer son. So it is believed that mistletoe symbolizes the death of the summer son while the winter son reigns. To decorate with evergreen, holly, and ivy is a long-time tradition in the homes during Yule, paying homage to the feminine elements. The prickly holly signifies the male, and the entwining, yielding ivy is the female. Together they remind us that nature never dies, but is waiting to be reborn again in Spring. The colors of these plants have significance as well: red for the sun, green for eternal life, and white for purity.

Another Attendant reads:

The sun-wheel is one of the oldest symbols of the mystic power of the sun. The sun-wheel is of key importance in Asatru Yule ceremony. The eight spokes of the wheel demonstrate the division of the year into the seasons, showing the movement of time. On the spiritual level, it is symbolic of the "seasons of the soul". The wheel of the year represents the journey of the soul as it moves through the cycles of the natural and the supernatural. Also represented in the spokes are the nine worlds of Yggdrasil with Midgard in the center forming an apex of the eight spokes. It is the wheel of nature representing the sacred circle.

Traditionally a wheel is prepared for the evening close of every Yule ceremony. The wheel is set on fire and rolled down a hill. This display is to demonstrate the image of fire and the return of the sun. It is important to know that the Santa Claus we all know and love today evolved to his present popularized form partly through the Allfather Odin. For a long time, the Odin celebrated at Yule was in the horned guise of Herne the Hunter, then known as Neck or Nick, meaning "spirit". The Christian church adopted the pagan shaman, canonizing him and changing his name to Saint Nicholas. The Americanized Santa of today is a commercialized consumer image that was created by the Coca-Cola Corporation advertisers in 1931 to promote the sale of their soft drinks.

Odin is known not only as a warrior god, but also as the bringer of sunshine and gifts. In return, sacrificial harvest gifts had to be left for his holy steed Sleipnir. Like today, these special gifts were left in socks, boots, and clogs.

During the chant a small sunwheel of wicker or wood is passed around the circle, turning continuously as each celebrant passes it to the next. An Attendant plays a drum beat before each stanza:

(boom) Odin, be in my thoughts,
And in my understanding;
(boom) Odin, be in my eyes,
And in my seeing;
(boom) Odin, be in my mouth,
And in my speaking;
(boom) Odin, be in my head,
And in my thinking;
(boom) Odin, be at my side,
In my departing.
(boom) The Wheel of life is turning
Through this winter night of darkness.
(boom) Wheel—symbol of endless dominion;
Wheel that binds immortal gods to men.
(boom) The Wheel of Life is turning,
Sun disk – Eye of Odin
(boom) Divine light!
Life giving fire!
(boom) Wheel of time, force, and motion,
By your power all creation turns.
(boom) In the dawn of newborn light
We celebrate the festival of Yule.
(boom) Hear us now, O Gods
As we pay honor to life's Majestic Radiance!

Bonfire dancing, everyone joins hands around the bonfire and moves in sunwise direction during the first two lines of the chant. On the second two lines of the chant, everyone steps inward towards the flame and back outwards. This continues until the time that a complete revolution has been made around the bonfire. If appropriate, two or more revolutions may be made. Godi will stop when the energy has culminated.

Golden Sun, star of light,
Return again into your height.
Golden Sun, the bane of night,
We call you now, give darkness flight!

An Attendant speaks:

The tree has had a place of prominence in most ancient myths. Its original mythic function was as the center of the world, a living axis topping the summit of the world mountain and reaching up to Asgard. The tree itself usually incorporates three levels: its roots grown down through Midgard to the underworld, while the trunk rises through the world of men here on Midgard, and holds up the crown of branches and leaves, fruits and nuts, toward the unattainable heights of Asgard. In mythic tradition, however, it is not only the "axis mundi", connecting the underworld with the realms of the Gods, it is also, the way by which the seiðkona or seiðmann ascends or descends on his ecstatic visits to the celestial spirits or the souls of the dead, which are known as Niflfarinn, or mist travelers. Because the tree grows green again every year and produces the seeds of the future, it is a major symbol of life, particularly the evergreen, which never dies, for which it has remained the single most identifiable life symbol for the Yule season.

The tree in general symbolizes the human soul and mind, where it has to do the unfolding of personality and the process of spiritual individuation. This type of tree stands at the source of life and bears fruit that grants enlightenment.

There is an ash tree, its name is Yggdrasil—
A tall tree sparkling with clear drops of dew
Which falls from its boughs down into the valleys;
Evergreen it stands besides the Norns' spring.

Godi or Attendant speaks:

Snow is always personified as a powerful fearful figure. A Russian folk song tells of an elderly childless couple who made a snow doll in their garden which a passing stranger blessed, whereupon it became a living child. The blue-eyed, fair-haired little girl was very precocious; she was like a child of fourteen by the time winter passed. As the snow melted form the fields in Spring, little snow child avoided the sun, in which she melted, and sought the shade of the willow trees. Most of all she liked heavy showers, and when there was a hailstorm she was as gay as if she had found a treasure trove. But on the 24th of June her friends took her on an outing and they were careful to keep her in the shade of the forest. As night fell they lit a bonfire and leapt across back and forth across it. Suddenly they heard a dreadful noise behind them. They could see nothing when they turned to look; Snow Child had disappeared. And though they looked for several days, combing the forest, tree by tree, they could find no trace of their little pale companion. The old couple was inconsolable and imagined that a cruel beast had carried Snow Child off. But, says the song, it was not a beast. When Snow Child followed her friends over the glowing embers she turned into fine mist and rose as a cloudlet to Asgard. The snow child, sweet and innocent as she is, represents the frosty winter, but for all the care that she takes to avoid the sun, she is vanquished in the end. It is interesting that it is not the sun itself which melts her, but the bonfire which in ancestral times was lit to celebrate the sun god at the height of his power, about the time of the Summer Solstice. In this Russian tale there is also a direct reference to the triumph of the rising sun god over the powers of the fading moon goddess.

Attendant speaks:
Ullr's realm is upon us,
And from the sky
Comes down enormous winter –
Rivers have turned to ice.
Dash down the frosty chill
Throw the Yule log on the fire,
Mix the ceremonial mead,
Hail to our Gods above!
There is great warmth within our spirits.
Equally do we honor the four seasons,
But now the moon has given way to the sun,

The day's light will be longer
And life's fertile bounty increase.
Godi speaks:
By firelight tonight,
I peer out into the still winter darkness.
It is the Mother night of Yule,
The sun's rebirth.
Bonfires and flaming wheels
Mark this ancient tradition,
In the distance – Sleipnir,
Odin's eight-legged steed,
Clamors above the night mist,
The sound of muted thunder
Now the moon goddess
Makes way for the awakening sun god,
The time of joyful celebration.
Horns of mead, we raise to our gods;
Oaths will be made and much feasting,
The spirits of Odin, Thor, and Freyr,
To their honor and life-giving sun
We pay homage and light the sacred Yule log.
Outside the snow is still falling;
Ullr's thick white mantle covers the land.
But the days of light will be longer now –
The great yearly cycle has been renewed.
Godi speaks:

Spirits of Asgard, we thank you for your presence here in this circle. We ask for your blessing and while you depart to your noble realm we bid you hail and farewell. I hereby release any Spirits that may have been imprisoned by this ceremony. Depart now in peace to your abodes and habitations. The Blót is now ended, let the sumbel begin.

Charming of the Plow Blót

Hallowing: Done in the same way as the Yule Blót. Once it is done, the Godi faces the altar, holding the ceremonial mead horn above his head and speaks:

I stand facing the North
And summon your favor, O Mighty Gods.
I summon great Odin
Allfather of our people.
I summon Heimdall,
Guardian of the Bifrost Bridge.
We ask that the Gods grant us
Fertile and abundant fields.
Gathered here,
We call to you from Midgard;
We call to you,
And in your honor we perform this sacred rite.

Godi places the horn back on stand. Standing in Elhaz position, Godi holds runestaff in his hands right above his head and faces the circle saying:

Nerthus, Nerthus, Nerthus, Earth Mother!
May the High Gods Frey and Njord
Grant you fields to increase and flourish,
Fields fruitful and healthy,
Shining harvests and shafts of millet,
Broad harvests of barley.
Hail to thee, Earth Mother of men!
Bring forth Nature's golden beauty,
Filled with life preserving goodness,
The sustenance of your people.
Goddess Sif, wife of Thor,
Your golden tresses, like flaxen wheat,
Emblem of earth and rich vegetation,
The promise of a prosperous season,
We call to you in Bilskirnir.

As you nurture us, so shall we nurture our children.
Grant us a promise of nourishing rain,

That fields may fruitful be,
And vines in blossom we may see,
That the grain be full and sound
And health throughout our people abound.
Godi now fills horn with mead and holds it over his head, saying:
Bless our fields. Noble Freyr, Son of Njord.
Thou who hast with Gullinbursti
Taught us to use the plow and furrow field.
We shall plan the new season's crop
In your honor.
Magic of earth, sun and sky,
By the name of Freyr
Do we pour this libation,
For the coming of the Spring planting good.

Godi pours libation on the ground. (For indoor celebrations, pour libation in bowl and pour onto ground afterwards.) Everyone is given two pieces of paper and a pencil. On one paper each celebrant writes a vice he or she wishes to give away; the other he or she writes the virtue they wish to gain. A bowli or caldron is placed on the altar. Each celebrant comes forward and to place both pieces of paper into the receptacle. The Godi sets the contents aflame. Attendant rings staller bell in five-second intervals until the flames are expired.

Attendant speaks:

As numerous references in the Rig Veda indicate, the land was the center of the universe to our ancestors, especially because it provided fields for their cultivation of crops and pasturage for the needed herds of cattle. From this sprang our great civilizations with their creative architecture, arts and sciences. Yet, even today, it is still the food planting and harvest that remains the key element to our very survival. No people have ever flourished mightily without abundant sources of grain. The simple crops and herbs provide us food for life, garments to clothe us and a wide variety of useful items too numerous to mention. We often take for granted just how essential our dependence remains on the planting and harvest seasons. The hunter-gather technique worked well for small tribes, but ultimately, as the population increased, the crop system was an inevitable means of food production. Once having mastered the basic secret of agriculture, the practice spread swiftly. Much attention and spirituality was attached to the sowing and the harvest seasons, making them two of the greatest ritual occasions of the year. At the end of a harvest, it was a long held tradition in some European countries to leave a few ears of corn left standing in a field. This, it was believed, served as a spiritual offering to Odin's horses, or to those who dwell under the earth.

The beginning of the planting season was celebrated on February 2nd, and long referred to as the "Charming of the Plow". This the first celebration of the new year, and a time when the days become longer, marking an end of winter's icy grip. It is a time of promise and preparation for fruitful crops, a time to honor our farmers and yeomen who work the fields, providing ample food and sustenance for our life survival. It is a time for the planting of seeds, not only in the physical, but the mental and spiritual realms as well.

Attendant speaks:

Days counted very little in the heart of the country, hours still less; the season alone mattered. The true countryman thought and moved in seasons. There was plowing time, sowing time, lambing time, harvest time, and hiring time. He moved through life in step with the seasons. And if his thinking has tended to become slow, it is often patient, unhurried, in touch and step with deep and abiding forces.

The traditional knowledge of old times was often perpetuated by catchy rhymes such as this:

When the elmen leaf is as big as a mouse's ear,

Then sow barley never fear;

When the elmen leaf is as big as an ox's eye,

Then says I, "Hie, boys! Hie!"

When the elm leaves are as big as a shilling,

Plant kidney beans, if to plant 'em you're willing;

When elm leaves are as big as a penny,

You must plant kidney beans if you mean to have

In celebrating the festivals and through acting out the rites of our ancestral tradition, we can reconnect with the living forces of the earth, and come to feel once again our realm of Midgard as a living being, revealed in the archetypal form of the Earth Goddess.

Godi gives each celebrant a candle. Attendant lights a candle and walking sunwise around the circle, lights everyone's candle. Attendant beats cadence on a sejdr drum. Godi speaks:

Like a fish in water,
Like a lapwing among the stars,
I breathe among my Gods,
I have lived among Gods countless years.
I am an old soul of man.
Many nights I have looked to the firs,
Felt the heat of their tongues,
Seen their faces,
Heard them speaking.
Many days I have stopped behind my plow
To gaze upward,
Blind with the sun and the Gods' power.
In my times,
And there have been many times,
I have come to know the Gods
By their silence.
I understand their presence;
O have quivered beneath their power
Of their hands on my head
And trembled in the powerlessness
Of their absence,
When they turned away
And left me to my destiny.
At dawn beyond the ring of trees,
The Great One comes
With the piercing solar eye,
Eye of wisdom and knowledge
Like the wind that moves boats,
His breath caught in a tattered white sail.
With invisible hands
He tugs on green shoots,
Causing corn and wheat to rise.

The first among us,
He willed himself to be
Then in loneliness dreamed
The company of others.
Because he willed it,
Ripples formed on the water
And clouds billowed in the sky.
Because he willed it
Stars spewed from his lips
And the sun and moon
Sprang from his eyes.
Because he willed it,
He gave powers to lesser Gods—
The way a mother gives bread
To her children.
They, in turn, to please him,
Made fish in the sea,
Birds in the air,
And wheat in the fields.
Because he willed it,
Men and woman leapt forth
And made children,
Tamed cattle, harvested barley,
Because it pleased him,
He made these things
And lay destiny upon them.
What passes, what is and what will be
Are the stuff of the Allfather's dreams.
When the serpents return at Ragnarok,
All he has made to flourish
Will wither and die.
And while Odin sleeps,
A new dream begins,
For even the Gods have destiny
And a veil will open to a glorious new age

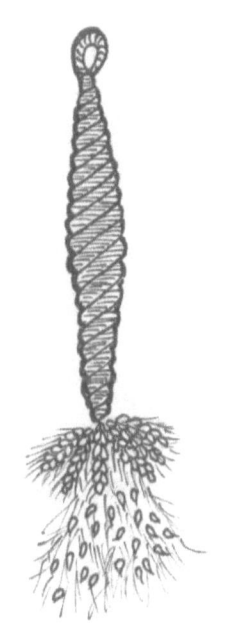

And hasten the coming of Balder Bright,
Son of Odin, son of the Sun.

In sunwise progression, one at a time, each celebrant comes forth to the altar to make a silent wish and to drop his or her candle into a bolli of water (or cauldron or bucket). Godi stands before altar and rings bell three times in five second intervals, and speaks:

Spirits of Asgard, we thank you for your presence here in this circle. We ask for your blessing and while you depart to your noble realm we bid you hail and fair well. I hereby release any Spirits that may have been imprisoned by this ceremony. The Blót is now ended, let the sumbel begin.

Ostara Blót

Hallowing: Done in the same way as the Yule Blót. Once it is done, the Godi lights candles, faces the altar and speaks:

We invoke thee, Ostara!
Grant us thy presence
In this our sacred circle,
That we have prepared for you.
It is in your honor
That we take this time of remembrance
For the coming season of warmth, joy, and life.
Ostara the Fruitful, we welcome you,
Comfort us with your timeless spirit.
Thou appearest in beauty in the dawn of each day.
O living Ostara, the beginning of life,
When thou risest in the eastern horizon
Thou fillest Midgard with the giving light of life.
Thou art gracious and radiant,
Glistening high over every land.
Thy rays encompass Midgard
To the bounds of all that the Gods have made.

The Godi dips evergreen sprig into the horn of mead and sprinkles each individual in the circle, in a sunwise progression saying:

I give you the blessing of Ostara.

Godi holds horn of mead overhead and continues:

The messengers of Spring

Have once again returned.

All hail to Lady Ostara, Goddess of Spring!

As the seasons blossoms by your holy grace,

May our spirits grow in strength

Ever stronger like the mighty oak,

In your praise and in your honor

Do we now pour this libation.

Godi pours mead form the horn onto the ground (or into a bolli when celebrating indoors to be poured outside later). Then, holding a runestaff, the Godi speaks:

Ostara, the goddess of Spring, of resurrection of nature after the long death of winter, was highly honored by all of the Norse people, even Christian zeal could not prevent her name from being immortalized in the word Easter—the period of Spring at which time the Saxons in England worshipped her. The memory of these olden times has long since passed away, although the "hare" still lays her "Easter eggs". We still perform the very old custom of giving each other colored eggs as a present at the time when day and night become equal in length—the Vernal Equinox—and when the frozen earth awakens to new life after the cold of winter is gone. The egg symbolized the beginning of life.

There are no existing legends about the Goddess of Spring. One monument alone is all that remains of the old worship, at the Externsteine, which are found in the Teutoburg Forest in Germany at the northern end of the wooded hills. There has been ample evidence that Ostara was kept on the memories of the people for hundreds, perhaps thousands of years, and shows how deeply rooted it was. There, as elsewhere, the pagan priests and priestesses of the Goddess assembled, scattering May flowers, lit bonfires and made sacrifices to her, and went on procession on the first night of May, which was dedicated to her.

Very much the same as this used to be done at Gambach, in Upper Hesse, where up until the early 1800's the young people went to the Easter-stones, on top of a hill every Easter to dance and hold sporting events. As with all ancient celebrations, Christianity incorporated Ostara intro its annual holy festivals in order to co-opt and replace traditional heathen practices.

Edicts were published in the eighth century forbidding these practices, but in vain—the people would not give up their old religion and customs. Afterwards, the priestesses were declared to be witches, the bonfires, which cast their light to great distances, were said to be infernal origin, and the festival of May was looked upon as the Witches' Sabbath.

The name Easter is derived for the Goddess Eostre, or Ostara. East is the direction of the first light and warmth of the dawning sun. Many pagans of old positioned their *horg* facing east in honor of Ostara. Ostara will never be eradicated, for it is she who gives new life to nature, is the divine protectress of youth and the giver of marital happiness.

Ostara is honored at the Equinox, when day and night are of equal length. At Ostara we take pleasure and reassurance from life's resurgence in the world around us. The fields are once again green, following winter's abuse, and young animals totter about on new legs. We think on the quickening of life and what it means for us—our role in the natural order.

Attendant speaks:

Bless us, O Queen of the Spring

Your beauty and bounty

Are in all living things.

Now the peak has been reached,

The change shall be made.

Let your warm light

Penetrate earth and sea

And stir our hearts and blood

All the celebrants join hands around the bonfire in readiness for the carole dance. Preceding the dance this song is recited:

"Where were you going, fair maid," said he,

"With your pale face and yellow hair?"

"Going to the well, sweet sir," she said,

"For strawberry leaves make maidens fair"

"Shall I go with you, fair maid," said he,

"With your pale face and your yellow hair?"

"Do if you wish, sweet sir" she said,
"For strawberry leaves makes maidens fair."

Music starts and dance begins. Celebrants move sunwise around the bonfire, at each quarter rotation stepping toward the fire and back again. When the carole dance concludes, Godi continues:

Now is the time of awakening,
Of healing and renewed strength,
A time of re-making
As Midgard unfurls
A new green mantle
 Of life and promise.
We hail to Frey,
To Thor and Heimdall.
To vitality, kinship
And the warm season ahead!

Attendant marks rhythm of sejdr drum as Godi recites:
Great Mother Ostara-high
Whose mercy lies all about us,
Your radiant beauty illuminates Midgard.
A dazzling display of crystal light enthroned on high.
Your presence gladdens our world.
You, too, contemn the cosmic laws,
Oneness of mind and being
For Aeons you have returned to us
Eternal creations eternally roll into being
As your might summons;
Beauty and love rejoice therein
Ebbing and exulting
On green meadows of everlasting joy.
From your pale blue eyes
Sparkling patterns of creation go dancing by,
A dance through eternity,
Going and coming in countless ranks,
O Mother, O Mildness.
Your every expression,

Your movement, your being
Lifts our hearts with joy.
We laud you, all-powerful and divine goddess,
We welcome you again to Midgard.

Godi anoints everyone in circle with scented oil, pressing a drop on the thumb and pressing it on the forehead of each celebrant, progressing sunwise around the circle saying:

May the blessing of Ostara be ever with you.

Godi stand before the altar and rings bell three times in five second intervals and speaks:

Spirits of Asgard, we thank you for your presence here in this circle. We ask for your blessing and while you depart to your noble realm, we bid you hail and fair well. I hereby release any Spirits that may have been imprisoned by this ceremony. Depart now in peace to your abodes and habitations. The Blót is now ended, let the sumbel begin.

Sumarsdag Blót

Hallowing: Done in the same way as the Yule Blót. Once it is done, the Godi faces the altar, holding high with both hands a runestaff and recites:

In the name of Odin, Balder, Freyr and Thor, we kindle the fire of cleansing and creation, the first mystery and the final mercy. Let flame be quickened by flame, that through darkness may we come to the light. And may the holy flame of our faith people, which ever burns, grow again to bathe Midgard in its sacred radiance. Hail our Gods! Hail our People! Hail Odin!

All respond: Hail Odin!

Godi fills ceremonial horn with mead. Holding mead horn in both hands, Godi raises it above his head and speaks:

Odin, God of Magic,
Possessor of knowledge,
Patron of song and poetry,
God of eloquence,
Hear us, Mighty Lord,
We invoke you and raise a horn in your honor.

Godi passes mead horn around circle for each celebrant to partake thereof, and says:

Odin, Sky Father,
Highest of the Gods in Asgard,
From Mimir's well you drank
For knowledge and wisdom,
A clear vision within,
A clear vision without.
Lord of Life and Death,
On Yggdrasill
Which spans all worlds, all life,
You hung in self-sacrifice,
And learned the sacred mysteries,
That do pierce the veil of all creation.
Mysterious and powerful are the ancient runes –
That you grasped unto yourself
And penetrated their deepest depths.

Godi passes runes sunwise around the circle for each attendant to take on and reflect upon. Godi continues:

The mead of inspiration you won,
And our inspiration comes from you.
May your cup be ever brimming for us to drink.
It is you, O Odin, who mastered the great knowledge.
Through your people it has been passed.
As a deep, deep knowing
Which calls to us
 And charges our spirit,
Let us hear this call and know you,
May the great ones of Asgard
Reside forever in our deepest essence –
And may we ever strive
To fulfill their image
Here on Midgard!

Godi passes bowl sunwise around the circle for each to return his or her rune and make a wish. Godi raises a sword above his head and speaks:

Allfather Odin—it is you who has filled the hearts and minds of our heroes, that they are renowned by legend and deed for their unquenchable thirst for knowledge and exploration. This is the fire which carried our ancestors to every part of the world, bearing the light of civilization.

Allfather Odin—may your sacred breath blow away the fog which now rests upon our people. Rouse them from their stupor. May we heed creation's laws and strive once more toward that immortal light of divine being.

Allfather Odin—grant us your inspiration, guide us and encourage us in our thoughts, words, and deeds. As time moves onward and outward, ever shall we work toward a new heroic golden age. Gods and Goddesses of Asgard, we give praise to you and the holy Norns who together weave our destiny. Hail Odin!

All respond: Hail Odin!

Attendant reads: As in ancient times, every month of April we draw our attention to Sumarsdag. In Iceland, Sumarsdag was the first day of summer. For Asatruar today it is not so significant as we celebrate Summer Finding, May Day, and Midsummer. April was traditionally a time of sacrifice to Odin for victory in the raiding and trading that began with the arrival of warm weather. This rite is known as the SigrBlót. We combine SigrBlót and Sumarsdag festivals for a single observance.

Another attendant anoints each celebrant with scented oil, pressing his thumb to the forehead of each celebrant, walking sunwise around the circle, and pronounces with each anointing:

I give you the blessings of the Norns. May they guide you always.

Godi speaks: Hear now thy rede and thy counsel ... *(pause)* Now, we honor mind and thought. In mind there is growth and diminishment, both we must accept, yet fight against diminishment. For it is truth that deeds start with a thought, and the power of thought is subtle, mysterious and potent. It is for each one of us to strive to learn, to gain knowledge and use that knowledge to aid our families, our people and our faith.

If the mind decay, shall spirit soar?

Shall great deeds be done?

A better tool than good sense a man cannot carry.

Be proud of knowing and doing.

Drink deep from the horn of the Gods,
Taste the magic mead Odhroerir.
Know beauty!
Cherish it—comprehend it!
Guard it remorselessly!
Let your wisdom shine in these dark times.
Let it aid our people and confound our foe.
Study the runes, they will serve you always.
Open your spirit and let the Gods abide within.

Attendant plays a drum cadence on sejdr drum. Godi recites from the Havamal:

I know that I hung,
On a wind-rocked tree,
Nine whole nights,
With a spear wounded,
And to Odin offered,
Myself to myself;
On that tree, of which no one knows
From what root it springs.
Bread no one gave me,
Nor a horn to drink,
Downward I peered,
To runes applied myself,
Wailing learnt them,
Then fell down hence.
Potent songs nine
From the famed son I learned
Of Bolthorn, Bestla's sire,
And a draught obtained of the precious mead,
Drawn from Odhroerir.
Then I began to bear fruit
And to know many things,
To grow and well thrive:
Word by word I sought our words,
Fact by fact I sought out facts.

Runes thou wilt find,
And explained characters,
Very large characters,
Very potent characters,
Which the great speakers depicted,
And the high powers formed,
And the powers' prince graved:
Odin among the Aesir,
But among the Alfar,
Dain and Dvalin for the dwarfs,
Asvid for the Jotuns: some I myself graved.
Drum cadence stops. One drumbeat (boom) sounds for each line:
(boom) Knowest thou how to grave them?
(boom) Knowest thou how to expound them?
(boom) Knowest thou how to depict them?
(boom) Knowest thou how to prove them?
(boom) Knowest thou how to pray?
(boom) Knowest thou how to offer?
(boom) Knowest thou how to send?
(boom) Knowest thou how to consume?
Attendant rings altar bell nine times in five second intervals. Godi speaks:
Like the winter sky,
The azure garbed and golden crowned,
The Gods of Valhalla sit enthroned.
Within the doorway stands each noble Norn,
Together bearing date's rune-written shield.
They made laws and chose life
For the Children of Ages and Wyrd of Men.
Attendant recites:
Odin! The morning mist of Midgard,
The silence of the trees,
The watching eyes of boar and bear,
And guardians of earth and air.
From raven's nest and dragon lair,
Cry out: Great Odin—Awake!

Awaken in my weary soul
The sky, the seed, the sun;
The hero I strive to be,
Hear us now, O High One!
Awaken in our weary world,
Enshrouded by night,
Your wisdom and your strength,
Awake—O Bearer of the Light!
Awaken, Great Odin
The honor we forsake
In glory and on majesty,
Mighty Odin – awake!

Godi turns toward altar and rings bell three times in five second intervals. Godi speaks:

Spirits of Asgard, we thank you for your presence here in this circle. We ask for your blessing and while you depart to your noble realm, we bid you hail and fair well. I hereby release any Spirits that may have been imprisoned by this ceremony. Depart now in peace to your abodes and habitations. The Blót is now ended.

Walpurgisnacht Blót

Hallowing: Done in the same way as the Yule Blót. Once it is done, the Godi dips evergreen sprig into the horn of mead and sprinkles each individual in the circle in a clockwise progression, saying:

I give you the blessings of Odin.

Raising the horn, the Godi speaks:

O Great Odin,
Sky-cloaked Wanderer
From the far ancient lands of our people
Chief of the Shining Ones,
Protectorate of our lands, our people and our families,
We call to thee to be with us here in this sacred circle.
We call to thee across all of time
And all the worlds of the Gods.
Thy people are still here, O Wise One,

Come to us again
And let us drink of thy cauldron of life and of inspiration,
That we may prosper once again.
Come to us now,
And be with us here, Odin Allfather!
Wise and mighty in the realm of the Gods!
Hail Odin!

All respond:

Hail Odin!

Godi passes the horn sunwise around the circle, for each celebrant in turn to sip of the holy mead. Then the Godi lights candles and speaks:

Gods of the Aesir and Vanir, we greet you.
We seek your working in all creation,
In the vibrant green growth,
In the wild woods
And the crop filled fields.
In all growing things,
We hear you in the wind
And the roaring thunder,
The laughter of the stream,
And the fall of the rain –
In all elements we see you and hear you.
In all, your presence is known to us,
By your guidance may we be prosperous,
Healthy and strong.

Attendant reads:

Walpurgisnacht is the night which we celebrate the ancient Goddess Walburga. It is the Night of the Wild Hunt. It is on this night that the witches associated with the cult of Freyr dance on the Brocken Mountain. The mysteries of death predominate when we think of the heroic dead. They are like layers of the past, their powerful lives continuing to shape the present through the acts, reputation and physical offspring they engendered while they were alive. Just as past events manifest among us, being constantly reborn, so the mound buried dead will eventually be reborn into their clan, to be with us once more. Seeds under the ground, actions that have not yet borne fruit, and souls waiting between incarnations, all deal with the essential idea of Walburga.

The Godi anoints each celebrant with scented oil, pressing his thumb to the forehead of each celebrant, walking sunwise around the circle and pronounces with each anointing:

May the blessings of Freya be with you.

Attendant sounds slow cadence on sejdr drum. Godi speaks:

Phantoms with shifting shapes
Thunder down to ground themselves,
Like fallen Valkyries
Toward a glowering light beyond the trees:
Walpurgisnacht!
If only Freya would ride with me tonight
To hear again the thunder-like roar
Which issues froth from clouds of nameless shadows
And forgotten bones...
Walpurgisnacht!
Would she still recall that special challenge
Offset by a full moon rising
To the bark of the North Wind
Or an amber sunset?
Walpurgisnacht!
And would she, then, stand patiently by
While each spectre waited like a great bird of prey
To swoop upon us, unbidden,
As we rode to clash like armies
Amongst the dirt and leaves of a darkening road
Into that radiant light of May?
Walpurgisnacht!
The wind is wandering wild,
Through this night's open ways.

Drum stops. Godi speaks:

On Walpurgisnacht we commemorate the death of Balder, son of Allfather Odin and Mother Goddess Frigga. Balder, beloved by every living creature—all animals, birds, trees, plants, mountains, lakes and rivers—sing thy praise today, as they cried bitterly upon the news of thy death.

Through Balder we are connected with all beings of this world and beyond, with those now living, those who came before us and those of our clan yet unborn.

Oh Balder, bright light of eternal justice and strength, your death informs us that injustice and oppression is part of the realities of this world. Your death shows us that the united will of every being on this living earth can be oppressed by the greedy acts of a minority. But your death, also, teaches us that injustice will not rule forever. As the forces of Walpurgisnacht meet the sun's rays of the new dawn, we feel the dynamic power inherent in us all build up towards the final victory of life.

Feel the freshness and vitality of Spring!

Breathe in the regenerated cosmic energy,

The essence of Balder,

Feel the growing warmth of Balder.

Breathe in the air of Spring with its promise of change.

Attendant speaks:

May Day. The word May itself sings of life, the results of gestation and deeds brought to fruition. It is a day to celebrate the visible world around us, and especially the life that animates it. Grim Holda has overseen death and germination, now glorious Freya reigns over nature and souls reborn—a day of rebirth!

Linked with the central cult of the sun and growth is the Maypole. This has a history long indeed, almost as far back as carole dancing itself. In warmer times and areas when a fire was not acceptable as a dance center, the erection of a pole in lieu of a natural and more awkward tree enabled a special dance to develop at sites considered sacred, for instance, above the fertility-inducing Long Man of Cerne. The Maypole originally represented the cosmic axis and the phallic power of the sky god. The pole itself represents the phallus and the streaming ribbons woven around the pole, its fertile seed confirming the inter-connectedness of all life.

May Day is the day to draw focus to the generative energy of our lives—the pole symbolizing cosmic order upholding the very laws of the universe. The Maypole represents Odin in the virile guise of the Green

Man, who personifies plant life as well as the powerful symbol of fertility. It is the embodiment of vegetation and the regenerative seed. The Maypole is positioned phallus like into the earth womb, the seed is given life, so that all forms of life may continue to flourish. The old European custom of burning a tree in the May bonfire hints at the sacrificial death of the God. In districts of Scandinavia, the May fires are still called balefires.

All in this pleasant evening, together—comers we,
For the summer springs so fresh, green and gay,
We'll tell you of a blossom and buds on every tree,
Drawing near to the merry month of May.
Rise up, the master of his house, put on your chain of gold,
For the summer springs so fresh, green and gay;
We hope you're not offended,
With you house we make so bold,
Drawing near to the merry month of May.
Rise up, the mistress of the house,
With gold along your breast,
For the summer springs so fresh, green, and gay;
And if your body be asleep, we hope your soul's at rest,
Drawing near to the merry month of May.
So now we're going to leave you, in pace and plenty here,
For the summer springs so fresh, green and gay,
We shall not sing you May again, until another year,
For to draw you these cold winters away.

Drum beats rhythm (boom-tah-dah-boom) three times. Godi raises sword and speaks:

I give honor to the lands of my Gods,
Ancient and good, and the power that is within them.
(boom-tah-dah-boom)
I give honor to the winds of my Gods,
Ever fresh and new, and the power that is within them.
(boom-tah-dah-boom)
I give honor to the warm sun of my Gods,
Ever giving of new life, and the power that is within them.
(boom-tah-dah-boom)

I give honor to the seas and lakes
And rivers of my Gods, and the power that is within them.
(boom-tah-dah-boom)
O Great Ones of high Valhalla,
I give honor to thee, for being with us here on Midgard.
(boom-tah-dah-boom)
May some of thy sacred spirits remain within us
As we leave, and be ever near us,
As well as with those who we call our people
To thee do we hail.

Drum roll, then stop drum. Godi makes sign of the hammer with sword and speaks:

Let flame be quickened by flame,
That through the darkness we may come to the light,
And may the holy flame of our faith
Which ever burns, grow again,
To bathe Midgard in its sacred radiance.
Hail Odin!

All respond:

Hail Odin!

Godi passes around packets of seeds and speaks:

Freya is the female counterpart to Frey and his sister. She is a goddess of fertility, like her father and brother. She is, also, a death goddess, and half of the souls of warriors who are slain in battle are carried to her estate Folkvang in Asgard. Here, too, go the women of Asatru whither they are lodged in her Castle of Sessrumnir.

Freya flies through the air with the feathered wings of a falcon, or as a Valkyrie. Most of the stories of Freya relate to the efforts of the Giants to carry her off. She is a goddess of fecundity, regeneration, sex and love. Her cult lasted into the Middle Ages in remote areas of the North.

Cauldron is passed sunwise around the circle. Celebrants pour their seeds into the cauldron, each saying:

Hail Freya!

Godi speaks:

We all hold hands.

Ancient Goddess of the Vanir,
Magical Freya, Valkyrie,
Rider of the Wind,
Use the power of generation
That we have invested in this cauldron.
May no danger threaten
And no harm be done
Through this vehicle of birth and re-birth.
Strong winds and high clouds,
Soft breezes and raging storms,
Harken well to what is said here,
And cast these seeds to fertile fortune.
Light now the flame of nature's wisdom
In life and triumph
Of thine ancient ways
Lady Freya, Goddess of Desire,
Stir the winds of Midgard,
Sow the seeds we cast,
In thy protection and thy knowing
On this Walpurgisnacht.

Godi pours the seeds of the cauldron on the ground, places the cauldron on the altar and rings bell three times in five second intervals, and then speaks:

Spirits of Asgard we thank you for your presence here in this circle. We ask for your blessing and while you depart to your noble realm, we bid you hail and fair well. I hereby release any Spirits that may have been imprisoned by this ceremony. Depart now in peace to your abodes and habitations. The Blót is now ended, let the sumbel begin.

Midsummer Blót

Hallowing: Done in the same way as the Yule Blót. Once it is done, the Godi lights candles and speaks:

Great Odin, we kindle the fire of cleansing and creation,
The first mystery and the final mercy.
Let flame be quickened by flame,
That through the darkness we may come to light.

And may the holy flame of our folk and future,
Which ever burns,
Grow again to bathe Midgard
In its sacred radiance.

The Godi faces the altar and fills ceremonial horn with mead. Holding the mead horn high with both hands, Gothi recites:

Hail to Balder—Sun of the seasons!
Hear us, as you travel in the skies high,
With your strong steps on the wing of heights.
Radiant as the stars above.
You sink down in the perilous ocean
Without hurt and without fear –
You rise up on the east wind
Like a young king in glory!
Hail life! And the wheel of creation.
Hail to all gathered here
Who pay tribute to our ancestors
And this Summer Solstice!
To your health and strength and beauty!
Great Balder, we honor you on this Mid-summer's eve!

Godi holds sword overhead, faces circle and speaks:

Noble Balder! We welcome you to this world of Midgard, shining one of the gods, instruct us in the ways of thy virtue. Hail Balder the bright, whose radiance lights a golden age, joy of god kin and mortal kin, it was you who was slain by darkness deceit, which despised your goodness. We pay homage to you, Balder, that you fell to rise again to an eternal hope of a greater and glorious time. We hail your speedy return. Show us the way of the warrior who walks in balance with goodness and justice in his heart. Your wisdom teaches us the mysteries of rebirth. May strength and honor be with you and all our people always.

Attendant speaks:

Summer Solstice, our longest day of the year, is marked by celebrating rituals which were used to ensure the cycle of year could continue. The three great features of the mid-summer throughout ancient times has been the traditional bonfires, the procession of torches around the fields, and the custom of rolling a fiery sun wheel down a hill. Midsummer is a time of dancing, festivities, divination, love, weddings, and merry making. The Summer Solstice is held in honor of Balder the Good, for it was considered the anniversary of his death and of his descent into Hel. On that day people congregated outdoors, making great bonfires and watching the sun, which in extreme Northern latitudes barely dips beneath the horizon before it rises upon a new day. From Midsummer the days gradually grow shorter and the sun's rays less warm until the Winter Solstice.

A wooden or wicker wheel is passed around, turning continuously among everyone within the circle, while Attendant reads:

The sun is risen quickly,
The summer days are long
The song of birds is splendid,
Unerring speechless beauty of earth.
Now I am golden grown
And fearless in battle.
I am a lion that flashes courage,
Resplendent in life's radiant flame.
All things are changing,
Nothing ever dies,
The wheel of life keeps turning,
The wheel of life keeps turning,
And in Nature's cycle spins creation,
Blazing like the sun's great disk,
Emanations of the High God Balder,
A time of sanctification.
The wheel of life keeps turning,
The wheel of life keeps turning,
I greet the Summer Solstice,
And the promise of a Golden Age.

Godi speaks:
We all hold hands.
Hail the sun, now at cycle's zenith.
From each day now, you will linger les,

Though your heart will grow more fierce
Earth will turn from your caress,
Till cold and dark have time
And we grow restless for your return.
Though you have fallen, O Balder,
You will rise a new!
As the sun sets to rise again,
For in this is creation and promise.

An Attendant hands everyone in the circle a candle. Another Attendant follows sunwise around the circle lighting the candles. Godi recites:

In cycle turns creation,
The weaver and the woven enmeshed.
Form golden age to vile age;
From purity to stained;
From innocence and corruption;
Till fearsome Ragnarok,
Awesome Mother, Father and mid-wife.
To a new golden time, comes crashing.
All hail now to creation,
For now is the high moon of men's year,
We labor and bask in good summer.
Hail to the sun and its golden rays!
May we drink from pure stream
A joyfully in creations flow.
Let the winter sky
In azure garbed and golden crowned,
The Gods of Valhalla sit enthroned.
Within the doorway stands each noble Norn,
Together bearing dates on rune-written shields.

Attendant reads:

The most cherished of and beloved of the gods is Balder, the symbol of light and truth. Son of Odin and Frigga, half-brother to Thor, he is known as the most handsome of the Aesir. His flowing blonde hair was thought to be the radiant sun, which warmed the earth and spirits of the Norse people. His skill with runes and his tremendous knowledge of healing herbs made him a prominent deity during times of illness on Midgard.

Balder's hall was called Breidablikk, where he lived with his wife Nanna, a goddess of vegetation. Breidablikk featured a golden roof supported by towering pillars of solid silver. It was said that no untruth could pass through its doors. Balder met his pre-destined death at the hands of his brother Hoder, who had been tricked by Loki, with the only element that had not sworn an oath not to harm him, a dart of mistletoe. With the death of Balder the gods and goddesses experienced their greatest sorrow. It is known that Balder would have his day of resurrection and usher in a new age of light form man after Ragnarok, ensuring new hope for the future. It is believed that both Balder and Hoder together represent the seed of Odin's soul.

Attendant reads:
Of all of the twelve found by Odin's throne,
Balder the Beautiful alone,
The Sun-god, good and pure and bright,
Was loved by all, as all love light.
But, in each human soul we find
That night's dark Hodur, Balder's brother blind,
Is born and waxeth strong as he;
For blind is ev'r evil born, as bear cubs be,
Night is the cloak of evil; but all good
Hath ever clad in shining garments stood.
Let busy Loki, tempter from of old,
Still forward treads incessant and doth hold
The blind one's murdering hand, who quick-launch'd spear
Piercing young Balder's breast, that sun of Valhal's sphere!
You fall to dark, O Balder, to rise anew!
As the sun falls to rise.
For in this is creation and promise.
Though the turning of day to week,
Month to year, decade to millennium and on,
To the great year, the greater yet,
We see in the light and light's return,

A future golden age
For those who will strive for it.
All hail to thee, Balder,
Shining God of Asgard!

Attendant rings altar bell nine times in five second intervals. Another Attendant passes rune bowl sunwise around the circle. Each celebrant takes one and meditates on it. Godi speaks:

Raise our spirits, Balder,
As the old gods raised our ancient stones.
Their silence speaks in volumes
In hushed and muted tones.
Power of North, memory and instinct,
Guardians of our fate
Guide and protect us
Till we pass through Midgard's gate.
Power of East, wind and sky,
Wisdom, thought and reason,
Hail to thee, Protector
Of the circle of the seasons.
Power of South, fire and flame,
Hearth and lantern burning,
Hail thou energizer,
Of the wheel and all its turning.
Power of West, of waters deep
Emotions ebb and flowing,
Hail to thee, Balder,
Of all that's green and growing.

Pass bowl around circle, each celebrant returning his or her rune. The Godi dips evergreen sprig into the horn of mead and sprinkles each celebrant in the circle in a sunwise progression, saying:

I give you the blessings of Balder.

Attendant beats a cadence on drum while Godi recites:

Streaming from the stars
Through everlasting space,
Whelming out of the Earth itself,

Singing in our hearts,
Surging in our people's blood and sinew,
The Odinic Force, the stuff of life,
Life is around and within;
It is the seed that rests in quiet dark.
It bursts forth seeking the light,
The ear ripens in the sun
And we make bread and eat,
And take in that life.
Let us remember
The bright beacons of the past,
Hold them dear and holy.
Brighter still determined
To build new beacons.
Look sunward and know
That our ancestors did this,
And swore themselves to a noble future.
Look sunward and behold the beauty
In a time of seeming chaos.
Look sunward and see the promise
Of a bright future that we can build.
Give thanks for true and loyal comrades,
Behold the sun and be glad.
Godi holds runestaff aloft and speaks:
In the name of Odin, Balder, Frey and Thor
And all our ancestral gods,
From Heidrun's breast to Lerath's bough,
My we obtain the food of Odin,
Which is wisdom;
Of Fiolnir, which is being and the blood of Kvasir,
Which is knowledge,
May we have the power of luck
And the honor of fellowship,
And may we be blessed with fine harvests
And all well-being in Midgard.

Godi stands before the altar and rings bell three times in five second intervals, then continues:

We shall rise again!

These things we sear in Odin's name!

Hail the Aesir and Vanir!

Spirits of Asgard, we thank you for your presence here in this circle. We ask for your blessing and while you depart to your noble realm we bid you hail and farewell. I hereby release any Spirits that may have been imprisoned by this ceremony. Depart now in peace to your abodes and habitations. The Blót is now ended.

Frey Faxi Blót

First, horse-shaped biscuits are passed out to all celebrants.

Hallowing: Done in the same way as the Yule Blót. Once it is done, the Godi lights candles and speaks:

Great Odin, we kindle the fire of cleansing and creation,

The first mystery and final mercy,

Let flame be kindled by flame,

That through the darkness we may come to light.

And may the holy flame of our people and our future,

Which ever burns,

Grow again to bathe Midgard

In its sacred radiance.

The Godi faces the altar, holding high with both hands a horn of mead and recites:

Hail to Thor!

Mighty in thy strength and prowess,

Friend to yeoman and warrior,

Hallow the sheaves of our harvest,

Hallow the golden grain,

Radiant as the locks of Sif, thy bride,

Harvest fruits have been gathered;

Sif's shining hair has been cropped;

Generous bounty of the Gods,

We give thanks to thee

And celebrate in thy honor!
We hail to Frey,
God of golden sunshine!
From thee we have learned to till the earth,
For your gifts we are ever grateful.
The first bread is baked,
The first mead is brewed,
Good is the harvest bestowed by our Gods,
Now bring forth the harvest fruits.

In sunwise order each celebrant brings his or her biscuit to the altar and places it into the basket and returns to his or her place in the circle. Godi speaks:

Shining sun of Balder bright,
Shining moon of Darksome night,
Midgard's fruit we now display,
Giving thanks this Harvest Day.

Godi fills ceremonial horn with mead and makes the sign of the hammer with the filled horn, then raises horn overhead with both hands saying:

Hail to Frey! To Thor and Sif!
A toast to you, O Noble Gods,
And a toast to Midgard's Bounty!
Hail the gods and goddesses!

Celebrants respond:

Hail the gods and goddesses!

Godi places evergreen sprig in blessing bowl and sprinkles the altar. Walking sunwise around the circle, Godi anoints each of the celebrants with mead, saying:

I give you the blessings of Sif.

Godi returns to altar and takes up the gandr. Godi assumes Elhaz position, faces the circle and speaks:

Goddess Frigga!
You, who are the natural mother of all things,
Mistress and Governess of all the elements,
The initial progeny of Midgard,
Chief of the powers divine, Queen of our folk,
Principal of the High Gods that dwell in Asgard,
Essence of nature, hear us now as we give tribute

For this season's bounty!

Attendant reads:

The horse was a sacred animal among our ancestors from the first moment of their appearance in history. The modern domesticated horse is of Indo-European origin, arriving in Europe and the Near East as part of the vast migration westward. The horse has had specific associations with these nomadic warriors and yeomen alike, and was often symbolic with the sun, one of the major powers of life.

Tacitus has related how in the shade of those woods and groves which served them for temples, white horses were fed at the public cost, which whose backs no mortal man crossed, whose neighings and snortings were carefully watched as auguries and omens, and who were thought to be conscious of divine mysteries. In Persia, too, the classical reader will remember how the neighing of a horse decided the choice for the crown. In England, we have only to think of Hengist and Horsa, the twin heroes of the Anglo-Saxon migration, as the legend ran—heroes whose name meant Horse—and the value of the White Horse in Berks, where the sacred form still gleams along the down, to be reminded of the horse of our forefathers.

The Eddas are filled with the names of famous horses, and the Sagas contain many stories of good steeds in whom their owners trusted and believed as sacred to this of that particular God. Such a horse is Dapplegrim, who saves his master out of all his perils and brings him to all fortune, and is another example of that mysteries connection with the higher powers which animals in all ages have been supposed to possess.

The festival of Frey Faxi has its origins in the root of Icelandic and Scandinavian harvest celebrations held traditionally in the month of August. It is a day of rejoicing the earth's offerings of bountiful grains, the baking of bread and the spirit of the diligent work ethic.

"Frey Faxi" or "Frey's Mane" lends to the symbolic characteristics of the god Frey and the various representative qualities of the horse, known as Frey Faxi. In the story of Hrafnkel of long ago, it was told that Hrafnkel loved no other God more than Frey, and gave to him joint possession with himself all his most valuable things. Among these was a horse, which on that account bore the name Frey Faxi. Another Frey Faxi belonged to Brand in Vatnsdal, and it is told that he had a high religious reverence for the horse. Horses owned by Frey are also mentioned as existing in Thandheim in the days of Olaf Tryggvason, about 996 CE.

Second Attendant reads:

In Northern European mythology Dag, the Teutonic God of Day, was transported through the havens by the white steed "Shining Mane", which spread his light across the whole living world. Odin's eight-legged horse was named Sleipnir. Gull-Faxi, the golden maned, belonged to the giant Hrungnir; Skin-Faxi, the glittering-maned, was the horse of the day; Brim-Faxi, dewy-maned, that of night. Roland's horse is said to still live in the Ardennes forest where it is heard neighing each year on John's Day, Midsummer Day.

Sometimes the heavens would be agitated into a fury of terrifying commotion, as if an army was marching through the clouds. Out of this was born the legend of the *Wildes Heer*—the Wild Hunt—the Allfather Huntsman Odin with his mighty horse Sleipnir and baying wolves searching for warrior kinsman for the Wild Hunt.

Horses were sometimes sacrificed in ancient societies, for a horse was considered a most precious possession which accorded this dreadful honor. In the festival held in Uppsala, horses as incarnations of Frey or Odin were suspended in a consecrated grave. In some tribes the horse sacrifice was important as a means to symbolically preserve the king's ebbing vitality in old age. The horse is also a symbol of fertility.

The horse, as an image, remains deeply imbedded in the tradition and fabric of Asatru. The giant who built the citadel in Asgard was helped by his stallion Svadifari. Loki was known to have turned himself into a mare to attract Svadifari. Loki as a mare gave birth to Sleipnir, Odin's eight-legged steed, the best of horses. The God Heimdall owned a steed named *Gulltop*, "Gold-topped".

The horse was a frequent sacrificial animal, and its head would be fastened to a tree or stake, known as the Nidhing Pole—the Pole of Scorn. The horse head was propped up with wood and was pointed in the direction whence an enemy, whom one wished to do harm, had to come.

It is worth noting that it was a long ancestral tradition for farmers' houses to have carved horses' heads on their gables. It is regarded as mere decoration today, but this custom has old roots. With the horse head's gaze directed outwards, it was believed that misfortune would be kept away from the house. As a supreme symbol of the victorious, the horse looms large in the Rig Veda and many Gods are referred to as horses.

Attendant rumbles on a drum, while two attendants carry simulated wooden horse heads into the circle. Drums stops and challenge is made between the Dark Horse and the Light Horse. Dark Horse speaks:

Your Golden Nag is getting old, his mane is turning grey. You cannot beat me now!

Light Horse speaks:

My stallion is at the full of his strength. Your mangy black colt cannot stand up to him! Come and try!

Drum beats change to slower meter. (Boom-boom-click, boom-boom-click.) Then drum beats faster meter. (Boom-click, boom-boom-click.) Horses lunge at each other with heads threatening and menacing. Light Horse finally overcomes Dark Horse and speaks:

The golden stallion is still King—Fair days for the harvest to come!

Drum rumbles until horses are returned to the altar. Godi hands penny to each celebrant and speaks:

Now unto the wells be worship given,
From which holy waters flow,
And unto the springs whence sprouts all that grows
And to the wights within!

Godi ties red ribbon around wishing bowl and speaks:

Deep in the water are wisdom's roots,
And Mimir sleeps within.
Cast for blessing the coin in your hand,
And think on what means most to thee.

Each celebrant drops a penny into the bowl and makes a wish Godi speaks:

Hail to the Gods!
Hail to the Aesir and Vanir!
Hail to Nature's giving abundance!

Godi empties blessing bowl into wishing bowl with pennies and the biscuits, also, and speaks:

Spirits of Asgard, we thank you for your presence here in this circle. We ask for your blessing and while you depart to your noble realm we bid you hail and farewell. I hereby release any Spirits that may have been imprisoned by this ceremony. Depart now in peace to your abodes and habitations. The Blót is now ended, let the sumbel begin.

Winter Finding Blót

Hallowing: Done in the same way as the Yule Blót. Once it is done, the Godi lights candles and speaks:

Great Odin, we kindle the fire of cleansing and creation,
The first mystery and final mercy,
Let flame be kindled by flame,
That through the darkness we may come to light.
And may the holy flame of our people and our future,
Which ever burns,
Grow again to bathe Midgard
In its sacred radiance.

The Godi faces the altar and fills the ceremonial horn with mead. Holding the mead horn high with both hands, the Godi recites:

As the sun wanes
Giving way to Winter
We bid the return of Thor
Divine god of strength and thunder,
Friend and protectorate of warrior and yeoman.
We call to the goddess Sif, wife of Thor,
Emblem of earth and its rich vegetation,
Whose beautiful golden tresses are liken to a golden harvest.
Our first bread will be baked in your honor,
As we have gathered in the store of Midgard's bounty,
With the added blessing of Frey.
May our crops sustain us through the wintertide.
As with this turn of nature's wheel.
We welcome the return of Ullr.
TO all the Gods of Asgard
We give thanks to the riches

Bestowed to us in Midgard,
For the fertile soil and nourishing rain,
For fruit trees, nuts, grains and corn.
For cattle and the reward of the hunt,
For ample waters from spring and stream,
For the abundant fish in rivers and oceans,
For the changing seasons.
For the sun divine
Which gives life and light
To all living things.
For all these gifts we give thanks.
All hail the Gods of Asgard
And guiding spirits of the Astral realms!
Grant us the strength,
The will, and the knowledge to ever provide
Life sustenance to our people
Here on Midgard.

Godi proposes a toast:
Nature is symbolized
By the Mother Goddess of Midgard.
Nature contains nature;
Nature rejoices in her own nature;
Nature surmounts Nature;
Nature cannot be amended, but by her own nature.
We raise a horn to the Mother Goddess of the world.
We raise a horn to Thor and Sif,
To Njord and Frey and to Bragi's full.
Let us now raise a toast
And give praise and blessings
To these gods of the harvest,
To their life and light and to the eternal good.
Hail the gods of the harvest!

All respond:
Hail the gods of the harvest!

Mead horn is passed around in a sunwise progression and all celebrants consume some. A small portion of what is left over is poured onto the ground for the gods and goddesses. Godi leads procession sunwise around bonfire, chanting:

Earth and sea—wind and rain
Make the fruit—make the grain;
Fire flame—and fire burn
Make the harvest—magic turn.

When the circle is completed each celebrant leaps over the fire. Godi returns to the altar. Attendant speaks:

Three men came out of the West
Their fortune to try,
And they swore a vow and solemn oath
John Barleycorn must die.
They took a plough and ploughed him down,
Threw clods upon his head,
And they had sworn the solemn oath,
John Barleycorn was dead.
But the cheerful spring came brightly on,
And showers began to fall,
John Barleycorn got up again,
And sore surprised them all.
The sultry suns of summer came,
And he grew thick and strong,
His head well-armed with pointed spears,
That no one do him wrong.
The sober autumn entered mild,
When he grew wan and pale,
His bending joints and drooping head,
Showed he began to fail,
They hired men with sickles sharp
To cut him off at the knee,
And the worst of all the severed Barleycorn,
They severed him barbarously.
Then they hired men with pitchforks
To pitch him onto the load,

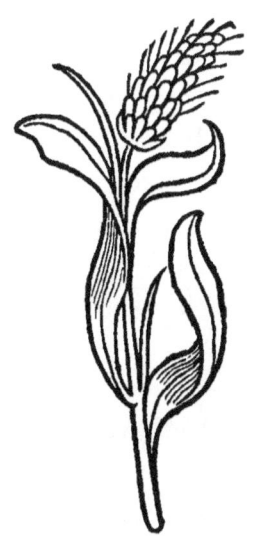

And the worst of all the severed Barleycorn
They bound him down with cord
Then they hired men with thrashers
To beat him high and low,
They cam smick-smack on poor Jack's back,
Till the flesh began to flow.
O, they put him in a maltin' kiln,
Thinking to dry his bones,
And the worst of all, they severed Barleycorn,
They crushed him between two stones.
Then they put him in the mashing-tub,
Thinking to scald his tail,
And the next thing they called Barleycorn,
They called him home-brewed ale.
John Barleycorn was a hero bold,
Of noble enterprise,
For if you do but taste his blood,
'Twill make your courage rise.
He'll make a maid dance around the room,
As naked as she was born,
He'll make a parson pawn his books,
And farmer burn his corn.
The whole world over worship him,
No matter friend or foe,
And where they be that make so free,
 He's sure to lay them low.
So, put your wine in glasses fine,
And cider in the can,
Put Barleycorn in the old brown jug,
For he's proved the strongest man!

Second Attendant speaks:

Long bitter winters imposed a seasonal rhythm on the life of our ancestors. For almost six months of every year they had to contend with deep snow and freezing cold on land and foul, icy weather at sea. Farming and maritime activity ceased and the men turned to trapping and hunting, and to the building and repairing of their ships. The winter months could prove fatal to those unprepared. Men and women had to rely on their wits and wisdom to survive.

Winter Finding is celebrated each year at the time of the Autumnal Equinox on September 20th—21st. As the days become shorter and nights become longer, it is a time for gathering up the summer harvest and preparing for the winter months ahead. This day is always marked with much joy, kinship and feasting. An old ritual after each harvest gathering was to leave a few ears of corn standing in the field. This was to show that the farmer had not exhausted the strength of the crop. Also, it was considered to be an offering for Odin's horses.

On the evening of the day that the last crop had been brought in, the farmer and his family would traditionally provide a great feast for the reapers, usually served in the barn which was specially decorated. It was the memory of this long-practiced tradition that the pilgrim fathers carried with them from Europe to America and naming it "Thanksgiving Day." The exact traditional day of Thanksgiving was not officially established until 1864 when President Lincoln set aside the fourth Thursday of November as the appointed day. Thanksgiving is a statutory holiday in Canada, celebrated on the second Monday in October.

According to mythological accounts. Frey was the son of Njord and brother of Freya. He had great personal beauty in addition to his divine powers. He rules over the produce of the earth, and it is good to call on him for peace and plenty. He, also, has power over the prosperity of men. Winter Finding is considered a holiday of major importance, second only to Yule and Midsummer.

Symbolically the harvest season is the most appropriate time for a God to die. Frey in the virile disguise of the Green Man ripens to a glorious golden figure known as Barleycorn of Autumn. Hence the tale of John Barleycorn is a traditional favorite at Winter Finding Celebrations.

First or Third Attendant speaks:

In the temple of Asgard stood a great golden statue of Odin. When Frigga was preparing to give a speech before the Gods, she spread out her best jewels to decide what to wear for the event. Not pleased with her choices, Frigga's handmaiden and confidant Fulla slyly convinced her to have a worthy necklace made out of some of the gold from Odin's statue. Skillful artificers were bribed to perform the deed. When Odin entered the temple his keen eye quickly spotted the missing gold. In a rage he raised Gungnir, his spear, ready to fling it at whoever had committed the evil deed. But his love for Frigga triumphed over all else; he determined another punishment.

He withdrew from Gods and men; he disappeared into distant regions, and with him went every blessing from heaven and earth. A false Odin took his place, who let loose the storms of winter and the ice giants over field and meadow. Every green leaf withered, thick clouds hid the golden sun and the light of the moon and stars; the earth, lakes and rivers were frozen by the raging cold, which threatened to destroy all forms of life. Every creature longed for the return of the god of blessing, and at length he came back. Thunder and lightning made known his approach. The usurper fled before the true Odin; shrubs and herbs of all kinds sprouted anew over the face of Midgard, which was now made young again by the warmth of Spring.

Godi speaks:
The light grows weaker
The ground is dark beneath out feet
The veil between the worlds is thin
As our ancestors before us
We prepare ourselves for the harsh season ahead.
Great lives are lived from patterns of great convictions.
Our daily conduct
Is based upon our convictions.
Our inward ethics have their source in our convictions.
Our Gods, time, space and the great laws –
These are what bind our universe together.
We stand before our Gods,
As our ancestors have stood before our Gods,
With boldness of spirit and unwavering perseverance
In all life's challenges.
Our family, hearth and home,
And the unity that binds our people

We covet above all earthly things.
Gods of Asgard, we give praise and thanks to thee
And perform this festive Blót in your honor.
Hail the Gods, hail the Folk,
And hail to the harvest good!

Godi faces altar and rings bell three times in five-second intervals, and speaks:

Spirits of Asgard, we thank you for your presence here in this circle. We ask for your blessing and while you depart to your noble realm we bid you hail and farewell. I hereby release any Spirits that may have been imprisoned by this ceremony. Depart now in peace to your abodes and habitations. The Blót is now ended.

Appendixes

Appendix I: Required Reading List

- *A Feri Witch's Guide to 21st Century Seiðr: A Workbook for the Modern Völva.* Ivy Mulligan (available on LULU only).
- *The History of Runic Lore.* Lars Magnar Enoksen, Google Books, 2016.
- *Galdrs of the Edda.* Lars Magnar Enoksen, Google Books, 2017.
- *Heathen Rites of Ancient Nordic Chronicles.* Lars Magnar Enoksen, Google Books, 2015.
- *The Icelandic Book of Fuþark.* Icelandic Magic Company, 2017.
- *Neolithic Shamanism: Spirit Work in the Norse Tradition*, Galina Krasskova and Raven Kaldera, Destiny Books, 2012.
- *Wyrdwalkers.* Raven Kaldera, Asphodel Press, 2007.
- *Wightridden*, Raven Kaldera, Asphodel Press, 2008.

Optional Reading

- *Elhaz Ablaze: A Compendium of Chaos Heathenry.* Elhaz Ablaze, Elhaz Press, 2018.
- *A Witch's Book of Silence.* Karina BlackHeart, KBH Enterprises, 2015.
- *Make Magic of Your Life.* T. Thorn Coyle, Weiser Press, 2014.
- *The Sorcerer's Screed.* Jochum Magnús Eggertsson, Icelandic Magic Company, 2014.
- *Remedies and Rituals: Folk Medicine in Norway and the New Land.* Kathleen Stokker, Minnesota Historical Society Press, 2009.
- *Elves, Wights, and Trolls.* Kveldulf Gundarsson, iUniverse Press, 2007.
- *The Ecstatic Experience: Healing Postures for Spirit Journeys.* Belinda Gore, Bear & Company, 2009.
- *Ecstatic Body Postures: An Alternate Reality Workbook.* Belinda Gore, Bear & Company, 1995.
- *Trance-Portation.* Diana Paxson, Weiser Books, 2008.
- *Teutonic Religion.* Kvedulf Gundarsson, Llewellyn Publications, 1993.
- *Witches and Pagans.* Max Dashu, Veleda Press, 2017.
- *The Viking Way: Magic and Mind.* Neil Price. Oxbow Press, 2019.

Appendix II: Rune Meanings

This rune chart includes both the Norse Futhark (the first 24 runes) and the extra 9 runes that turn the Futhark into the Anglo-Saxon Futhorc. You may work only with the first 24, or with all 33, as you choose. Both systems are useful and beautiful. This chart is reprinted with permission from the book *Candles In The Cave: Northern Religion for Prisoners*. (Asphodel Press, 2017)

FEHU (pronounced *fay-hoo*)
Saxon name: FEOH (pronounced *fay-oh*)
Alphabet sound: F
Keyword: WEALTH
Symbol Origin: Horned cattle
Deity: Freya, the goddess of fertility and love, or her brother Frey
Meaning: The Rune of cattle, on its surface, symbolizes wealth and riches, but its deeper meaning speaks of what you value, and how much you value it. Where is your true wealth—in material objects and money, or elsewhere?

URUZ (pronounced *oor-ooz*)
Saxon name: UR (pronounced *oor*)
Alphabet sound: U as in flute
Keyword: STRENGTH
Symbol Origin: The aurochs, the "wild ox" or European buffalo, long ago hunted to extinction
Deity: Thor, Thrud, Gefjon, Vili
Meaning: Strength and endurance. Untamable wildness of might.

THURISAZ (pronounced *thoor-ih-sahz*)
Saxon name: THORN
Alphabet sound: Th
Keyword: THORN
Symbol Origin: A thorn

Deity: Thor or Loki, whichever you prefer; Hlin

Meaning: Thorn in the foot. Nasty little obstacles that trip you up and bedevil you. Constant difficulties.

ANSUZ (pronounced *ahn-sooz*)

Saxon name: AESC (pronounced *ask*)

Alphabet sound: A as in "father" for the Futhark, Aah as in "fat" for the Futhorc

Keyword: MESSAGE

Symbol Origin: A bird flying through the air

Deity: Odin

Meaning: This is the rune of the Messenger, and it means that Someone is trying to tell you something, and you had better listen.

RAIDO (pronounced *rah-ee-do*)

Saxon name: RAD (pronouced *rade*)

Alphabet sound: R

Keyword: ROAD, PATH

Symbol Origin: Walking traveler

Deity: Hermod, Mordgud, Gna

Meaning: Travel. Movement. Getting "on your path".

KANO (pronounced *cahn-o*)

Saxon name: KEN

Alphabet sound: K

Keyword: FIRE, TRUTH

Symbol Origins: Blacksmith's hammer and tongs

Deity: Loki, Logi, Wayland the Smith

Meaning: Truth. This is the Rune of Fire, which burns away all falsehoods. Say its Saxon name over and over—ken, ken, ken—and you hear the sound of the blacksmith's hammer hitting the hot steel again and again. Truth forges us anew even as it burns us.

GEBO (pronounced *gay-bo*)
Saxon name: GYFU (pronounced *gif-oo*)
Alphabet sound: hard G
Keyword: GIFT
Symbol Origin: Crossroads
Deity: Iduna, Freya, Lofn, Sjofn, Nanna

Meaning: This rune means Gift. Its meaning is partnership, hospitality, and gifts that come with mutually fulfilling obligations. Its symbol is the crossroads, representing the paths of two people crossing.

WUNJO (pronounced *woon-jo*)
Saxon name: WYN (pronounced *win*)
Alphabet sound: W or V
Keyword: LIGHT
Symbol Origin: A torch
Deity: Baldur, Hoder, Mani, the Alfar

Meaning: Happiness. A light in the darkness.

HAGALAZ (pronounced *hog-a-lahz*)
Saxon name: HAEGL (pronounced *hay-gle*)
Alphabet sound: H
Keyword: HAIL OF TROUBLES
Symbol Origin: Falling hail
Deity: Fenris, Thor, Kari

Meaning: The Rune of Hail means chaos, misfortune coming from nowhere which hits you at random. Don't bother trying to figure out why it happened—it happened because it was going to happen to someone, and you were there.

NAUTHIZ (pronounced *now-theez*)
Saxon name: NYTH (pronounced *neeth*)
Alphabet sound: N
Keyword: NEED or NO
Symbol Origin: Firebow for making fire

Deity: Nidhogg, Sigyn, Narvi, Vali, Snotra, Vár

Meaning: That which you need, even if you hate it. The annoying daily chores, the necessary commitments. Duty. Obligation. Responsibility. Nauthiz can also be a big No—look at the surrounding runes for clarity.

ISA (pronounced *ee-sa*)
Saxon name: IS (pronounced *ice*)
Alphabet sound: I as in "ice" or as in "sit"
Keyword: FREEZE
Symbol Origin: Icicle
Deity: Skadi, Holda

Meaning: The Rune of Ice means that things are frozen in place, and nothing that you can do will move them. Everything has come to a standstill. Be patient and wait for the thaw.

JERA (pronounced *yair-ah*)
Saxon name: JER (pronounced *yair*)
Alphabet sound: J
Keyword: HARVEST
Symbol Origin: Grains of scattered wheat
Deity: Jord, Nerthus, Freya, Frey

Meaning: Reward only after hard work-the harvest after laboring.

EIHWAZ (pronounced *ay-wahz*)
Saxon name: EOH (pronounced *ay-oh*)
Alphabet sound: A as in "hay"
Keyword: DEFENSE
Symbol Origin: Quarterstaff of yew, swung in a circle
Deity: Heimdall, Ullr, Syn, Eir

Meaning: Defense of what you value. Standing firm against attack. Possibly being overly defensive out of fear.

PERTH (pronounced *pairth*)
Saxon name: PEORTH (pronounced *pee-orth*)
Alphabet sound: P
Keyword: MYSTERY or RANDOM CHANCE
Symbol Origin: Either the mouth of a cave, or a dice cup.
Deities: The Nornir, Holda, Vor, Mimir
Meaning: That which is hidden and mysterious. The mysteries of the universe. Taking a chance on the unknown. Taking a gamble on one's intuition.

ALGIZ (pronounced *all-gheez*) or ELHAZ
Saxon name: Eolx (pronounced *ay-olks*)
Alphabet sound: Z in Futhark, X in Futhorc; I use it for either one
Keyword: CHALLENGE
Symbol Origin: Either an elk's head, and/or a hand held up in a "stop" position
Deity: Ullr, Vár
Meaning: A challenge awaits, and you must take it. Or you could be the challenger, saying, "No further. This must stop."

SOWELU (pronounced *so-well-loo*)
Saxon name: SIGIL (pronounced *sij-ill*)
Alphabet sound: S
Keyword: JOY
Symbol Origin: Lightning bolt and/or sun's rays
Deity: Thor, Sif, Sunna
Meaning: Joy. Victory. Inspiration striking. Awakening.

TEIWAZ (pronounced *tay-wahz*)
Saxon name: TYR (pronounced *teer*)
Alphabet sound: T
Keyword: WARRIOR, COURAGE

Symbol Origin: Spear and/or arrow
Deity: Tyr, Vidar, Váli
Meaning: Time to be a warrior and fight bravely and honorably for what you believe in and value.

BERKANA (pronounced *ber-cahn-ah*)
Saxon name: BEORC (pronounced *bee-ork*)
Alphabet sound: B
Keyword: GROWTH
Symbol Origin: Breasts, birch tree
Deity: Frigga, Jord, Laufey
Meaning: This is the rune of fertility, which means growth and flourishing of all things.

EHWAZ (pronounced *ehh-waz*)
Saxon name: EH
Alphabet sound: For the Futhark, any "E" sound. For the Futhorc, E as in "bed"
Keyword: PROGRESS
Symbol Origin: Horse
Deity: Nott, Daeg, Hermod
Meaning: The Rune of the Horse's shape is a horse plodding along, and its meaning is movement and progress. Even though a horse can run fast, it has to walk every mile of the road between here and there. You will get there, but only by slow and steady progress.

MANNAZ (pronounced *mahn-ahz*)
Saxon name: MANN (pronounced *mahn*)
Alphabet sound: M
Keyword: PEOPLE
Symbol Origin: A man and woman holding crossed hands, as in a handfasting
Deities: Ask and Embla, Forseti

Meaning: Your people. Your tribe. Your community. The human race.

LAGUZ (pronounced *lah-gooz*)
Saxon name: LAGU (pronounced *lah-goo*)
Alphabet sound: L
Keyword: FLOW
Symbol Origin: Waterfall
Deity: Njord, Aegir, Ran, the Nine Sisters

Meaning: Laguz, the Rune of Water, suggests a river flowing forever onwards. Go With The Flow. Don't resist. Let things fall into place.

INGUZ (pronounced *ing-gooz*)
Saxon name: Ing
Alphabet sound: Ng
Keyword: SACRIFICE
Symbol Origin: Bound wheat sheaf
Deity: Frey, who is also called Ingvi

Meaning: Ing is the Corn God, John Barleycorn, the one who is sacrificed in the fields so that we may live. His rune's meaning is that of a sacrifice for the greater good.

DAGAZ (pronounced *dahg-ahz*)
Saxon name: DAEG (pronounced *dahg*)
Alphabet sound: D
Keyword: BREAKTHROUGH
Symbol Origin: Sun dawning over mountain or standing stone on the Summer Solstice
Deity: Daeg, Ve
Meaning: Light of dawn rising from the long night, the triumph of good, and the breakthrough after a long period of confusion.

OTHILA (pronounced *o-thee-la*) or alternately **OTHALA** (*o-thah-lah*)
Saxon name: OETHEL (pronounced *oy-thel*)
Alphabet sound: For Futhark, any O sound; for Futhorc, O as in "cog"
Keyword: HOME or HERITAGE
Symbol Origin: Man holding shield
Deity: Fulla
Meaning: Home and family. Inheritances, both good and bad.

Hela's Aett, for the Futhorc:

EAR (pronounced *eer* or perhaps *ay-ar*)
Alphabet sound: E as in "reed"
Keyword: DEATH, GRAVE
Symbol Origin: A singletree, the thing you hang carcasses on to be butchered. This is the Rune of the Grave.
Deity: Hela
Meaning: Loss. Endings. Transformation after destruction.

AC (pronounced *Ack*)
Alphabet sound: A as in "father"
Keyword: ENDURANCE
Symbol Origin: Person holding an oaken staff
Deity: Angrboda, Thor, Mengloth
Meaning: That which endures many blows and still emerges victorious. Strong as an oaken staff.

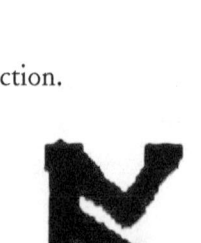

IOR (pronounced *yor*)
Alphabet sound: Y as in "yes"
Keyword: BOUNDARIES, LIMITS
Symbol Origin: Serpent swimming
Deity: Jormundgand
Meaning: The limits of the situation.

The boundaries of Reality, of Midgard, around which everything must work. Working with what you have rather than what you cannot have.

OS (pronounced *ohss*)
Alphabet sound: O as in "cold"
Keyword: SPEAK
Symbol Origin: A man gesturing with his arms
Deity: Bragi, Odin, Loki
Meaning: The Rune of the Bard. Communication. Story and song. Words, and their power to make magic and make things change.

YR (pronounced *yeer*)
Alphabet sound: Y as in "funny"
Keyword: FOCUS
Symbol Origin: Bow and arrow
Deity: Aurvandil, Ullr, Skadi
Meaning: Focus like an archer on the one important target.

CWEORTH (pronounced *cwairth*)
Alphabet sound: Q
Keyword: PURIFY
Deity: Surt
Meaning: Rune of the Funeral Pyre. Shedding. Transformation and purification through an ordeal of destruction.

CHALC (pronounced *calc* or *khalk*)
Alphabet sound: Ch or Kh (gutteral H)
Keyword: QUEST
Symbol Origin: Chalice
Deity: Gerda, Saga
Meaning: This is the Rune of the Chalice, the Holy Grail, not in the Christian sense, but in the much-older sense of the quest for the sacred.

STAN (pronounced *shtan*)
Alphabet sound: Sh
Keyword: CRUCIAL
Symbol Origin: A keystone
Deity: Nerthus

Meaning: The heart of the issue, the most important, unavoidable thing. Stan symbolizes the keystone in the center of the arch, the foundation stone under the building, the bedrock beneath our feet. It is the center of the problem, which must be dealt with. Like Ansuz, it is an indicator rune; look to the next rune to find the important thing.

GAR
No phonetic sound
Keyword: NOT FOR YOU TO KNOW
Symbol Origin: The World Tree, from the top, or Odin's spear rushing at you
Deity: Odin

Meaning: The Gods Have Spoken! This rune is outside the ordinary alphabet, and has no value except as a "mystery" rune, often used as a blank rune these days. "Gar" means Spear, and refers to Odin's spear, which he crafted from the World Tree, and so this rune is a "kenning", or riddle, for the World Tree itself. This means that the Gods have decided that all this is not for you to know at this time; it will mean more to you if you have to figure it out by yourself.

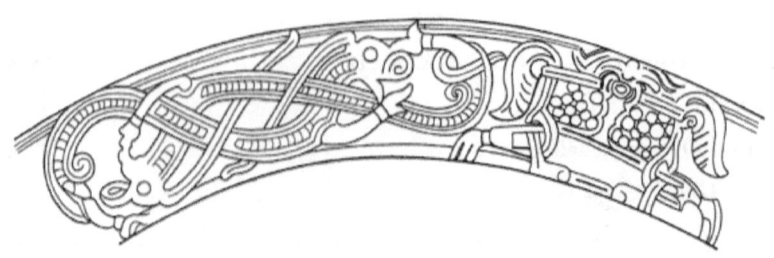

About The Author

I have been a practicing Heathen and Priestess since the early 1980's; and I have had the honor of meeting, knowing and working with some of the early pioneers—not only in the Goddess Movement, but also in the U.S. Heathen reconstructionist faith.

I grew up in the Adirondack Mountains, the remote high peaks region of northern New York. I am an avid outdoor enthusiast, an instructor of wilderness survival, a naturalist, herbalist, Reiki Master, crystal therapist and certified Life Coach. I work with NOLS and teach outdoor survival, as well as advanced first aid for he American Red Cross. I have participated as a leader, healer and Priestess in the Pagan community since 1995.

Walking the path of a Northern Shaman, I became initiated as a Master Core Shaman, and was taught a Sami form of Core Shamanism by the late Ailo Gaup from 2010-2012. I was introduced to the arts of the Seið-practitioner in 2005 by a Völva from Norway, and today I have taken two consecutive summer sessions of weeklong Norse Mysteries intensives with Inger Borg and Lindy Fay Hella when they visit the states. I joined the Troth in 1998; I became a Gythia, and performed many public Blóts, rites of passage, and teaching circles from 1998 till today.

I discovered The Asatru Community three years ago now. I have written a couple of books, and somehow, I got the privilege of helping to create the Clergy Training Program for TAC. After a time, I was then asked to be Director of Religious Affairs, which I adored; after the death of Sage Nelson, I became the Vice President at the end of 2018.

With my long-time spiritual sister, I run the 21st Century Heathen and the Germanic/Teutonic Center for Cultural Arts websites which promote the memory, use, and re-constructing practices of our Ancestors way of living, transposed onto a modern high-tech world; thereby ensuring the continuing evolution of our cultural heritage arts.

My lifestyle of living close to the natural world as well as my dedication to Earth Spiritualism led me to become an active Heathen steward in the protection and furtherance of our planet and its future. I am a landscaper, master gardener and plant whisperer. Currently I live with my husband and our dog Basil in western Washington.

www.ingramcontent.com/pod-product-compliance
Lightning Source LLC
Chambersburg PA
CBHW021820300426
44114CB00009BA/253